Also by Frances Mayes
and published by Bantam Books

UNDER THE TUSCAN SUN

BELLA TUSCANY

The Sweet Life in Italy

Frances Mayes

BANTAM BOOKS

London • New York • Toronto • Sydney • Auckland

BELLA TUSCANY
A BANTAM BOOK : 0553 81250 5

Originally published in Great Britain by Bantam Press,
a division of Transworld Publishers

PRINTING HISTORY
Bantam Press edition published 1999
Bantam Books edition published 2000

1 3 5 7 9 10 8 6 4 2

Set in 12/14 pt Bembo by Falcon Oast Graphic Art

Bantam Books are published by Transworld Publishers,
61–63 Uxbridge Road, London W5 5SA,
a division of The Random House Group Ltd,
in Australia by Random House Australia (Pty) Ltd,
20 Alfred Street, Milsons Point, Sydney, NSW 2061, Australia,
in New Zealand by Random House New Zealand Ltd,
18 Poland Road, Glenfield, Auckland 10, New Zealand,
and in South Africa by Random House (Pty) Ltd,
Endulini, 5a Jubilee Road, Parktown 2193, South Africa.

Reproduced, printed and bound in Great Britain by
Clays Ltd, St Ives plc.

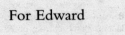
For Edward

ACKNOWLEDGEMENTS

My great thanks to Peter Ginsberg, my agent, and Francesca Liversidge, my editor at Bantam Books. Special thanks to Patrick Janson-Smith at Transworld, and to Shirley Stewart and Dave Barbor, both of Curtis Brown Ltd. Lucy Bennett designed the joyous cover. To her and to Emma Dowson—*grazie*.

Many friends were important to me while I was writing this book: Josephine Carson, Susan MacDonald and Cole Dalton, Ann and Walter Dellinger, Robin and John Heyeck, Kate Abbe, Rena Williams and Steve Harrison, Todd Alden, Toni Mirosevich and Shotsy Faust—you're welcome to pull up a chair at my table anytime. All thanks to my family and to Ed's—Bramasole's *portone* always will swing open to greet you.

The people who live in Cortona have given me this book; all I had to do is write. My thanks to Donatella di Palme and Rupert Palmer, Giuseppina Paolelli, Serena Caressi, Giorgio Zappini, Giuseppe Agnolucci, Ricardo and Amy Bertocci, Nella Gawronska, the Molesini family, Riccardo and Sylvia Baracchi, Giulio Nocentini, Antonio Giornelli, Lucio Ricci, Edo Perugini, and to our great neighbors, the Cardinali family: Placido, Fiorella, and Chiara. We are fortunate to have landed in their midst. With tremendous gratitude, I thank il Sindaco, Ilio Pasqui, and il Consiglio Comunale di Cortona for conferring on me *la cittadinanza onoraria*, honorary citizenship.

My thanks to the editors of *National Geographic Traveler*, *Attaché*, *San Francisco Magazine*, *The San Francisco Examiner*, the *Lands' End* catalogue, and *Within Borders* for publishing portions of this book in their pages.

CONTENTS

BELLA TUSCANY

PREFACE

Stepping inside the *forno*, I'm suddenly surrounded by the warm aromas of just-baked bread. 'Welcome back,' a Cortona woman greets me. Maybe I look dazed, having arrived last night from California, a twenty-hour ordeal, because she asks, 'What do you do for jet lag?'

'I usually just wait it out. I'm so happy to be here that I don't notice it very much — just get up at four in the morning for a few days. What do you do?'

'I stare at the sunset. Then the body knows.'

I merely smile, but mentally I make a little bow to her. Maybe it's a small world, maybe we're in a global economy, and maybe we're slowly melting into one pot, but everyday life is still radically particular in rural Italy. Cut a slice anywhere: It remains purely *Italian*.

When Beppe, who helps in our garden, tells me, '*La luna è dura*,' the moon is hard, and that we must harvest the onions today, I'm reminded that the moon holds sway. 'But we must wait', he continues, 'and plant lettuces *quando la luna è tenera*, when the moon is tender.'

Walking down into town for coffee, I see a waiter bring out a bowl of water for a customer's dog. Overhead I hear, '*Buon giorno, una bella giornata*,' good morning, a beautiful day. An ancient man, who has slipped into a happy dementia, leans from his second-storey window, waving and shouting. Everyone greets him with equal enthusiasm. Shop owners are sprinkling water around their entrances with watering cans, nipping into the bars for a quick coffee, their shops untended, the doors open. After a leisurely half-hour with a cappuccino and a novel, I start to pay and am told that Simonetta has paid. Simonetta? The very quiet woman who owns a *profumeria* where I sometimes buy soap and lotion. This gentle courtesy happens frequently.

At Matteo and Gabriella's *frutta e verdura*, I see the first basket of hazelnuts still in their ruffs. The season is changing and soon all the luscious peaches and peppers of summer will give over to citrus and cauliflower, an entirely different selection. 'Look,' Matteo says, 'the green walnut.' He cracks it, carefully peels the skin, and hands me a smooth piece, the color of ivory. 'You must eat them in three or four days. After that they are too dry.' The taste of green walnuts is not unknown to me. When I was a child, our cook Willie Bell used to squeeze the juice and rub it into my hands if I got ringworm or poison ivy. The new walnuts are gold balls, slightly damp. 'Very good for low blood pressure,' Matteo continues, 'but don't eat too many or you'll have a rise in temperature.'

And so another day begins in this Tuscan hilltown. I came to Italy expecting adventure. What I never anticipated is the absolute sweet joy of everyday life – *la dolce vita*.

Under the Tuscan Sun, my first memoir, chronicled the

discovery of Bramasole, an abandoned house situated beneath an eighth-century BC Etruscan wall. Getting to know the superb hilltown of Cortona, the excitement of cooking in a foreign country, the intense labor of rescuing a house from ruin and the land from brambles, and meeting the people here—these pleasures paralleled the deeper pleasure of learning how to live a new life. Even the name of the house drew me here: *Bramasole*, something that yearns for the sun, and, yes, I did.

I walk from window to window, taking in the view: When I wrote the last line of *Under the Tuscan Sun*, I wrote the first line of *Bella Tuscany*. I knew I was at the beginning of my experience of Italy, the inner experience as well as the outer. Views – they are so various. From my upstairs window, I see a green sweep of the Apennines. As the wooded slopes angle toward the valley, olive orchards begin, and mellow stone farmhouses with tile roofs anchor each farm to the land. There is no entrance of time into this view, except for a turquoise postage stamp far below, the swimming pool of friends. Looking out – looking into Italy! North, south, east, west is the allure of the whole country. I know more now, after several seasons of travels. I've been to the heel, to Sicily, to the watery reaches of the Veneto, those revealing extremes of this country. I've fallen in love with Verona, the Basilicata and Marche regions, Bellagio, Asolo, Bologna, and more and more with the castle towns around Lago Trasimeno, which I can see from my land.

Travelling the circles, concentric from Bramasole, enlarges my perception of the endless complexity and richness of this country. At the same time, my travels bring me back to this rose and apricot house facing the valley. Because it seems like paradise, I continue to work to make it so. Gardening is something I always enjoyed on a capricious level. I was interested not so much in gardening as in the effects of gardening – the flower beds that bloomed on cue and the design of the yard – where to place big pots and how to see a fine range of colors from the windows. I bought flats of just-about-to-bloom flowers, and plopped them in the ground. Now I am a convert. I've fallen into the sustained rhythm of the garden. I compost the coffee grounds and the potato peels. I've learned to double-dig.

With two men who know everything about the land, Ed and I have created extensive herb and vegetable plots. We acknowledge the distant future by planting chestnut, cypress, and evergreens – trees for the long haul – as well as the more winsome and immediate pomegranate, cherry, and pear trees. No trip to a nursery ends without the purchase of still another fragrant rose. Rain reactivates another fragrance, the acrid, steamy smell of sheep dung, delivered by a canny Sardinian shepherd to the second terrace just above the living room. We can't move the stuffed bags, so when it rains, *we* move to the other side of the house.

Buying a house seven thousand miles from home once felt like an enormous risk. Now we just live here. How to quantify happiness? Any loved house you've personally slaved over feels like an extension of yourself. Many people have told me that when they arrived in Italy, they've surprised themselves by thinking, *I'm home.* I, too, had that sensation when I first came here. By now, that feeling has magnified. And, as for a loved one, I have that scarier feeling, *I can't be without you.* Meanwhile, the house just stands here, indifferent, facing the changing light and weather.

Cortona
1 September 1998

PRIMAVERA

Fortunate that cypress shadows fall in wide bands across the sunlit road; fortunate that on the first day back in Cortona I see a carpenter carrying boards, his tabby cat balanced on his shoulders, tail straight up, riding like a surfer. The carpenter tosses the wood on sawhorses and begins to whistle. The cat bends and leans as he moves – a working cat. I watch for a few moments then walk on into town for a cappuccino. *Thank you*, I think. Fortunate that yellow blazes of forsythia light the hills. After seven summers on this terraced land, Ed and I feel a rush of happiness on turning the front-door key. I'm enchanted by the rounded Apennines, this quirky house that takes in the sun, and the daily rhythms of life in a Tuscan hilltown. He's far in love with the land. By now he knows the habits of every olive tree.

Fortunate. Otherwise, we might want to post a For Sale sign on the gate ten minutes after arrival because neither well pump is working: a grinding noise in the switch for the old well, a buzz for the new well. We peer into the cistern – at least there's enough water for a few days.

When the pump went down into the new well six years ago, I never expected to see it again. Now, on our first morning, three plumbers are hauling up ropes, their heads down the well. It's a beast. Then Giacomo stands on the well wall, the others beside him. They're counting, *uno*, *due*, *tre*, giving the heave-ho. Soon they're stripped to their pants, cursing and laughing. Up it comes, and Giacomo almost falls backward. They carry it to the truck.

The old well's pump – replaced just last year – they yank out easily. The contraption comes up with fig roots dangling and is pronounced dead on arrival. Why? They begin to dig for wires. By noon, the walkway is torn up, the lawn is carved into ditches and the mystery is solved. Mice have eaten the insulation around the wires. Why would they eat plastic when they can eat hazelnuts and almonds? The pumps have shorted out.

The new well's pump, it turns out, is also dead. Fizzled. Kaput. By the third day, we have new pumps, new wires sealed with silicone, which the original electrician neglected to do, lots of water, a patched walkway, and a depleted bank account. If mice eat plastic, what's to keep them from eating silicone?

Fortunate that we are served pheasant with roasted potatoes for dinner at the trattoria up the mountain, and that the early March dark spills forth a million twirling stars, because otherwise Ed's scrawled list might seem daunting: new grass, prune trees, build a shed for tools, remodel two old bathrooms, new septic system, paint shutters, buy desk and something with space to hang clothes, plant trees, extend garden.

★

Primo Bianchi, a stonemason who has done extensive work here during our restoration, arrives to discuss the projects. He can start in July. 'I was on your roof in January,' he tells us. 'Your friend Donatella called and said there was a leak.' We've seen the dripping stain on the yellow wall of my study. 'It was the wind. You lost some tiles. When I was working in the afternoon, the wind came again and blew down my ladder.'

'Oh, no!'

He laughs, pointing both forefingers at the ground, that gesture meaning *Let it not happen here*. Dark comes early in winter. I imagine him, his back against the chimney, sitting on the cold tiles, his pale blue eyes squinting at the road below, the wind standing his hair on end. 'I waited. No one came by. Then a car but he did not hear me. After perhaps two hours a woman walked by and I called for help. This house was empty so long – she thought I was a spirit and let out a scream when she saw me waving on the roof. You need to think of a new roof soon.'

He walks off a measurement of pipes we'll need for the new drainage system. It looks like a plan for trench warfare. 'Hurry and order the furnishings for the bathrooms if you want everything here by July.'

Fortunate that the place is restored – central heating, new doors, finished kitchen, one lovely bath, refinished beams, barrels of new paint, rebuilt stone walls, refitted *cantina* for oil and wine. Otherwise, these new projects might seem like restoration itself. 'You may think you're through with old houses,' Primo tells us, 'but they are never through with you.'

19

Soft spring air, an elixir of joy simply to breathe in and out. Quick streams are opening on the terraces. I take off my shoes and let the cold, cold water bathe my feet. The rocky hillsides sprout ferns, glossy green. A new lizard runs across my toes and I feel the clutch of the tiny feet.

★

Primavera, first green, and the wet grasses shine. A European spring, my first. I only have read of Proust's chestnuts flowering, Nabokov's linden lanes, Colette's double-red violets. But no one ever told me about quince, their sudden pink flares against stone walls. No one said the spring winds can turn murderous. No one mentioned lilac, and somehow during my summers in Italy, I never noticed the heart-shaped leaves. Now I see the Tuscan hills spattered with enormous white or smoky-lavender bushes. Near our house, a hedge of lilac leads to an abandoned farm, and in the rain I cut wet armfuls to fill all my pitchers and vases. More than any flower, the mesmerizing perfume seems to be the very scent of memory, hauling me back to college in Virginia and my first breath of lilac, which didn't grow in the warm latitude of my childhood home in Georgia. I remember thinking, *How could I have lived eighteen years without knowing this?* I had a terrible crush on my philosophy professor, married with three children, and over and over I played Harry Belafonte, *Green grow the lilacs all sparkling with dew.* My dorm window overlooked the James River through a tangle of brush. *Springtime is here and it's here without you.* That he wore drip-dry shirts I crassly blamed on his wife; that he combed a long strand of hair over his pate I tried to ignore.

Violets, the suffocatingly sweet-scented ones, bloom along the spontaneous springs. Naturalized double daffodils, *tromboni* in Italian, mass along the terrace edges. The faint mists of hawthorn (*biancospino*, white thorn, or, locally, *topospino*, mouse-pricker) drift along the upper terraces and, below, the fruit trees continue to outdo themselves. We won't mow – the luxurious grass is overtaken by white camomile and marguerites.

What is this happiness that keeps coming in waves? Time, the gift of time, the free running of time – and Italy owns so much of it. Being from the South, I'm used to people talking about The War Between the States as though it were a decade ago. In the South the long dead and buried are talked about, too. Sometimes I thought Mother Mayes would come walking in the door again, bringing back her powdery lavender scent, her spongy body I could feel beneath the voile print dress. Here, it's Hannibal. Hannibal, who passed this way and fought the Roman Flaminio in 217 BC. All the hilltowns celebrate jousts or weddings or battles which occurred hundreds of years ago. Maybe having so much time behind them contributes to the different sense I absorb in Italy. Gradually, I fall into time. At home in California, I operate *against* time. My agenda, stuffed with notes and business cards, is always with me, each day scribbled with appointments. Sometimes when I look at the week coming up, I know that I simply have to walk through it. To be that booked-up, blocked-in feels depleting. When I make the weekly list of what needs to be accomplished, I know I'll be running double-time to catch up. I don't have time to see my friends and sometimes when I do, I'm hoping to cut it short because I need to get back to work. I read about an American doctor who pumps her breasts in freeway traffic so she can continue to breast-feed her baby and still keep up with her medical practice. An ad in *The Wall Street Journal* offered engagement rings by telephone for couples who don't have time to shop. Am I that bad?

Sabbatical, what a civilized idea. All jobs should have them. This year both Ed and I have this blessed time-out, which, combined with summer vacation, gives us the chance to spend six months in Italy. Since this is my first leave in twenty years of teaching, I want to bask in every day. To wake up – without having to go anywhere – and wander the terraces to see what is coming into bloom seems like *paradiso*. Soon the wild irises will open. Their pointy, bruise-blue heads seem to push up taller as I watch. Narcissi, just on the verge of glory, run rampant. Already, yellow light emanates from the buds.

I am, every day, shocked by something new and shocked that this house and land, which I thought I knew from my summers and Decembers, continue to astound me. We stepped off the plane in Florence on March 15 to seventy-degree weather and it has held, except for occasional blasts of wind. Now, the pears are turning from flower to leaf. As white petals drop or flurry – I remember hearing 'peach-blow' as a child – new leaves shoot out with force. That energy has swollen the limbs of all the old fig trees and the branches of the spindly pomegranate we have just planted.

Happiness? The color of it must be spring green, impossible to describe until I see a just-hatched lizard sunning on a stone. That color, the glowing green lizard skin, repeats in every new leaf. 'The force that through the green fuse drives the flower . . .' Dylan Thomas wrote. 'Fuse' and 'force' are excellent word choices – the regenerative power of nature explodes in every weed, stalk, branch. Working in the mild sun, I feel the green fuse of my body, too. Surges of energy, kaleidoscopic sunlight through the leaves, the soft breeze that makes me want to say the word 'zephyr' – this mindless simplicity can be called happiness.

*

A momentous change has occurred at Bramasole. 'Can you find someone to take care of the place?' I asked signor Martini at the end of last summer. We were leaving and had no one to keep the rampant forces of nature at bay in our garden. Francesco and Beppe, who've worked this land for several years, only want to care for fruit trees, grapes, and olives. Once we asked Beppe to cut the grass. He wielded his weed machine as though clearing brambles, leaving the yard looking like a dust bowl. When he and Francesco saw the lawn mower Ed bought, they took a couple of steps back and said, '*No, no, professore, grazie.*' They, men of the fields, did not see themselves pushing the little humming mower across some lawn.

Signor Martini, who sold us the house, knows everyone. Perhaps some friend would like a part-time job.

He pushed back from his desk and pointed to his chest. '*Io,*' he pronounced. 'I will make the garden.' He took down something framed above his desk, blew off the dust on top, and held out his agricultural diploma. A small photo stuck in the corner of the frame showed him at twenty with his hand on the rump of a cow. He grew up on a farm and always missed the country life he'd known as a boy. After World War II, he sold pigs before moving to town and taking up real estate. Because he is eligible for a pension, he planned to close his office at the end of the year, he explained, and was moving to a large estate as caretaker. Because so many Italians start work in their teens, they become *pensionati*, pensioners, while still relatively young. He wanted to make a mid-course correction.

23

Usually we arrive at the end of May, when it's too late to plant vegetables. By the time we've cleared a space, turned the soil, and bought seeds, the planting season has left us behind. We look longingly at the *fagiolini*, string beans, climbing tepees of bamboo in our neighbors' gardens. If a few tomato plants happen to survive our ineptitude and lateness, we sit staring at the runty green blobs the morning of our leaving for San Francisco, shaking our heads at the unfulfilled dream of snapping luscious tomatoes from our own labor.

Now, signor Martini has metamorphosed into a gardener. A couple of times a week, he comes here to work, often bringing his sister-in-law as well.

★

Every day involves a trip to a nursery – we've visited every one within twenty miles – or a walk around the terraces and yard sketching possible gardens. Winter rains have softened the soil so that I sink slightly as I walk. Since we're here in time, I aim to have the most riotous, flamboyant, flourishing garden this side of the Boboli in Florence. I want every bird, butterfly, and bee in Tuscany to feel drawn to my lilies, surfinias, jasmine, roses, honeysuckle, lavender, anemones, and to the hundred scents drifting from them. Even though the risk of freeze is still a consideration, I barely can restrain myself from planting. In the nursery greenhouses, the humid air and the narcotizing effect of bright geraniums, hydrangeas, petunias, impatiens, begonias, and dozens of other rosy pinks and corals, entice me to load the car immediately.

'Whoa, slow down,' Ed says. 'We should buy only what we can plant now, the lavender, rosemary, and sage.' These replace what was damaged by the paralyzing winter storm, when it snowed, melted, then froze all in one day.

'And more trees can be planted immediately. There's plenty of time.'

Plenty of time. What a musical phrase.

Five cypresses, two pears, a cherry, a peach, and two apricots delivered from the nursery line the driveway, awaiting Francesco and Beppe, who already have argued over where each will receive the right amount of sun. They have pruned the olives, which also suffered in the hard freeze. They whipped around the terraces with a ladder, ruthlessly cutting off freeze-burned limbs, then took us on an inspection tour, examining each tree for damage. We stand before a scrawny olive on the first terrace. They shake their heads sadly, as over the deceased body of a friend. Ed grieves, too, since the casualties are his three-year-olds. On the surviving young ones, the usually glistening leaves are dry. The worst sign is split bark; the farther down the tree a split occurs, the more damage. Those split at the base cause the men to shake their heads and say in low tones, '*Buttare via.*' Get it out. We will have to dig out at least ten; others they're iffy about – wait and see. A few scraggly leaves on one, shoots at the bottom of another, offer just enough hope to leave it. On the lower slopes of town and in the valley, many groves look dead, and grim-faced men are sawing off thick branches. Hard as it is, the lesson from the record-low 1985 freeze was to prune severely and the trees will regenerate in time.

Nothing is more sacred than the olive. Francesco eyes two oaks on the olive terraces and shakes his head. 'Good for the fireplace. Too much shade for the olives.' Ed is careful not to disagree but also to point out emphatically that, because of me, the trees have to stay. I have a log bench under one and like to read there. Otherwise, we might come home one day to find the trees cut, Francesco having assumed we agreed. I'm blamed for all deviations of the weed machine around flowers and for any decision that interferes with the self-evident rights of olives and grapes. Ed certainly would lose face if they suspected that he will transplant a wildflower in the tractor path. The men prune and fertilize all morning. Beppe and Francesco tie each new cypress to a giant stake. Between the stake and the tree they stuff a handful of grasses to keep the stake from sawing into the slender trunk.

Although the December freeze totally killed my hedge of herbs and the floppy blue plumbago by the cistern, the balmy, delicious early spring compensates. The laurel hedge Ed doesn't like but doesn't have the heart to eliminate, has, of course, thrived. We work all morning, chopping, digging out, and clearing the dried plants. I feel my neck and arms start to turn red. Is the breeze balmy? Or do I feel its sharp origins in the Swiss Alps?

The worst loss by far is one of the two palm trees on either side of the front door. One looks better than ever. The other is now a tall trunk with a fan of brown, drooping forlornly. From my third-floor study window, I can see a green frond emerging. A hand-span wide, it does not look promising.

★

Signor Martini is now Anselmo to us. He arrives in his real estate clothes, driving his big Alfa and shouting into his *telefonino*, but soon he reappears from the *limonaia* transformed into a farmer – tall rubber boots, flannel shirt, and a beret. What I did not expect is how completely he would take over. 'Don't touch!' he warns. 'If you touch while the dew is wet on the leaves, the plants will die.' I'm startled; he's so emphatic.

'Why?'

He repeats himself. No reason. Usually, these pronouncements have some basis. Perhaps certain funguses are transmitted more easily – or something logical.

'What is that?' I ask him, gesturing to the thriving, knee-high plants he has put in on the third terrace. 'There are so many of them.' I scan the rows; eight rows of ten – eighty plants. He has neglected to consult with me about expanding the garden exponentially. Formerly, we had potatoes, lettuces, basil.

'*Baccelli*,' he answers. 'To eat with fresh pecorino.'

'What are *baccelli*?'

He is uncharacteristically silent. '*Baccelli sono baccelli*.' They are what they are. He keeps chopping weeds, shrugs.

I look up the word in the dictionary but it says only 'pods,' so I call my friend, Donatella. 'Ah, *si, i baccelli*, as we call them – they are the *fave* he has planted, but in the local dialect, '*fava*' means penis so I am sure he would not say the word to you.'

The *baccelli* flowers are tender white wings with a second pair of petals inside, each marked with a purple-black dot. I examine the leaves, looking for the dark veins forming the letter θ, which made the Greeks consider the fava dangerous and unlucky because *thanatos* (death) also starts with theta. So far, these are simply green and vigorous.

In our absence, Anselmo has planted enough vegetables for several families. He has converted two terraces to an enormous garden. A Sardinian shepherd sold him fifteen great bags of sheep manure, which he works into the soil. So far, I've counted, besides the eighty fava plants, forty potato plants, twenty artichokes, four rows of chard, a patch of carrots, a large bed of onions, enough garlic for all the *ragù* in Cortona, and a beautiful triangle of lettuces. He has put in asparagus, too, but he says not to pick the scraggly spears coming up. Asparagus is ready after two years. Zucchini, melon, and eggplant are germinating in the *limonaia*, and sharpened bamboo stakes for tomatoes – quite a few stakes – he has stacked at the end of the garden until the weather stabilizes. I may have to set up a stand and sell zucchini flowers at the Saturday market. Since he is paid by the hour, we dread to know how many he already has spent.

He also has pruned the roses, cut down three of my favorite wild plum trees that were in the way of the garden, and has begun to espalier a line of plums along the edge of the terrace. They look tortured. When he sees me looking at them, he shakes his finger, as though to a child contemplating a dash into the street. 'Wild trees,' he says contemptuously. Whose land is this, I suddenly wonder. Like Beppe and Francesco, he considers anything that interferes with his domain to be a nuisance. And like them, he knows everything, so we do as he says.

'But the best yellow plums . . .' I will have to keep my eye on these trees. One morning I may wake to find them stacked in the woodpile, along with the oaks Francesco would like to attack.

★

Even the spring night is shocking. The silence of the country sounds loud. I'm not yet accustomed to the shrieks of owls tearing apart the stillness. We're coming from burrito-and-a-movie nights, order-out-for-Chinese nights, seventeen-messages-on-the-answering-machine nights. I wake up at three or four and wander from room to room, looking out the windows. What is this quiet, the big, moony night with a comet ball smearing my study window and the dark valley below? Why can't I erase the image my student wrote: *the comet, like a big Q-tip swabbing the sky*? A nightingale practices some nightingale version of scales, lingering on each note. This seems to be a lone bird; no answer comes to the plaintive song.

★

Late every afternoon, Ed hauls in olive wood. We have supper on trays in front of the fire. 'Now, we're back,' he says, raising his glass to the flames, perhaps to the humble god of the hearth. Happiness, divine and banal word, a complex proposition which shifts its boundaries constantly, and sometimes feels so very easy. I pull a blanket around me and doze over Italian idioms. A wind comes up. Which one? The *tramontana*, tinged with frigid air from the Alps, the *ponente*, bringing rain, or the *levante*, blowing hard and fast from the east? The cypresses outlined by moonlight seem to swirl their pointed tops in all directions. Certainly it is not the *libeccio*, the warm, dry wind from the south, or the summery *grecale* or *maestrale*. These winds in the chimney are serious, reminding me that, in March, spring is only an idea.

BITTER GREENS OF TUSCAN SPRING

Sheer excitement wakes me up early. This is the first market day since I arrived. As I dress, I catch a glimpse from the back window of someone moving along one of the upper terraces. A fox? No, someone leaning down, gathering something. A woman, I think, making out through the milky fog a rounded form and dark scarf. Then she's gone, hidden by the *ginestre* and wild rose bushes. 'Probably someone looking for mushrooms,' Ed guesses. As I drive away, I think I see a movement in the hawthorn above the road.

Three closed trucks from way south in Puglia and Basilicata have arrived at the Thursday market in Camucia. They're open at the back and sides to reveal their bounty – artichokes, still attached to stalks. The drivers pull out enormous mounds and stack them under signs that say twenty-five for 8000 *lire*, about eighteen cents apiece. Women cluster around, buying in quantity. Most favored are the purple-streaked smallest ones. These artichokes, even the peeled stalks, are greatly tender. Too small for a choke, the whole thing is edible, except for a few outer leaves. They're sold on foot-long stalks, tied in a cumbrous bundle so heavy that my market tour must end right here. I struggle home, trying to decide how I will use the twenty-five artichokes I have somehow hoisted under my arm. As I haul them into the kitchen, I see another huge bundle of tiny purple artichokes on the counter. 'Oh no! Where did you get these?'

Ed grabs some of my bags. 'I was up at Torreone and a pick-up packed with artichokes pulled up to the bar. Everyone ran out to buy from this guy, so I bought some, too.' Fifty artichokes. Two people.

All the restaurants and trattorie have fried artichokes on the menu. In homes, they're often eaten raw, with seasoned olive oil, or quartered and cooked with potatoes, spring onions, lemon juice, and parsley. The textures and flavors complement each other. Steamed briefly and drizzled with olive oil, their astringent taste seems just right on any spring day.

The winter rape is at the end of its tenure but one farmer still shouted out '*Polezze*,' the dialect word. I've seen it already, flowering in home gardens, at first mistaking it for mustard, which is waving its yellow blooms at home in California wine country right now. When the *rape* flowers, it's too late to savor its particular flavor. Picked early, cleaned of stems, steamed, then sautéed with garlic, the buds and leaves taste like an untamed cousin of broccoli, somewhat bitter and distinct. *Rape* (both syllables are pronounced) tastes good for you; it must be packed with iron and nitrogen. When I eat it, I feel that I rise from the table a stronger person.

Bitter is a popular taste in Italy. All those herbal after-dinner drinks and *aperitivi*, collectively known as *amari*, bitters, that the Italians knock back are definitely an acquired taste. 'Italians seem to have *acquired* more tastes than many of us,' Ed observes. The first time I tried Cynar, based on artichoke flavor, I remembered my mother chasing me around the house trying to get me to take cough medicine. Even an orange soda is labeled '*amara*.' At the *pasta fresca* shop, they're making ravioli with ricotta and *borragine*, wild borage. Ravioli stuffed with anything and ricotta is usually mellow. With borage, the little pillows prod the taste buds. Dandelion, turnip, and beet greens – all are savored in this season. Even the hated nettles, which we battle on a hillside all summer, have a snappy taste when picked as soon as the leaves unfurl, blanched, then stirred into risotto or pasta and topped with toasted pine nuts.

The green that looks strange and new to me is *agretti*. It must exist somewhere in America but I've never seen it. Tied with a weed, a bunch of it looks like wild grasses, something to hand-feed a horse. Thrown onto a hard and fast boil for a few moments, it then gets a turn in the sauté pan with oil, salt, and pepper. When I first saw *agretti*, I thought, uh oh, one of those acquired tastes. While cooking, it had the smell of dirt – that earthiness you recognize when beets are cooking, but with a verdant freshness, too. An Italian friend recommends lemon juice but, as soon as I smelled it, I wanted to taste it unadorned. Because the 'grass' is about the same thickness as *vermicelli*, I later tried it tossed with that pasta and slivers of *parmigiano*. Spinach is the closest taste, but while *agretti* has the mineral sharpness of spinach, it tastes livelier, full of the energy of spring.

I am surprised to find that the legendary wild asparagus also is extremely bitter. Chiara, a neighbor, is out on her land with a handful of the weedy little spears. She pushes back spiny strands to reveal the plant, which looks like a coarser, meaner asparagus fern. She is eloquent on the subject of frittata with chopped wild asparagus. Eloquent, that is, in gesture. Her quick motion, like pulling a zipper in front of her mouth, means something is extra-delicious. Had she placed her thumb against her cheek and rotated her fist back and forth, we would have seen how words fail to describe just how good something to eat can be.

The early riser I saw up on the terraces must have been after the asparagus. Now someone has raided the daffodils, too. After a morning of looking at toilets and tile for the remodeling project this summer, we come home to find about two hundred *tromboni* gone from the hillside. Only a few, drooping and past their prime, are left for us.

All along the road in late afternoons, women walk with their sticks and plastic bags, gathering both asparagus and *mescolanza*, wild greens, most of which are bitter, for their dinner salads. I'm just learning about this *insalata mista* for the taking. They look for *tarassaco*, which resembles dandelion, several kinds of *radicchio*, chicory, borage, *barbe dei frati* – friars' beards – and many others.

What else is bulging in those bags? Why do they suddenly stop and study a piece of ground for a few minutes, poking at it with a stick? They bend over and dig with a penknife – some roots, a few leaves, mushrooms – and move on. We've even seen the well-dressed stop their cars, scamper up a hill, and come down waving two or three bunches of mint or fennel for roasting meat, or some medicinal plant, dirt falling off the roots.

I, too, go out hunting for asparagus. Ed cuts what we think will be the perfect stick for me, a magic stick, as if I will be divining water. Odd how something can be invisible to you, then when it's pointed out, you find it everywhere. The upper terraces flourish with prickly wands. They seem to like growing under a tree or next to a hillside. Right away, I learn to look in hidden places, although sometimes there's a feathery renegade just growing out in the open. Usually a tangle of weeds is between my hand and the dark spears poking out of the dirt. A spear here, one there. Asparagus must have appeared early in the food chain. Cultivated asparagus, despite its many elegant preparations, looks primitive; the wild form is even more so. Some stalks are as thin as yarn and the color ranges from viridian to purple. Those thorns your hand must find its way among are needle-sharp. This is slow work, but good.

I cook my thirty spears to go with roast chicken and neither of us likes the wry, almost medicinal taste. Then, at the market, a strange woman barely four feet tall holds out a newspaper cone full of wild asparagus. She looks as if she just materialized out of a fairy tale and might say, 'Come to the woods, children.' But 'Genuino, genuino,' she repeats. The real thing. 'Fifteen thousand lire' (about nine dollars). Because I have the feeling that I will not be seeing her kind at the market many more times, I hand over the money. Just to be in her presence a little longer, I ask her how to prepare it. Like my neighbor, she likes it cut finely into a frittata.

Ed tries the frittata, bolstering it with spring garlic, but the asparagus taste almost disappears, just a crackle of the bony stem to remind us it is there.

On the street in Arezzo, I see another of these woodsy women. The word strega, witch, comes to mind, or that old source of wisdom in the South, a conjure-woman. Who could resist? I buy some from her basket, too. A

34

crescent-shaped knife lies in the bottom, its blade worn thin. She is almost toothless, bundled in sweaters with bits of straw sticking out of the wool. 'Where did you find so much?' I ask. But she just raises her finger to her lips; her mouth is sealed on that subject. She limps away and I notice she is wearing bright white running shoes. She hoists herself up to the arcade level on the Corso, where sophisticated businessmen at a *caffè* table madly buy her asparagus.

Usually I roast asparagus in the oven – arrange the stalks on a baking sheet, drizzle with oil and salt and pepper and run them in the oven. That's the best asparagus can taste. Without contact with water, even steam, the asparagus retains all succulence and texture without absorbing a watery taste, or worse, going limp. But wild asparagus turned tough as string in the oven, so I learn to steam them very slightly, then roll them around in olive oil. The quality of the oil is crucial; without the best, I'd use butter. With each bite, I imagine the woman foraging in the countryside, her secret hillsides above the vineyards, the years she has attended to this ritual, the surety of her thumb against the curved knife.

When I show Beppe, master grape pruner, the patches of asparagus on the land, he's pleased. He cuts off the dry arching branches. 'Like this, cut low under the dirt and more will come next year,' he explains. When he leans to show me, he discovers that someone already has begun this pruning process. Old wands have been cut on the diagonal, not snapped off. The mysterious forager. Or some spirit who lived here a century ago and revisits in spring? Or some canny soul who sells both flowers and asparagus at the market? A woman with a curved knife? Beppe starts to eat a raw asparagus and hands me one: a taste to sharpen the teeth. I'm beginning to like this spring treat.

I've been surprised during winter visits to find the food so truly different from what I'm used to in summer, the season I'm usually here. Now, as spring continues to unroll, almost every day brings some new taste. At Matteo and Gabriella's *frutta e verdura*, I see a basket holding something I've never seen before. Gnarly dwarf kiwi? Moldy walnuts? No, *mandorline*, Matteo tells me, a special treat in the Val di Chiana, the expansive valley below Cortona. Matteo bites one then holds out the basket to me. Ah, bitter *and* sour, not like anything I've ever tasted. I know immediately that I will like this new almond in its casing. He eats the whole thing slowly, fuzzed skin and all, relishing the crunch. Beneath the sage-green exterior, there's a neon-green layer, then a yellow layer, then the tender, embryonic nut, still soft and delicately touched with the taste of almond.

At home I go out on my own land where wild almonds grow, but none seems to be the right variety of the *mandorline*. The shells are hardening. I crack one with a rock and taste the nut: hint of rose, hint of peach, and the aftertaste which reminds me that prussic acid also comes from almonds. When ripe, these almonds retain their intense perfume but the acid tamps down to a twist of bitterness.

The land is a mystery to me. After seven years, I think I know it and then, suddenly, I don't. I am watching the season's benefactions. Rivers of wild irises are about to debut along the terraces. These we share with the forager, too, and with the porcupines, who feast on the rhizomes. Symbol of Florence, the iris used to be widely cultivated in Tuscany for the use of its dried root (orris) for the sensuous, deep violet-grape scent in perfumes. Such an unlikely wildflower. In San Francisco, I buy tight bunches of five at the grocery store, the attenuated buds barely able to open. Now I'm almost alarmed to see so many just volunteering and blooming with blowsy abandon.

As we walk back toward the house after the asparagus expedition, Beppe pulls up a slick, thick-leaved plant. 'Boil this. It's good for the liver.'

'What's its name?'

'In this moment, I do not recall. Look.' Beppe points to a spreading ferny plant with tiny fan-shaped leaves. '*Morroncello*.' I have no idea what this is. The dictionary does not tell me. I'll try it — another new greeny green of spring.

★

Very early, I hear voices in the road below the house and look out to see three women, hunter-gatherers, gesturing up to our land. They must see some new plant, I think. They're down there a long time and I don't see any movement toward the side of the hill. Finally, they walk on.

While dressing, I hear a skid of brakes, and two beeps of a horn, but when I look out, a blue Fiat is speeding on down the road. We're going to Petroio today, the home of handmade terra-cotta pots. As we start down the driveway, I sense something. Coming closer, we see the road littered with large stones. We look up. The tall stone wall which supports the shady part of our garden has collapsed in the night, leaving a fifteen-by-fifteen-foot gap, uglier than missing front teeth. We push the stones off the road and go up to look. The lovely clear springs surging forth from the hills saturated the ground, undermining the wall. Sins come back to haunt. The fey builder we hired to reconstruct the major terrace walls six years ago did not leave enough drainage holes. Our long yellow picnic table leans precariously where the wall tumbled.

We call our trusted Primo and he comes immediately.

'*Mah*,' he shrugs. 'Walls fall.' He comes in the house and calls his crew.

We don't know what else to do, so we take off for Petroio, over in the Siena province. We want to buy large terra-cotta flower pots for the walls – those still standing. We go into the perched, medieval town first for something to drink but everything is closed and the car barely can squeeze through the narrowest street we've yet encountered. Just outside town are several *fabbricanti*, manufacturers, with hundreds of pots of all sizes. One is as large as a California hot tub. The place we choose makes theirs by hand. We've bought the mass-produced ones before and they're attractive too. A ruddy, actually terra-cotta–colored man comes out looking puzzled. We ask if we may look and he explains that he sells only wholesale. Fortunately, he likes to talk about pots. We're taken in a warehouse above the kilns, hot as a sweat lodge. The jars for olive oil, glazed on the inside, come in many sizes. They make herb pots, garden columns, sundials, classic urns and amphoras. Flower pots of every shape known and others unknown are stacked in rows. These handmade ones have rounded edges, a touch of honey color that looks warm and alive, and an occasional thumb print. He shows us the initials or signs of the maker on the bottom.

When he leans over to move a pot, his glasses slip from his pocket and fall out on the floor. One lens breaks out of the frame but does not shatter. We all kneel in the fine clay dust to look for the tiny screw. After the owner and I give up, Ed continues to search until he spots it in the shadows. Twisting the screw with his little fingernail, he repairs the glasses. We thank the owner for his time and start to leave.

'Wait, how many did you want?' he asks.

'Oh, a few – just for flowers at our house.'

'Not for resale?'

'No. Three or four.'

'Well, you see, I'm not allowed, but three or four, what's the harm?' He gives us a price list and says to deduct forty percent. We select an urn to go with three along our wall and three large pots, all with garlands and swags. When we start to pay, we find that we don't have nearly enough money. He says there's a Bancomat in town so we head back toward the twisted streets, this time parking outside and walking in. Petroio means 'large villa,' and the town is hardly larger than a huge castle. No one is about. We walk all over the tiny town and see no bank. The oldest church, San Giorgio, is closed tight. We spot a man walking his dog and he leads us to a doorway we wouldn't have found. No sign at all and the Bancomat is hidden away in a little closet opening.

Back we go to the shop, where the owner helps us pack the pots in the car. We take off and I fish the map from under the seat. 'We're near the Abbadia a Sicille, supposed to be a refuge and inn for pilgrims on their way to the Holy Land. Embedded in the wall is a Maltese Cross and an emblem of the Knights Templar—'

'Are we avoiding the wall?' Ed interrupts. No need to answer.

Primo's men are loading the Ape (pronounced AH-pay, which means 'bee,' and is a useful small vehicle, something like a covered scooter with a pick-up bed behind it). They've neatly stacked the fallen stones along with bags of cement. A new bottom row already is in place, boulders with cuneal openings for water to escape. Up top, we find they've dug trenches and laid pipes from the hillside to the terrace edge. I point my two forefingers to the ground. 'Let it not happen here. Again.' Such a useful gesture.

The streams now have channels, creating several waterfalls over the edge. We squish up to our ankles. '*Tutto bagnato*,' Primo says, all wet. Everyone passing stops to view the disaster. A woman tells us that many years ago a small child fell in a well here and drowned, that her cries can be heard at night in the house. This news is unsettling. 'That's why the house was abandoned for thirty years. I was afraid to walk by at night when I was a girl.'

'We've never heard cries,' Ed tells her. I wish she hadn't told us. Now when I'm alone, I'm sure I'll be listening.

When she walks on, Primo says, 'All old houses are haunted.' He shrugs, turns out both hands. 'Spooks do nothing. Water is what to worry about.'

In the night I wake up but all's quiet except for the little Niagaras plummeting into the ditch.

SFUSO: LOOSE WINE

Gita, one of my favorite words, a little trip. This morning, I expected Ed to head to the olive terraces with his hoe but instead, he looked up from Burton Anderson's *The Wine Atlas of Italy*, which he often reads at breakfast, and said, 'Let's go to Montepulciano. Our wine supply is getting low.'

'Great. I want to go to the garden center there to buy plumbago to plant under the hazelnut tree. And we can pick up fresh ricotta at a farm.'

Isn't this what we came to Italy for? Sometimes, in the long restoration, I've thought that I came to Italy only to rip ivy from walls and refinish floors. But now that the main projects are over, the house is – well, not finished, but at least looking more like home.

We will restock our *sfuso*, loose wine. Many vineyards

produce a house wine for themselves, their friends, and local customers. Most Tuscans don't drink bottled wine on an everyday basis; either they make their own, they know someone who does, or they buy *sfuso*. In preparation, Ed washes out our enormous green glass demijohn and also our shiny, stainless steel container with a red spigot, an innovation that threatens to replace the traditional demijohns.

To protect wine from air after the demijohn is filled, we learned to pour a splash of olive oil on top, forming a seal, then jam in a fist-sized cork. The new canister has a flat lid which floats on top of the wine. A drizzle of neutral oil is poured around the tiny space between the lid and the side of the canister. A second tight lid then goes on top. As you open the spigot at the bottom and pour your wine into a pitcher, the lid and sealing oil lower too, keeping the seal intact.

When families have seven or eight demijohns, they usually store them in a special cool room, a *cantina*, then uncork each demijohn as they need wine. We've done that, hoisted the demijohn to a table and tipped it, filling old wine bottles through a funnel, then sealed our twenty or so bottles with olive oil. We became adept at tossing off the oil with a jerk when we opened a bottle. But always a few drops floated on the surface. Already, I've consigned two demijohns to decorative functions in corners of rooms. We found our three abandoned by the recycle bin; someone else had given up. But how could they throw the bottles away? I love the curvaceous, globular, pregnant shape and the green glass with bubbles trapped inside. We scrubbed them with bottle brushes made for the job and bought new corks. 'Do we really want to use the demijohn again?' I venture.

'You're right. But don't tell the men.' He means, of

course, Anselmo, Beppe, and Francesco, who scorn any change regarding olives or wine. We load two twenty-liter plastic jugs into the trunk – handy for transporting, but we must transfer the wine into the canister as soon as we come home. A plastic taste can seep quickly into wine.

★

It's great being a tourist. Guidebook and camera in my bag, a bottle of water in the car, the map spread out on my knees – what could be finer?

The road from Cortona to Montepulciano, one of my favorites, levels from terraced olive groves to luxive, undulating hills, brilliant with golden wheels of wheat in summer, and now, in spring, bright green with cover crops and long grasses. I can almost see the July fields in bloom with *girasoli*, giant sunflowers, the hallelujah chorus of crops. Today, lambs are out. The new ones look whiffey on their faltering legs, while those just older cavort about the mothers' udders. This is the sweetest countryside I know. Only occasional blasts of pig barn odors remind me that this is not paradise. In shadowed dips of the hills, shaggy flocks sleep in big white clumps. Wheat fields, fruit orchards, and olives, perfectly cared for inch by inch – all gradually give way to the vineyards of Vino Nobile of Montepulciano.

Chianti, Brunello, and Vino Nobile, the three greatest wines of Tuscany, share a characteristic full-bodied, essential grape taste. Beyond that, Tuscans can discuss endless shades of difference far into the night. Since production of Vino Nobile began in the 1300s, they've had a long time to get it just right. The name of the Tuscan grape, Sangiovese, suggests much older wine production; the etymology is from *sanguis*, Latin for 'blood,' and from Jove – blood of Jove. The local strain of

Sangiovese is called 'Prugnolo Gentile,' nice little plums.

We turn into a long alley of lofty cypresses lining a *strada bianca*, a white road tunneling under the trees. We drive through bolts of pale green light angling down through gaps between trees. Ed only nods when I remember a line from Octavio Paz, 'Light is time thinking about itself.' It seems true to me on one level and not on another. The Avignonesi vineyards surround one of those sublime properties that set me to dreaming of living another life in an earlier time. The villa, the family chapel, the noble outbuildings – I'm in a heavy linen dress in 1780, sweeping across the courtyard, a white pitcher and a ring of iron keys in my hands. Whether I'm the contessa of this *fattoria* or the maid, I don't know but I have a flash of my steps years ago, the outline of my shadow on the stones.

Avignonesi's winemaker, Paolo Trappolini, a startlingly good-looking man who looks like a Raphael portrait of himself, tells us about the experiments at the vineyard. 'I've been searching out almost-extinct rootstock around Tuscany and saving old strains.' We walk out in the vineyard and he shows us new bushy vines planted in the *'settonce'* pattern, a Latin way of placing one vine in the center of a hexagon of other plants. He points uphill at a spiraling planting pattern, *la vigna tonda*, the round vineyard. 'This also is an experiment in using different densities to see the effect on wine quantity and quality.' He shows us the aging rooms, some of which are covered in thick, gray mold, and the *vin santo* room, deliriously perfumed with smoky, woody scents.

Avignonesi makes many fine wines, which can be tasted here or in their Palazzo Avignonesi in the center of Montepulciano. Ed is especially interested in their *vin santo*, the smooth, nutty wine sipped with *biscotti* after dinner. In homes, at all hours, we've been offered *vin santo*, have had *vin santo* forced on us. It's ready, in every cupboard, and you must try it because it's homemade. Avignonesi's is special, one of Italy's finest. We are able to buy only one bottle; their limited quantity has been sold. A friend has given us two special old bottles of *vin santo*, a 1953 and a 1962 Ricasoli, bought in New York and now transported back to their place of origin. Anselmo also has given us a bottle of his own. With the Avignonesi, we'll invite friends for a tasting after a big feast one summer night.

★

Next is Tenuta Trerose. Most of their vineyards are planted the usual way, in staked rows, but a large field is planted as a low arbor, the Etruscan style of planting. The offices are in a modern building behind a villa in a cypress grove. A young man, surprised to see visitors, gives us a price list and shows us their wines in a conference room. Ed, having consulted the most recent *Vini d'Italia*, his trusty yearly guide, selects a case of Salterio Chardonnay and a mixed case of reds. We follow the man out onto a catwalk overlooking a warehouse of stainless steel tanks, some oak barrels, and cases and cases of wine. He shouts, and a woman appears from behind boxes. She starts to put together our cases, leaping, as gracefully as a lynx, over and on stacks of boxes. The beautiful cases cost about forty dollars each, with many smiles and *arrivedercis* thrown in.

Inconspicuous yellow signs point the way to vineyards — Fassato, Massimo Romeo, Villa S. Anna (produced by women), Fattoria del Cerro, Terre di Bindella, Podere Il Macchione, Valdipiatta. We know the names, having popped many a cork from their heroic wines. We're headed to Poliziano for our *sfuso*. Ed waves to someone in a field, who meets us in their warehouse. 'The best *sfuso* in a decade,' he tells us, as he sets out two glasses on a stack of wine boxes. Even at eleven a.m., we're pleased by the hearty red color and the light hint of strawberries in the taste and, what, oh, almost a fragrance of mimosa. We've found our house wine. He fills our jugs from a hose attached to an enormous vat. By law he must seal the jugs and dutifully record our names in his computer. As he pulls up Ed's name, he sees we've been here before. 'Americans like our wine, no?' he asks, so we answer yes, for all Americans. Ed wedges the tanks behind the seat, hoping they won't leak as we negotiate the unpaved roads.

★

The anguine town of Montepulciano stretches and winds as though it were following a river but it climbs a long ridge instead. Henry James's impression, a view caught between arcades, was of 'some big battered, blistered, overladen, over-masted ship, swimming in a violet sea.' Tuscan hilltowns often give one the sense of an immense ship sailing above a plain.

On the roof across from Sant'Agostino, an iron *pulcinella* has hit the clock with his hammer to mark all the hours since the 1600s. I stop to buy candles in a small shop. There, among the potholders, key rings, mats, and corkscrews, I find a dim opening into an Etruscan tomb! 'Oh yes,' the owner says as he flicks on spotlights, 'many store owners find these surprises when they renovate.' He leads us over to a glass-covered opening in the front of the shop and points. We look down into a deep cistern hollowed from stone. He shrugs. 'The roof drained here so they always had water.'

'When?' Ed asks.

The owner lights a cigarette and blows smoke against the window. 'The middle ages, possibly earlier.' We're always amazed by how casually Italians accept their co-existence with such remains of the past.

The street up to the *centro storico*, historic center, jogs off the main shopping street so that the *piazza* is somewhat removed from the bustle of daily shopping. The un-finished front of the massive church adds to the abandoned feeling. A sheepdog on the steps is the most alert being in the *piazza*. We don't go in this time, but, walking by, I imagine inside the polyptych altarpiece by Taddeo di Bartolo, where Mary is dying in one panel, then surrounded by lovely angels while being swooped into heaven, with apostles weeping down on earth. White plastic *caffè* chairs lean onto their tables in one corner of the *piazza*. We have the whole grand, majestic square to ourselves. We look down into the bottomless well, presided over by two stone lions and two griffins. It must have been a pleasure to shoulder your jug and go to the town well to meet your friends and haul up pure water.

In the fine *palazzi*, several vineyards have tasting rooms. Inside Poliziano's, there's a portrait of the Renaissance poet for whom this distinguished vineyard is named. The woman who pours liberal tastes highly recommends two of their *reserve* wines and she is right. Three of their wines are named for poems of Poliziano's: Le Stanze, Ambrae, and Elegia. Stanzas and Elegy we understand but what does the white wine's name, 'ambrae,' mean? She pauses then shakes her head. Finally she waves her hands, smiles, '*Solo ambrae, ambrae.*' She gestures everywhere. Ambiance is my best guess. We buy several *reserve* and the poet's wines.

As a poet, Poliziano made it big in Montepulciano. A bar on the main street is named for him, too, though the decor is strictly nineteenth century instead of the poet's period. Beyond the curved marble bar are two rooms of dark wood and William Morris–style wallpaper with matching upholstered banquettes and proper little round tables, a Victorian tearoom, Italian style. Both rooms open onto the view, framed by flower-filled iron balconies. We have a sandwich and coffee then hurry to the car. The day is slipping away. I stop for a quick look at a church interior I remember, the Chiesa del Gesù, with its small *trompe l'oeil* dome painted to look like an encircling stair rail around another dome. The perspective only makes sense to the eye from the center of the front entrance. From any other, it goes wonky.

The flower nursery takes its name from the massive church, San Biagio, which we skirt quickly in our rush to buy the plumbago before closing. San Biagio is one of my favorite buildings in the world, for its position at the end of a cypress-lined drive, and for its golden stones, which radiate in afternoon sun, casting a soft flush on the faces of those looking up at the austere planes of the building. If you sit on one of the ledges around the base, the light pours over you, while also seeming to seep into your back from the walls. A walk around the building, inside the warm halo surrounding it, gives me a sense of well-being. As we wind around San Biagio on the road going down, we see the church from changing angles.

We find an apricot bougainvillea to replace one that froze, two plumbagos promising soft blue clusters of bloom under the trees, and a new rose, Pierre de Ronsard, a climber for a stone wall. A French poet to join Poliziano in the car.

'Oh, no.' Ed hits his fist on the steering wheel.

'What?'

'We forgot to stop for ricotta.' The ricotta farms are near Pienza, miles down the road.

The mingled scents of plants and sloshing wine wash through the car, along with the deep grassy smell of spring rain which has begun to fall as we head toward Cortona.

For dinner tonight, we've stopped at the *rosticceria* and picked up some divine *gnocchi* made from semolina flour. I've made a salad. Ed brings out the Ambrae from Montepulciano and holds it up to the light. *Ambrae* is not in my dictionary. It must be Latin, possibly for amber. I take a sip — maybe it *is* ambiance, the way dew on lilacs and oak leaves might taste. *Wine is light, held together by water.* I wish I'd said that, but Galileo did.

FOLLOWING SPRING: THE PALMS OF SICILY

I'm not off the plane in Palermo five minutes before I have an *arancino* in my hand, ready to taste *the* signature dish of Sicily. Ed has gone to find the rental car office and I head to the bar right in the center of the airport. There they are, a line of the deep-fried *risotto* balls formed into the size and shape of oranges. 'What's inside?' I ask.

A man with those amazing black, Sicilian, deep-as-wells eyes points to the round ones. '*Ragù, signora*. And the oval ones — *besciamella e prosciutto*.' His eyes fascinate me as much as the *arancini*. All through the airport I've seen the same Byzantine, hidden, historical eyes. At the bar, savoring the crisp creamy texture of the rice, I'm watching a parade of these intensely Italian-looking Italians. Women with gobs of dark curls cascading and flowing, slender men who seem to glide instead of walk. Tiny girls with miniature gobs of the same dark curls, and old men formed by stoop labor, carrying their hats in their hands. Crowds surge to meet planes coming in from Rome, which is only an hour away. They're all waving and shouting greetings to deplaning Sicilians who probably have been gone a few days, judging from their carry-on bags. Ed comes back, bearing keys. He, too, polishes off an *arancino* and orders an espresso. He looks startled when he sees how small it is, barely a spoonful, with rich *crema*. One taste and he's transported.

The waiter sees his surprise. He's about 5' 3". He looks up at Ed, almost a foot taller. 'The farther south you go, *signore*, the smaller and the stronger.'

Ed laughs, '*È fantastico.*' He wheels our bag to the green Fiat and zooms out of the garage.

Along the coastal road to Palermo, we glimpse the sea and cubical North African–style houses in a rocky land-scape. The instant we enter Palermo, we're in wild traffic, careening traffic, traffic moving too fast for us to locate where we are going. Lanes disappear, avenue names keep changing, we turn and turn in mazes of one-way streets. 'That *barista* should have said "smaller, stronger, and *faster*,"' Ed shouts. At a light, he rolls down the window and calls desperately to a man revving his motorcycle in anticipation of the green, '*Per favore*, which way to Hotel Villa Igiea?'

'Follow me,' he shouts back and he's off, spiraling among cars and glancing back now and then to see if we're behind him. Somehow we are. Ed seems to be in his wake, just going. At highway speeds on city streets, cars are neck-and-neck. On all four sides, we are two inches from other bite-sized cars. If someone braked, we'd be in a hundred-car pile-up. But no one brakes. At an intersection, the motorcyclist points to the left then waves.

He swerves right so hard his ear almost touches the ground. We're tossed into a roundabout, spun, and emptied suddenly onto a quiet street. And there's the hotel. We creep into the parking lot and stop.

'Let's don't get in this car again until we leave. That was absolutely the worst.'

'Suits me,' Ed agrees. He's still gripping the wheel. 'Let's take taxis. Everywhere. This is more like the running of the bulls than driving.' We grab our bag, lock the Fiat, and don't look at the car again until we check out.

★

Because we have ended up with 'the most beautiful room in Palermo,' according to the manager, I am ready to fill the tub with bubbles, open the minibar for cold water, and recuperate. When the weather turned on us in Tuscany, we decided to follow spring south. The delicious days of early March turned stormy and freezing rain hit the windows. Primo managed to stabilize our sliding hillside wall, and now has moved his men to an indoor job in town until the ground dries. We were toasting in front of the fire when Ed said, 'I bet it's already warm in Sicily. Wouldn't it be fun just to take off – go tomorrow?'

I looked up from my book. 'Tomorrow?'

'It's close, really. Drive to Florence, quick flight – we'll be there in three hours total, door-to-door. It's no more than going to Seattle from San Francisco.'

'I've never been to Seattle.'

'That's beside the point. We'll go to Seattle. But the forecast here is for rain all week. Look at the sun all over Sicily.' He showed me the weather report in the newspaper, with gray slants covering central Italy and yellow smiley faces dotting Sicily.

'But I have Fear of Palermo. What if we get caught in

Mafia crossfire at a funeral and end up on the evening news?'

'We won't be going to any funerals. We don't even know anyone in Sicily. The Mafia is not interested in us.'

'Well,' I paused for about fifteen seconds, 'let's pack.'

★

A day later, this corner room has four sets of immense doors opening onto a balcony. Balmy air, palms, and blue, blue, blue water. The twenty-foot ceilings match the grand scale of the Napoleonic furniture. Tile floors, a big sleigh bed – a fabulous room, totally unlike the first one we were shown in another wing of the building. That one was depressingly dark with a carpet I did not want my feet to touch. The bellman opened the shutters to a view of a wall. 'No palms,' I said.

'Here there is no palm,' he agreed.

I loathe complaining and Ed hates it more than I, but after an hour we went downstairs and I asked for the manager. 'The room we have is not beautiful. In such a lovely hotel, I expected something more... Is there another available? We'd like to see the palm trees.'

He looked up our room number and grimaced. 'Come with me,' he said. Then he took us miles down marble corridors and came to this one. He flung back the draperies, pushed open the doors, and light off the water bounced into the room. '*Ecco, signori, Palermo!*' He showed us an octagonal sitting room with gilt ballroom chairs, as if we should have a chamber music quartet playing while we slept.

'Now I'm happy,' I told him.

★

The taxi arrives quickly and we launch into the bumper-car traffic. Yes, it's always like this, the driver tells us. No, there aren't many accidents. Why? He shrugs, everybody is used to it. We sit back, and he's right, we begin to feel the double-time rhythm of driving here. Drivers look alert, as though engaging in a contact sport. He drops us in the center near an esplanade closed to traffic. Out of the street's chaos, we're greeted by the scent of flowers. Vendors are selling freesias in all the Easter colors, purple, yellow, and white. Instead of the puny bouquets I buy at home, these are sold in armfuls, wrapped in a ruff of brazen pink foil and trailing ribbons.

Not wanting to take time for lunch, we sample *sfincione*, pizza with big bread crumbs on top, then keep going – palms, outdoor tables filled with people, small shops of luxurious bags and shoes, waiters with trays aloft carrying pastries and espresso.

Pastries! Every *pasticceria* displays an astonishing variety. We're used to dry Tuscan pastries; these are mounded with cream. A woman arranges her shop window with realistic marzipan pineapples, bananas, prickly pears, lemons, cherries, and, for the Easter season, lambs complete with curls. Inside, her cases display almond cakes, wild strawberry tarts, *biscotti*, and, of course, *cannoli*, but in all sizes, from thumb-sized to a giant as large as a leg of lamb. Two bakers pause in the kitchen doorway and all the customers step back as they gingerly balance and step. They bring out a three-foot tree made from small *cannoli*, a stiff pyramid like a French *croquembouche* at Christmas. *Sfince*, rice fritters filled with ricotta, cinnamon, candied oranges or strawberries, honor San Giuseppe, whose *onomastico*, name day, is March 19, when Italians also celebrate Father's Day.

The freezers glow with *sorbetti* – pistachio, lemon, watermelon, cinnamon, jasmine, almond, as well as the usual fruits. Most children seem to prefer *gelato*, not in a cup or cone, but stuffed inside a brioche. Just looking at the almond cake is almost enough satisfaction, but instead we split one of the crisp *cannoli* lined with chocolate and heavenly, creamy ricotta. No harm done; we're planning to walk for the rest of the afternoon.

On the first day in a new place, it's good to wander, absorb colors, textures, and scents, see who lives here, and find the rhythm of the day. We'll crank into tourist mode later, making sure we don't miss the great sights. Dazed by actually coming to Palermo, by the flight, the espresso, and the day, we just take the appealing street, turning back if it begins to look dicey. Palms are everywhere. I wish I could take one back to Bramasole to replace the one December's freeze probably killed. Not only do I love palms because they mean tropical air, I love the image Wallace Stevens made: 'the palm at the end of the mind.' To imagine the end of the mind and to see not a blank wall or a roadblock or an abyss but a tall swaying palm seems felicitous to me.

We come upon a botanical park, dusty and empty except for cacti, carob, mulberry, agave, and shrubs with primitive, broad leaves. The palm looks native but was brought by Arabs in the ninth century, along with their fountains, spices, arabesques, ice cream, mosaics, and domes. Palms and domes – gold, pomegranate, aqua, verdigris – characterize Palermo. How bold to color the five domes of San Giovanni degli Eremiti a burnt red. Inside, aromatic citrus blossoms and jasmine suffuse a cloister garden, a secretive respite from the tortured road outside.

On the map, we see that the Palazzo dei Normanni is nearby and decide to go in its famous Cappella Palatina today. The subjects of the mosaics, the guidebook says, seem to have been chosen with reference to the Holy Spirit and the theology of light. I'm intrigued, since these two concepts seem identical in my mind.

Originally built by those busy Arabs in the ninth century, the palace was expanded by the Normans in the twelfth century and established as the residence for their kings. Later residents and royalty left their bits and pieces, and today the styles have so long overlapped that the architecture simply looks like itself. Byzantine Greeks began the mosaic decoration in the twelfth century. Tessera by tessera, it must have taken them forever; every Bible story I ever heard glitters around this room. The floors, too, are mosaic or inlaid marble in designs like Oriental rugs.

The Holy Spirit and the theology of light are only a layer. A lot is going on. It's like Palermo – each square inch occupied with life. I love the word 'tesserae.' It seems to shower silver and gold on its own. There's the whole Adam and Eve saga, the flood, there's Jacob wrestling with the angel, and in the dome and apse, Christ. In the dome he's surrounded by foreshortened angels, each in intricate clothes. Christ offers a blessing in the apse. In both mosaics, he has long, long fingers. Looking through my opera glasses, I focus for a long time on his right hand, just this one small moment in the entire chapel – the hand held up, the thumb holding down the next-to-last finger, the other three straight, all formed with delicacy and subtle coloration. Late afternoon sun has a weak hold on the walls but still the gold around him sings with burnished amber light.

The rest of the Palazzo is closed. Walking back toward the center of Palermo, we pass rubble-filled lots still un-restored since World War II bombings. We look in open storefronts, where hideous junk is sold, and step off crowded sidewalks with fry-stations selling chickpea fritters. People are out gathering last-minute food for dinner. About their business, the people look contained, silent, often weary, but when they meet an acquaintance their faces break into vibrant expression. In the taxi back to the hotel, we hardly notice the near-death encounters.

★

The first two restaurants Ed selects for dinner are nixed by the hotel desk clerk. Dangerous areas, he tells us, making the motion of someone slicing a throat. He takes a ball-point and scribbles out whole areas of our map. 'What about this one?' Ed asks, pointing in our Italian restaurant guide to the highly regarded, unpronounceable *N'grasciata*. 'And what does that mean?'

'In local dialect that means "dirty" but don't be alarmed, just a way of speaking.'

Speaking of what? I think. Dirty means dirty. 'Your highest recommendation?'

'*Sì*. Authentic. They have their own fishing boat. You won't see tourists there. I will call and they will expect you.'

We're dropped off at a plain place which is even plainer inside. No tablecloths, a TV somewhere, no decor, no menu, harsh lighting, and the buzz of bugs hitting the zapper. The waiter starts bringing out the food. I'm crazy about the *panelli*, chickpea fritters, and the platter of fried artichokes. Then comes pasta with *pomarola*, that intense, decocted tomato sauce, and baby octopus. I'm not so sure about this dish. I chew for a long time. The platter comes round again and Ed has more. We're offered another pasta, this one *bucatini* with sardines, currants, and fennel. The next dish is a grilled *orata*, which my dictionary trans-lates as 'gilthead,' surrounded by fried *frutti di mare* – just

57

various fish. I'm slowing down. I like a little bit of fish, not a lot. Ed loves anything that comes from the sea and is so obviously relishing the food that the waiter starts to hover, commenting on each morsel. He's pouring wine to the brim of the glass. His dolorous eyes look like Jesus's in the mosaic dome. His long fingers have tufts of black curly hair on each digit, and a mat of hair escapes the collar of his shirt. He has the long, four-inch-wide face I associate with newspaper photos of hijackers.

I revive briefly for the spicy *melanzane* – here's a touch of the Arabic, eggplant with cinnamon and pine nuts – but balk at the appearance of the stuffed squid (all those suction cups on the arms) and the sea bream sausage. Is he bringing us everything in the kitchen? Next comes a plate of fried potatoes. '*Signora*,' our waiter says. '*Signora*.' He can't believe that I have stopped eating. He pulls up a chair and sits down. 'You must.'

I smile and shake my head. Impossible. He rolls those dolorous eyes to heaven. '*Ho paura*,' I'm afraid, I try to joke, pointing at the squid. He takes me literally and eats a bite himself to prove there's no cause for alarm. Still, I shake my head no. He takes my fork, gently grabs a handful of my hair, and starts to feed me. I am so astonished I open my mouth and eat. I really hate the texture, like tenderized erasers.

As an afterthought, he brings out *involtini*, veal rolled around a layer of herbs and cheese, but even Ed has stopped by now. He's thanking the waiter. 'The best fish in Palermo,' he tells him.

'How do you know?' I ask him on the way out. The waiter bares his teeth in a big grin. No, he looks more like a wolf than Jesus.

'It had to be. That was a down-home place.'

★

We're out early. In the Vucciria quarter, the market is stupendous. I've been to markets in France, Spain, Peru, San Francisco, all over Italy. *This* is the market. For the senses, ecstasy and assault. Because Palm Sunday is this weekend, perhaps it is more of an assault than usual. Lines of lambs, gutted and dripping, eyeballs bulging, hang by their feet. Their little hooves and tails look so sad. Their little guts look so horrifying. The rainbows of shining fish on ice, the mounds of shrimp still wiggling their antennae, painted carts of lemons, jewel-colored candied fruits, bins of olives, nuts, seeds – everything is presided over by dealers who shout, sing, cajole, joke, curse, barter, badger. They're loud and raucous. Could it be true, as I've read, that the Mafia runs the heroin trade out of here? A vendor holds out a basket of eels that look like live sterling silver. He gyrates his hips to emphasize their movement. This feels more like a carnival than the decorous Tuscan markets we're used to. I wish for a kitchen so I could gather some of the lustrous eggplants and clumps of field greens. My stomach is growling so loud it sounds like a tiny horse neighing. Cooks here are in paradise. I'll never eat lamb again.

Ed refuses to go to the Catacombe dei Cappuccini, where 8,000 desiccated corpses are on exhibit. I have already bought a postcard of a red-haired girl under glass for decades, her delicate nostrils still stuffed with cotton, a ribbon in her hair. We have visited the same sort of place in Guanajuato, Mexico. I was fascinated; he was revolted. We decide on the Museo Archeologico, and we don't come out until it closes. I find this one of the best museums I've ever visited – so much of what interests me is gathered in this old convent. Phoenician anchors and amphoras dredged from the sea lie around the courtyard. Mysterious stelae painted with portraits were found on ancient grave sites in Marsala. Etruscan treasures, some with traces of paint, from the tombs at Chiusi, near us in Tuscany, somehow have ended up in Sicily. Here we get to see the sixth- and fifth-century BC metopes (panels of the temple frieze) removed from the Greek site at Selinunte, one of the most important ruins on the island. We find Demeter, the Cretan bull; Perseus, Hercules, and Athena star in various triumphs. Hera marries Zeus, and Actaeon becomes a stag. Seeing the familiar mythic players as they actually were on temples brings the legends closer to my imagination. These images come from the time when they were real to people, not just characters from the pages of a history of myth — an astounding telescoping of distance. The enormous scale, too, prepares us for the dimensions of the ruins we'll see.

We can't look at all 12,000 of the votive figures also excavated at Selinunte but we look until we can't look anymore. That only leaves rooms and rooms of Roman sculpture, Greek vases, and more and more. We meander through, stopped by painted fragments from Pompeii, a fantastic third-century BC bronze ram, and a blur of mosaic pavements. Then, out. Onto the plain sidewalk, dazed and dazzled by what we've seen.

*

All of Palermo is a grand feast. Not an easy city but a challenging one. You keep your wits about you; you're not lulled or allowed to be passive. It's a place to encounter, which makes it memorable. We spend three days among the Palermitani, engrossed in their street life, saturated by their Sicilian Baroque, which out-Baroques Baroque, stiff-necked from looking up into domes. Does the baby in the womb experience light, the way I can see through my hand held to a strong light? If so, to the emerging infant, perhaps the last blurred look back from the birth canal resembles the inside of the bricked Moorish dome at San Cataldo, a concentric expansion of pale light.

The surprise of Palermo was Sicily's fling with Art Nouveau, called 'Liberty' in Italy. The metal kiosks around the Quattro Canti, the main intersection at the town center, had all the charm of the famous metro signs in Paris. Our hotel was decorated with extensive paintings by Ernesto Basile, who also finished the decoration of the Teatro Massimo, designed by his father, which recently reopened after over twenty years in restoration. What a father and son duo. Spotting their sources in the Byzantine, Moorish, and Greek motifs around town was an added pleasure. A frustration was how many places were closed. No sign, just closed.

As the freesias begin to wilt in our room, we decide to start our tour of the island tomorrow morning. We have a glass of blood orange juice on our balcony. All we can hear is the rattle of palms below us in the breeze and the jingle of rigging on the sailboats in the bay. 'Do you want to come back?' I ask.

'Yes. We haven't seen whole areas of Palermo.'

'It's hard to get a sense of the place. So layered, so crude, so complex – a daunting city.'

'My core impression is of a chaos everyone here has learned how to survive.'

'I don't think I could live here. Besides the horror of the Mafia, I'd never be able to drive anywhere.' I don't even like to drive the East Bay freeways.

'Yes, you would. You'd get a used mini-car and if you got a few dents a day you wouldn't care.'

'What about dents in my head?' Chaos, I think. Yes, it's here. But I suddenly remember a story a woman I met in Milwaukee told me about someone she knew. 'This Midwestern soldier in World War II was on a ship which was bombed by retreating Germans in the harbor of Palermo,' I tell Ed. 'He survived even though almost everyone else was killed. He swam to shore and was stranded here. I think the Germans were retreating by then. One night he went to the opera – he'd never been before. At the end, he was so moved by the music he began to cry. All the horrors caught up with him. He just stood there during the applause and afterwards, openly crying. The audience started to file out. A man looked at him, paused, and touched him on the head, as though he were bestowing a benediction. As all the people passed him, each one stopped and touched him on the head.'

'That's one of the best things I've ever heard. So that's Palermo.'

★

Each succeeding conqueror of Sicily – Greeks, Carthaginians, Romans, Arabs, Normans, and all the rest – must have brought pocketfuls of wildflower seeds. The countryside in *primavera* is solidly in flower, rivers of yellow, purple cascading around rocks, roadsides lined with tiny blue-eyed blooms, and almond orchards whose long grasses are overtaken by white daisies. We made an easy exit, considering. We were only lost half an hour. Even though Ed was intimidated by traffic in Palermo, once we were out on the open road, I noticed his new skills, learned from the back seat of the taxis. He's relaxing into the concept that lanes do not exist much; the road is an open field for getting where you're going. The white line is the center of an imaginary lane to be used as needed.

Driving along the coast and meandering inland, the Mar Tirreno seven shades of blue out one window, and rampantly flowering hills out the other, it is easy to see why all those conquering hordes wanted this island. The landscape is everywhere various or dramatic. Anytime the perfume of orange and lemon groves wafts in the window, the human body has to feel suffused with a languorous well–being.

Soon we come to the turnoff for Segesta, first of the many Greek temples we hope to see in Sicily – the number rivals Greece itself. The Doric temple rises, just off the highway, where it has loomed on the hillside since the fifth century BC, which is close to forever. Along the climbing path, we see gigantic fennel growing, ten feet, even more. I always wondered how Prometheus took fire back to the Greeks in a fennel stalk. In these you could stash quite a few coals. In the process, maybe he invented grilled fennel.

The guidebook says of Segesta: 'It is peripteral and hexastyle with 36 unfluted columns (9m high, 2m wide at base) on a stylobate 58m by 23m. The high entablature and the pediments are intact. The bosses used for maneuvering the blocks of the stylobate into position remain. Refinements include the curvature of the entablature and the abaci.' Well, yes, but it's beautiful.

So is the equally ancient theater a short hike away. Greece was the first country I ever wanted to see. My longing was produced by a total immersion in Lord Byron when I was a senior in high school. In college, my friend Rena and I took a course in Greek drama. We wrote for brochures from Greek freighters and decided to drop out and see the world. We wanted to book passage on the Hellenic Destiny, until our parents said absolutely not. I've never yet been to Greece. A few years ago I saw the magnificent temples at Paestum in the south of Italy and the longing was reawakened. 'The mountains look on Marathon/and Marathon looks on the sea/and musing there an hour alone,/I dreamed that Greece might still be free.' Something like that – it seems to scan into iambic tetrameter.

Like Paestum, Segesta is stripped down to pure silence, its skeletal purity etched against the sky. No one is here. We're alone with history and swallows swooping from their nests.

★

We check into a country inn with a damp bed where we huddle during siesta. The young spring sun has not yet penetrated these walls. A charming courtyard with luxuriant sage and rosemary, and the room with colorful handmade rugs and iron bed do not compensate. Nor does the view of the sea. It's freezing. A weak square of sunlight reaches halfway across the floor. Bedside lamps with the wattage of Christmas tree bulbs preclude reading. At four, we're back in the car heading for Erice, a craggy medieval town, whose early name was Eryx. Where is everyone? We're alone, as we were at Segesta. Even the well-known pastry shop is empty, except for a languid clerk who seems intent on his cigarette. The almond cake and thick lemon pie topped with roasted almonds sustain Sicily's reputation for sublime pastries. I wish I could take the rest of that lemon pie with me; with the local almonds on top, it's better than my grandmother's Deep South recipe. Even though Erice is small, the village feels disorienting. We look in the few shops, and walk the perimeter. All the churches are closed. We know better than to judge the life of an Italian town by one visit. At a different time on a different day, Erice may be lively. Places have their odd closing days, their individual rhythms.

Finally the restaurants open. This early, we're alone. Ah, chickpea fritters again. We order *cuscus alla Trapanese*, couscous cooked with fish broth in the North

African–influenced style of nearby Trapani. The waiter recommends *spigola al sale*, sea bass in a salt crust, a dish I sometimes make at home. Under his arm, he brings a bottle of Còthon, a red wine of Marsala, and holds out the platter with the encased fish on a bed of fennel leaves.

After dinner we emerge and find that we have no idea where we left the car. We cross, recross the town, enter a dark park, go down- and uphill. The streets shine like polished pewter in the moonlight. No one is out. Where is the restaurant? Eerie Erice.

Back at our room, the sheets are cold again. I open my notebook and write: Erice — radio towers, unusual stone streets. Then I fall asleep.

We're out of that damp *tomba*; this will be an all–Greek day. Selinunte, more ruined than Segesta, spreads from a broad hilltop down to the sea. The name Selinunte, Ed reads, comes from the Greek word for wild celery. Hundreds of colossal broken columns fill one area. Fallen, lying in pieces, they look even more massive. We take a walk downhill toward the ruins on the edge of the sea. This approach shows us the outline of the sixth-century BC golden columns against blue water. In soft air, we sit on a rock and stare at surely one of the great classical scenes in the universe. The names 'Temples C, G, E' seem ludicrous. Again, we are alone at the site. Having seen the metopes in Palermo, it's easy to imagine them positioned around the top but not easy to imagine how the Greeks managed to get them up there.

★

Fancy thoughts of paradisiacal spring don't last long. Soon the scene out the car window changes to fields totally encased in hideous plastic. Growing vegetables under plastic-covered hoops surely extends the growing season and improves farm economy, but it blights the landscape. The growers have been thorough – as far as you can see, the sheen of plastic. No vegetable is as tortured and managed as the tomato. Those grown under plastic look better than they taste. Only direct sun infuses tomatoes with flavor, awakens the full taste. Good Sicilian cooks must wait for summer to make their tomato sauce.

Many of the towns we dip into are hideous. A fifty-year ban on cement should be imposed. Historic centers are often smothered by postwar concrete, mainly in the form of apartment towers, which form instant slums. The oil and chemical plants don't add to the *bellezza* either. Much of the coast we pass is ruined – everywhere, the phenomenon of buildings started then abandoned halfway along. Plenty of money must be paid for start-up and somehow the project dissolves. Too many payoffs?

How much is the Mafia to blame? Fear in the air probably stops most people from having normal initiative; better to lie low. Having only been here a few days, I feel waves of rage about the Mafia. I can't imagine what it must be like actually to *live* under the pall of their serious evil. I never hear the word 'Mafia' from anyone; as a tourist, I wouldn't. Even leading questions are routed around so that answers don't have to involve speculations about 'Our Thing.' Small rocks on Mars can be inspected. Babies can be made in glass dishes. I don't understand why the Mafia can't be stopped. Imagine Sicily without the Mafia, imagine the spirits of the people lifting . . .

★

I'm glad I don't have to take a test on Agrigento. For an American used to a comparatively straightforward history, all the Italian past seems hopelessly convoluted. The saga of the Greek ruins multiplies this complexity. Agrigento, since its Greek founding in the sixth century BC, has been tossed among Carthaginians, Romans, Swabians, Arabians, Bourbons, and Spaniards. Subjected to a name change during Mussolini's zeal to Italianize all things, the old name Akragas became Agrigento. I've seen the same zeal on the plaque outside where John Keats lived in Rome, cut off from his love and dying from tuberculosis. He's called Giovanni Keats, which somehow makes him seem more vulnerable than ever.

Akragas/Agrigento was Luigi Pirandello's birthplace. Travelling in Sicily casts his plays and stories, with their quirky sense of reality, in quite a natural light. The co-existence of the Greek ruins, the contemporary ruins, the tentacles of the Mafia, and the mundane day-to-day would skew my sense of character and place, too. The sun, Pirandello wrote, can break stones. Even in March, we feel the driving force on our heads as we walk in the Valley of the Temples.

All over a valley of almond trees and wildflowers stands a mind-boggling array of remains from an ancient town, from temples to sewer pipes. You could stay for days and not see everything. Unlike other sites, this one is quite populated with visitors. The Temple of Concordia is the best-preserved temple we've seen. Patch up the roof and the populace could commune with Castor and Pollux, to whom it probably was dedicated.

Five days ago I knew almost nothing about these ruins. Now the ancient dust covers my feet through my sandals; I have seen the unlikely survival of these buildings through rolls and rolls of time. The temples, men selling woven palm fronds for Palm Sunday, schoolchildren hiding among the columns, awed travellers like us with dripping *gelato* – all under the intense Sicilian sky. I'm thrilled. Just as I think that, Ed says, 'This is the thrill of a lifetime.'

Still, at dinner, we find that one temple is beginning to fade into another. Maybe we've seen enough of Agrigento this time.

By the time we're back at the hotel, I've begun to descend into what I've come to call traveller's melancholy, a profound displacement that occasionally seizes me for a few hours when I am in a foreign country. The pleasure of being the observer suddenly flips over into a disembodied anxiety. During its grip, I go silent. I dwell on the fact that most of those I love have no idea where I am and my absence among them is unremarkable; they continue their days indifferent to the lack of my presence. Then an immense longing for home comes over me. I imagine my bed with a stack of books – probably travel books – on the table, the combed afternoon sunlight coming through the curved windows, my cat Sister leaping up with her claws catching the yellow blanket. Why am I here where I don't belong? What is this alien place? I feel I'm in a strange afterlife, a haint blowing with the winds. I suspect the subtext to this displacement is the dread of death. Who and where are you when you are no one? Downstairs in the hotel courtyard, a wedding dinner is in progress. The shouts, bawdy toasts, and slightly disheveled bride intensify my state. Usually I would savor the position of the almost invisible observer at the window, but tonight I am nothing to them. They belong. I'm a free radical. As the band starts up after a break, two small girls in frilly, silly dresses began to dance together. I could be anywhere on the planet, or not on the planet, and they would dance and dance. *With or without.* The groom would turn over his chair. The grandparents in their stiff country clothes would look as startled. *With or without.* The moon would shed its ancient light on the singular columns scattered over the valley, as it has and will.

Ed already is sleeping. I walk downstairs and watch the party break up. Kisses and embraces. I go in the bar and order a glass of *limoncello*, concentrate hard on the lively citrus taste, conjure to my mind the lovely face of my daughter seven thousand miles from here.

*

We drive on in the morning, passing some dire ugliness along the way. Petrochemical — what a hideous word. Poor Gela — I see that it has interesting remains somewhere in this labyrinth but it is so intensely ugly that we speed through. Ed remembers that Aeschylus died here when an eagle flying above him dropped a tortoise on his head. Fate, as in a foretold prediction. A mythic way to go. I'm sure Pirandello as a child was influenced by this story.

Ragusa — we'll spend the night. This hilltown feels like Sicily as I imagined it — provincial, and so privately itself. Like several other towns in the environs, Ragusa was rebuilt in the Baroque style after the terrible earthquake of 1693. There's an old town and an older town, Ragusa Ibla. By now we just expect to get lost and we do. We hit Ibla at a moment of celebration. How this many cars can squeeze into streets hardly wider than an arm's length is hilarious. We crawl, turning a dozen times, trying to get out. We glimpse the church of San Giorgio, more fanciful than a wedding cake, which seems to be the focal point of whatever is going on. Is the Saturday before Palm Sunday a special day? Finally, we escape Ibla and find our way to a pleasant hotel in the upper town, which is newer but looks old to us. It's drizzling. We sit in the bar with espresso, looking at books and maps. *Americani* are a novelty here. Two men in suits come up and speak to us, obviously intrigued when we say we're from San

Francisco. They want to know if we like Sicily, if we like Ragusa. '*Sì*,' we both answer. They insist on buying the coffee.

Walking in the rain, we admire iron balconies and watch the locals dashing into the cathedral for Saturday mass. Surrounding the great carved door are displays of intricately woven palm fronds for sale by boys. Everyone buys one so we do, too. Ed sticks it behind the mirror in our room. Because today is my birthday, we set out for a special restaurant ten or so miles away. Soon we're lost on unmarked roads. The restaurant seems to be an illusion. We turn back and have dinner in a fluorescent–lit pizza place with orange plastic chairs.

*

Meandering, we stop at a cypress–guarded cemetery near Modica. Extravagant tombs are elaborately carved minia-ture houses laid along miniature streets. Here's the exuberance of Modica's art of the Baroque in microcosm. Through the grates or gates, little chapels open to linen-draped altars with framed portraits of the dead and potted plants or vases of flowers. At thresholds, a few cats sun themselves on the warmed marble. A woman is scrubbing, as she would her own stoop. With a corner of her apron, she polishes the round photo of a World War I soldier. A girl weeds the hump of earth over a recent grave in the plain old ground. These dead cool off slowly; someone still tends flowers on plots where the inhabitants have lain for fifty years. Cortona's cemetery, too, reflects the town, although not as grandly. A walled city of the dead situated just below the live city, it glows at night from the votive lights on each grave. Looking down from the Piazza del Duomo, it's hard not to imagine the dead up and about, visiting each other as their relatives still do right up the hill. The dead here probably would want more elaborate theatrical entertainments.

Next on our route, Avola retains some charm. One-room-wide Baroque houses line the streets. Could we take home at least a dozen of the gorgeous children in their white smocks? On the corners men with handheld scales scoop cockles from a mound on the sidewalk. Open trucks selling vegetables attract crowds of women with baskets. We keep turning down tiny roads to the sea. We can't find the beaches we expect – the unspoiled littoral dream of the island's limpid waters – only bleak beach towns, closed and depressing out of season.

It's only in Siracusa that I finally fall in love. In my Greek phase in college, I took Greek and Roman History, Greek and Roman Drama, Greek Etymology. At that point, my grandfather, who was sending me to college, drew a line. 'I am not paying for you to stick your head in the clouds. You should get a certificate for teaching so you have something to fall back on.' The message being, if your husband – whom you have gone to college to acquire, and no Yankees, please – dies or runs off. Meanwhile, I was loving Aeschylus, the severe consequences of passion, pure-as-milk marble sculptures, the explorative spirit of the Greeks. Siracusa, therefore, is tremendously exciting to visit. Mighty Siracusa, ancient of ancients. Second to Athens in the classical world. We opt for a super-luxurious hotel on the connecting island of Ortigia, with a room surrounded by views of the water. We're suddenly not tired exactly, but saturated. We spend the afternoon in the huge bed, order coffee sent up, pull back the curtains and watch the fishing boats nosing – isn't that a Greek blue – into the harbor.

After siesta, we find Ortigia in high gear for Easter. Bars display chocolate eggs two feet tall, wrapped in purple cellophane and ribbons. Some are open on one side to reveal a marzipan Christ on the cross. Others have a surprise inside. I'd love to buy marzipan doves, lambs in baskets, chocolate hens. The lambs are like stuffed animals, large, decorated from nose to tail with fanciful marzipan curls. At the Antica Dolceria, they've gone into marzipan frenzy: Noah's ark complete with animals, the Greek temples, olives, pencils. Marzipan – called *pasta reale* – we realize is a serious folk art form. For me, three bites will suffice; maybe you have to have been born in Sicily to be able to eat more.

Ortigia is fantastic. The vague, intuitive sense of oppression I've felt in Sicily entirely lifts. Is the Mafia not in control here? People seem more lighthearted, playful, and swaggering. They look you in the eye, as people do in the rest of Italy. In the late afternoon, we walk all over the small island. It has its own Greek ruins just lying in a grassy plot at an intersection. An inscription carved into steps identifies the site as a temple to Apollo. Dense ficus trees along a walkway bordering the water are home to thousands of birds singing their evening doxology. Views across the water, Baroque iron balconies, Venetian Gothic windows, boarded up *palazzi*, and intricate medieval streets – layers and layers of architecture and time. Suddenly the streets intersect and widen at the Piazza del Duomo. The Baroque façade and entrance of the church in no way prepare you for the stunning surprise inside. Along one wall, the building incorporates a row of twelve majestic columns from the fifth century BC Tempio di Atene, Temple of Athena. At evening, spikes of sunlight fall across the *piazza*, lighting the faces of those having an *aperitivo* at outdoor tables. Ordinary people, with the sun, like the sheen of gold mosaics, transforming their faces.

★

Unlike the *Lotophagi* – lotus eaters – Homer wrote about, I have not tasted anything that would make me lose the desire for my native land, not even the tomato sauce, which is the best in the world. The food, everywhere we've eaten, is great, the best. The coffee simply exists in a league by itself. Those who love seafood never will get over Sicilian food. Ed researches restaurants thoroughly before we go somewhere, not wanting to waste a precious night. But tonight we're drawn into a trattoria simply because it looks like someone's Sicilian aunt's funky dining room, with painted cupboards, bits of old lace, family photos. We're waved to the last available table. No menu arrives. Carafe wine is plunked down on the table. A woman and her daughter are in animated conversation in the slot of a kitchen. The husband tends the dining room. He's holding a glass of wine aloft as he floats from table to table, taking a few sips as his customers order. Soon a plate of antipasti appears – little squid, a vegetable tart, olives. We eat everything then wait. And wait. Ed holds up the small carafe. More wine? The husband is flustered; the wine has not been delivered. He scurries around to other tables and scrounges from half-filled carafes. The diners look somewhat astonished. 'Soon it will come,' he assures us. Suddenly three men in dark suits arrive and the husband practically bows. They enter the kitchen. The women stand at attention. We can see them from our table, drying their hands on their aprons, rolling their eyes to heaven. Is this a Mafia visit? A demand for payment? But the men open cupboards, bend to the floor, lean over the stove. One takes out a notebook and confers with the others. For a moment they seem to argue. One looks sullen. The wife piles something on plates and hands them around. Everyone goes silent while they eat, then they shake hands with the husband, give him a slip of paper, nod to the women and exit. The dining room is hushed. The husband watches them disappear around the corner then lets out a whoop. A stooped man about four feet tall with a demijohn of wine enters. The husband whoops again, uncorks the bottle and fills the pitchers of all the tables. He lifts his own glass and the women emerge from the kitchen, laughing. The health inspectors have made a surprise visit and everything was O.K. We all toast and more wine is poured. Service after that is chaotic. The vegetables appear ten minutes before the main course. We get someone else's grilled fish but by then we don't care. It's all good anyway.

The next morning when I am out walking alone early, a car whizzes by me and stops. The woman chef from the restaurant jumps out of her car, takes my hand, and tells me how lovely to see me again, that I must come back. She has trailing scarves and stacks of jewelry on her wrists. I definitely would go back.

★

We're ready to put in a full day on foot. In the museum on Ortigia, Caravaggio's painting of the burial of Santa Lucia, a local virgin martyr in 304, who cut out her own eyes when a suitor admired them, occasioned a lecture from the guard worthy of any docent. And where are we from? Ah, he has a cousin in California; we should meet him when we return. Ed loves Annunciation paintings and the peeling one by da Messina enthralls him. Small local museums are my favorite kind. They stay close to the source, usually, and deepen a tourist-level connection with a place.

We walk across the bridge, through a park, then through a honeycomb of streets. The Museo Archeologico in Siracusa proper is world class. Intelligently arranged and exhibited, the art and craft of succeeding waves of life in this area are displayed. Beginning with prehistory, we trace the eras through one stunning room after another. Artifacts, statues, lion faces from the temple in ruins in Ortigia, Greek ex-votos, and an amazing bronze horse – oh, so much.

The amphitheater in Siracusa – what fabulous siting. The stone cup of the hill was chopped out into natural seating, a 300-degree arrangement focusing on a stage. Corridors were carved out for gladiators to enter and exit. In summer, the Greek plays are still performed here. What fun it would be to act in one. The ruins we've seen are the major ones; hundreds of other temples, foundations, baths, and unknown stones cover the island. This must be the ideal time to see them because hardly anyone is around. The solitude of these places sharpens the experience of happening upon them, the sense of discovery that for me lies at the heart of travel.

We vaguely hear a thunderstorm in the night but are so thoroughly exhausted from our day that nothing really wakes us until about three o'clock. The room's wrap-around glass creaks ominously in its frames and the bed feels as though someone is shaking the headboard. Earthquake. We leap up and look out at the harbor, where quiet boats just seem to be rocking with the water. We wait, as we have on other nights in San Francisco, for whatever comes next. We've experienced so many by now that we can judge the force on the Richter scale, although the 7.5 quake of October 1989 was so far beyond what we'd felt before that we had no idea. I think of what must have existed in Sicily before the earthquake of 1693 knocked down whole areas. But tonight's was only a hard jolt, perhaps 3.4, a reminder that the earth has its own rhythms having nothing to do with us.

In the inland Baroque town of Noto, we come upon my fearful fantasy of the Mafia funeral. Maybe it is only a local patriarch laid to rest but we turn the corner and are among mourners with big jewelry and two Mercedes-Benz sedans. A coffin is hauled into the church on the shoulders of men who could play parts in a refilming of The Godfather. Three women weep behind veils. I grab Ed's arm and we turn around quickly.

We've backtracked to visit Noto, not only for another taste of the interior of the country but for the taste of ice cream. A gourmet guide to Italy promises the best ice cream in Sicily is here on a back street. I try the tangerine, melon, and jasmine sorbets. Ed chooses almond, coffee, and pistachio gelato. In Italy, one always orders several flavors in the same cup. He tastes all of mine and I taste all of his. We're convinced. A cold slanted rain begins. We get our raincoats and umbrella out of the car and walk anyway. Might as well get soaked – who knows when we'll ever get back to Noto.

★

Briefly lost in Catania, we find the airport and fly out. Below us the coast gradually enlarges so that we see a slice of the eastern edge of the island. 'What are you writing?' I see Ed is making one of his lists.

'Reasons to come back – we didn't see the mosaics at Piazza Armerina, the Arab baths at Cefalù. I can't believe we didn't make it to Taormina. A week was short. Let's go to the Aeolian islands – for the name if nothing else – and Pantelleria for the *moscato* dessert wines. What else?'

A wisp of lemon scent escapes from my bag under the seat stuffed with lemon soap, a ceramic platter decorated with lemons and leaves, and a small bag of real lemons.

'More of the groves along the coast.' I remember the hills outside the Baroque towns, criss-crossed with intricate stone boundary walls. 'More of the inland part. We never even looked at tiles for the bathroom. And we have to go back to Siracusa; the map listed forty-eight points of interest. We didn't see half.' I glimpse the slopes of Mount Etna then we bank into clouds, losing Sicily entirely.

A SICILIAN MENU

After our trip to Sicily, we're inspired to adapt some of the tastes from that island to our own kitchen. We prepare a dinner for three Cortona friends. Oddly, not one has been to Sicily. We get a glimpse of how they feel about it from Massimo, one of our guests. We use the same plumber he does, and Ed asks him, 'You know that man who works for Carlo, the skinny one who talks so fast? Is he Italian?'

'Oh no,' Duilio answers, 'he's Sicilian.'

Ed lugged bottles of Moscato and Passito home in his carry-on bag, along with capers, almonds, and the marzipan fruits we couldn't resist. With dessert, we bring out a plate of them. Everyone admires the verisimilitude but at the end of the evening we still have the adorable peaches, pears, and plums.

For Sicilian recipes from the source, I've enjoyed *La*

Cucina Siciliana di Gangivecchio by Wanda and Giovanna Tornabene, which is published in English and adapted to American ingredients.

*

MENU

Caponata

I've made *caponata* for years. The Sicilian version was more flavorful than mine. Why? The concentrated tomato *estratto* (tomato paste made from sun-dried tomatoes) available in Sicily, a freer hand with seasoning, the saltiness of anchovies. Spread this on bread or crackers. It's one of those perfect *hors d'oeuvres* to have on hand for guests. At lunch, a couple of tablespoons turns a plain ham or tomato sandwich into something special, and it's also a great pasta sauce — just toss with *penne*.

Bake two medium-sized eggplants on a piece of foil in the oven at 350 degrees for half an hour. Coarsely chop ½ cup each of pitted green and black olives. Sauté one large chopped onion and three or four cloves of minced garlic. Cut the eggplants into small cubes, add to the onions and cook to blend. Lacking the intense tomato sauce of Sicily, add five or six minced sun-dried tomatoes to ½ cup of tomato paste and one cup of tomato sauce. Stir into eggplant mixture. Chop three or four anchovy fillets. Add those, 2 T. of capers, a handful of chopped parsley, and the chopped olives to the eggplant. Season with oregano, salt, and pepper. Like many tomato-based recipes, caponata is best if made a day early. It will keep in the fridge for a week. Makes about five cups, depending on the size of the eggplants.

*

Olive Piccanti

Mince two small hot peppers — one red, one green — and sauté with a small minced onion. Mix with two cups of large green olives, moisten with a little olive oil and lemon juice. Let rest in the fridge overnight.

*

Pasta al Limone

If I had to say what one ingredient I must have in the kitchen, it would be the lemon because the flavor, both assertive and enhancing, is like liquid sunshine going into the food. Anselmo brought me two lemon trees in pots. As an essential of the Italian garden, lemons are so valued that most old houses have a *limonaia*, a glass-walled room for storing the pots over the winter. Our *limonaia* functions as a storage room for mowers and tools but this winter reclaimed its function with the two pots taking a sunny spot. In spring we dragged them out in front of the house again, to a place near the kitchen door — very handy for grabbing one for this extremely easy and tasty pasta. When I make this in California, I often add a half pound of crab, but it's a marvelous pasta by itself. With a green salad, it's the lightest dinner imaginable, perfect the day after a crippling feast.

Boil pasta — spaghetti or tagliatelle — for six. Squeeze enough lemons for ½ cup of juice. Drain pasta, season, and toss with ½ cup of chopped Italian parsley, the lemon juice, and grated parmigiano to taste. If you like, sauté a pound of crabmeat in 2 T. of butter or olive oil. Add a big splash of white wine. Bring to a boil for an instant, stir the lemon juice mixture into the crab and toss with the pasta.

*

Sea Bass in a Salt Crust

Don't expect a salty fish – the crust seals in the juices but only slightly penetrates. In San Francisco, I go to a fish market on Clement Street for sea bass. They net the fish from a tank, then knock it on the head with a mallet. Not my favorite moment of shopping. Here, we are two hours from both the Mediterranean and the Adriatic. Fishmongers come to the Thursday market in Camucia where the fish are safely dead and on ice.

Ask the fishmonger to clean and prepare for cooking a large sea bass, about 3½ to 4 pounds. Dry the fish well and stuff the inside with slices of lemon, wands of rosemary, and a few sprigs of thyme. Mix the juice of two lemons with 6 T. olive oil and brush the fish all over. Season with pepper and thyme. To the remaining oil and lemon, add some chopped thyme and parsley and reserve this for serving later. For the crust, you'll need about 5 pounds of coarse salt, depending on the size of the fish. Layer the bottom of a baking dish (one that can go to the table as well) with an inch of salt. Place the fish on top then mound the rest of the salt over the fish, completely covering it. Pat in place around the fish. Make a mask of ¾ c. flour and enough water to thin the flour. Brush the salt with this mixture. Bake in a preheated, hot oven, 400 degrees, for 40 minutes, or until the salt looks toasted. Present the fish at the table, cracking or sawing into the hard crust, then take it back to the kitchen and remove the fish to a platter for serving. Heat and pour the reserved lemon and oil over the fish. Serves six generously.

*

Zucchini with Mint

Thinly slice or grate eight slender zucchini. If you grate, squeeze out the liquid. Quickly sauté in hot olive oil with some minced garlic. Stir in chopped parsley and mint, season with salt and pepper. Serve warm or at room temperature.

★

Lemon Pie with Roasted Almonds

I'll never forget the lemon pie of Erice. The crunch of almonds added a wonderful complement to the familiar, luscious textures of lemon meringue pie – the flaky pastry, airy meringue, and the creamy lemon custard. The almonds of Sicily have a perfume and a complex aftertaste. Because fresh nuts make all the difference, at home I order pecans from the South every fall and store the bags in the freezer. I can taste a change in the texture after a couple of months, but still, the nuts keep much better in the freezer. In San Francisco, we have access to fresh walnuts and almonds from California groves through the Saturday farmers' market. Here's my grandmother's lemon pie, enhanced with the Sicilian touch of almonds – and further enhanced when served with the fragrant Moscato of the islands off Sicily. Actually, it's my grandmother's sister Besta's recipe. Besta was otherwise known for her fuming blackberry cordials, which my father refused to drink for fear of going blind.

Beat the juice and zest of four lemons with 1½ cups of sugar. Mix 2 T. melted butter with 4 T. flour, ¼ t. of salt. Beat 4 egg yolks. Whip the yolks into the butter and flour and whisk in the juice and sugar. Gently pour in 2 cups of hot water, beating all along, and place on a moderate flame. Cook the custard until very thick, stirring constantly. Keep the flame adjusted so that the mixture cooks but doesn't boil. When thick, add 2 T. cream. Slightly cool. Separately beat 4 egg whites until stiff, whisking in 2 tablespoons of sugar at the end. Toast 1 cup of halved almonds in a 350-degree oven for five to seven minutes, shaking once or twice. Nothing is as easy to burn as nuts! Sprinkle them with a little sugar. Pour the lemon filling into your favorite baked pie shell, arrange nuts on top, then spread the egg whites in a swirling pattern and bake at 350 degrees until the meringue browns.

RESURRECTION

Beppe stops digging and cocks his head. '*Senta*,' listen, he says, '*Il cuculo*.' He removes his wool cap and runs his hand over his tight gray curls. 'They arrive for Easter.' The light two-note call of the cuckoo repeats. 'Exactly on time this year.'

With forbearance, Beppe is planting lavender along the walk to the lake view, where earlier he and Francesco installed five new cypress trees. Planting cypresses is important work but mere flowering bushes do not interest him. At his place, he and his wife hold to the separation of *campo* and *cortile*, field and courtyard. Flowers – woman's work. He's fast. Is it knowing exactly how to angle the shovel so that three or four movements are all it takes? I shake the plant from the plastic pot, and place it in the hole. Quickly, he pushes the shovel back and forth; it's done. While I seem to have to use my whole body to dig, I see him work with his shoulders, not with his lower body. Sort of the opposite of Latino dancers, who stay so still above the waist but are all action below. He lifts the shovel and shoves hard. No leaping on and off, wiggling it back and forth, no back-wrenching lifting of heavy soil. He raises it as easily as I lift a wooden spoon from cake batter. Whack! Down through the dirt. On to the next one.

Beppe was born in the isolated mountains east of Cortona. He has taken us to his now-abandoned childhood home, an aerie in a tiny *borgo* consisting of a cluster of small, almost windowless stone woodcutters' houses. All his sixty-odd years he has worked the land. Unlike Francesco who is tough (at eighty), wiry, and works with a concentrated vengeance, Beppe's way of working fascinates me. He's upright, and lean. His corduroys and sweater suspend loosely from him as though from a clothes hanger. He works with no wasted motions at a steady pace. I especially like to watch him swing the scythe through long grasses. His rhythm is like a pendulum; he could be marking time in a book of hours rather than cutting weeds.

At ten he pauses and takes a sack from the back of his new green Ape. Time for *spuntino*, a snack. He also takes out a jug covered with woven osier, which he fills with well water. He upends it and takes a long swig, proclaiming it '*Acqua buona*,' as he always does.

While he pauses, I haul water out to the twenty-five lavender plants. '*Un bel secchio d'acqua, signora*,' he calls to me. Idiomatically, he probably means just a good amount, but I hear him literally, a beautiful bucket of water, which makes the carrying easier. Beautiful water, I silently tell the plants, loosen your tight roots, trauma is over, you're home.

The car is full of five-gallon marguerites to be planted in the rose garden. I won't ask him to help me plant the smaller bedding flats or the geraniums for all the pots. The cosmos and hollyhock seeds I've started in the *limonaia* don't get his attention. He wouldn't refuse to help me plant, but he would be in mortal pain. I unload two marguerites. 'Would you mind helping me with these big ones?'

To my surprise, he smiles. 'Ah, Santa Margherita.' She is the loved patron saint of Cortona and still lies in a glass coffin in the church at the top of this hill. We intersperse her white flowers, about to bloom, with the well-established lavender and roses, softening the line of thorny roses just coming into leaf, and hiding their scrawny legs. Contrary to usual practice, which is to grow roses by themselves, I'm going to try filling the beds profusely and see what happens. '*Venerdì sera*,' Friday evening, 'at nine, a procession commencing at Santo Spirito goes up to Santa Margherita,' Beppe tells me. 'A long procession.'

Today is Maundy Thursday. The shops in town are filling with life-sized chocolate hens, huge eggs wrapped in bright foil with prizes inside, a mild display compared with Sicily. 'What do you eat on Easter?' I want to know. But I'm thinking, what does 'maundy' mean?

'*Tortellini*, a good shoulder of lamb, potatoes, spinach, *insalata*, a little wine.' Beppe heads up to the olive terraces to help Ed, relieved to quit the *fiori*, I am sure. I bring more beautiful water to Santa Margherita's namesakes. I open the trunk and take out lobelia, ageratum, snap-dragons, dahlias, and the ashen-lavender flowers no one knew the name of. I have a bag of sunflower seeds and packets of creeping thyme, trailing nasturtium, and morning glory. Ed will help me plant them tomorrow. Beside a climbing yellow rose on the main wall (called the Polish

Wall because it was restored by Polish workers), I plant the bush with velvety, purse-shaped pink flowers. No one at the nursery knew the name of them either.

Death is coming again to the pinned body on the cross. Strange, I always thought it was important whether or not I believed in the factual truth of 'on the third day He rose.' My hand around the ball of pale roots, crescents of dirt under my nails, I'm content to believe or not, but to feel a rise in my blood as the sun makes tracks across the equator bringing back my favorite season, the long summer days.

Maybe we were smart enough to make the gods. What better way to explain the darkest moment of the year and how it swings toward light, except by the metaphor of a birth. How to face the incredible rejuvenescence of spring except in a story of a miraculous rising. 'Well,' I'm quoting myself aloud to the drooping leaves of the nameless pink plant,

> . . . if there's a God dotting lines along spheres for
>   the sun
> to cross, good. And if not, we are more
> than we know. I can hold the windflower and
> the crucifix nail in mind at once. I wanted truth
> and find we form the words we need from flesh.

I dig a hole for a gray-green santolina, which they used to toss on the cathedral floors in the Middle Ages to keep down the human smells.

I splash water around the roots. 'Rise,' I command.

★

Hail — banging my tender new plants, hopping off the stone wall like popcorn. This tempestuous weather for

Good Friday – where is *primavera* now? The hail stops and wind drives rain sideways against the house so that it seeps in my study window, soaking my notes on Sicilian history into swirls of blue ink that look more like tide pools than facts about the Normans. Several louvers sail into the linden trees, smacking the stone wall. From the bedroom window, I watch columns of rain 'walking' across the valley, heading straight for us. When sun breaks through, we dash out the door, trowels in hand, plant flowers until rain starts to pelt again and we're driven back to the front door, where we dry out under the balcony.

By evening the air clears. We're stir-crazy and go into town for a *prosecco*. The streets are packed – everyone from miles around has come in for the procession of the stations of the cross. We try four *trattorie* before we find a table at the cozy Osteria, where opera arias fill the small room, and I can have the *strozzapreti*, priest-strangler, pasta with a cream and hazelnut sauce. The waitress, Cinzia, seems always amused. She gestures with her hands constantly, lights the candle with a large swoop. The owner glides around serenely. Once I asked her if she was local and she said no, she was from Castiglion Fiorentino, five miles away. Ed is about to order a bottle of wine but Cinzia puts her finger to her lips, raises her shoulders almost to her ears, and points with her other hand to a Chianti that is half the price. The other, a 1994 – she shakes her head and ticks her finger at him. Ed orders the homey beef braised in red wine, a true *casalinga* dish. We split a chocolate charlotte and think with longing of the peach charlotte they make in summer.

Down the hill to Santo Spirito, a church I've never seen open. The doorway is outlined in lights and, as we arrive, eight robed and hooded men are hoisting the crucified figure of Christ onto their shoulders. They look scary to me; I flash on the robes worn by the Ku Klux Klan. As a child, I once saw a Klan meeting around a bonfire. 'What is that?' I asked my mother. 'A bunch of old fools,' she answered. 'And there are no fools like old fools.' I remember I've seen these odd peaked hoods in Italian paintings, worn by plague doctors along with bird-beak masks. Behind them, eight women are shouldering a figure of grieving Mary, who looks to weigh about a ton. They walk out, accompanied by people carrying torches and we join the procession up Via Guelfa. The town band is playing a tinny dirge. As we go, more people join us.

At each church, we stop. More sacred figures are brought out and blend into the procession through the darkened town. Some people sing with the music and many carry candles, sheltering the flame with a cupped hand. Through roving clouds, the full moon comes and goes. I have the strange feeling of having slipped behind a curtain of time and entered a place and ceremony both alien and familiar to me. The music sounds atonal, shrill, almost something you could imagine hearing after death. The faces of the people stay private, except for the teenagers who are jostling and jabbing each other. We're all bundled in shapeless raincoats and scarves, further erasing connections with present time. Without the signs of haircuts and glasses, we almost could be in the fifteenth century.

For most local people, this service is one of their yearly rituals. I'm short on rituals myself, especially ones involving torches, hoods, and the agonized Christ aloft in the streets. Good Friday, I realize, is major. In the South of my particular childhood, all emphasis was on Easter Sunday, with the main event for me being my carefully chosen new dress and shoes. I remember the thrill of a blue organdy with hand-embroidered daisies around the hem and on the ends of the sash.

When they start to climb through upper Cortona, along the steep way of the stations of the cross made in mosaic by Gino Severini, and on to Santa Margherita, we drop out and go to a bar for coffee. The raw wind has numbed my ears. How can they carry those beams on their shoulders? Quite quickly it seems, we hear the mournful music again and we rush uphill to join at San Marco, then wind back to the *piazza*, where the bishop delivers a long sermon. It's almost midnight by now and we have a mile to walk back to Bramasole in the dark so we leave the throngs of people who have more stamina than we.

*

Into the spirit of the Easter festivals, we decide to drive over on Easter Saturday to Sansepolcro, Piero della Francesca's hometown, to see his stupendous painting of the resurrection. The countryside between here and there rolls — green valleys and wooded hillsides, a curvy road interrupted by few villages, bucolic Tuscany. Roadsides are flush with dandelions and purple wildflowers, the first poppies are springing out in the grasses, wisteria is climbing over pale stone farmhouses. In this blissful landscape, we are suddenly stunned to see a tall African woman, dressed in tight striped pants and a revealing red shirt, standing on the roadside. Around the next bend we see another, this one equally statuesque and curvaceous. She stares. Every few hundred feet these women are stationed along the road. They stand or sit on wooden crates. One eats from a bag of potato chips. Then we see a parked car, with no woman near her crate. This is surreal. Prostitutes out in rural Italy. Some of the women are regal, with elaborate plaited hair and full red lips. All are wearing red and black.

Who would stop? Surely not local men, who might be seen by their neighbors. And this isn't exactly the autostrada. How many delivery trucks could there be? We must have passed fifteen women just poised on the side of the road, more women than cars. Bizarre and disturbing because this makes no sense in the Arcadian valley of the upper Tiber, which appears in the backgrounds of paintings, this dreamy route known as the Piero della Francesca trail.

I like to come to Sansepolcro. On the way we stop either at Anghiari, for its pitched medieval streets, or at Monterchi, an intact and tiny hilltown with a shady *piazza*. Piero della Francesca's mother was from Monterchi so the presence of his painting *Madonna del Parto*, Mary about to give birth, has a personal significance. No longer in the cemetery chapel, the painting is now housed in a building of its own just below the town walls. It has lost some of its former allure because it is now behind glass, and it has lost the tension that came from its location in a place of death. But, still she is staring down, not only remote and austere, as some have described her, but with a quiet inward focus. I don't know of another painting of the Madonna about to give birth. Her hand rests lightly on her stomach. Has she just felt the first mild contraction? It's an unnerving painting — the moment women recognize, when nothing ever will be the same again.

We're so used to hills. The town named for the Holy Sepulchre is flat. It's easy to imagine Piero della Francesca walking diagonally across the *piazza*. His work was here, in Urbino, and in Arezzo. He was a strictly provincial person creating art at the highest level. Walking on Sansepolcro's level streets, feeling the linear perspectives of the *piazza*, and the shadows cutting across upright buildings, I can sense how the town layout influenced his vision.

In the Museo Civico, which we usually find almost empty, some Italian tourists have had the same urge to visit today. It's a typical regional collection, except that the local painter was Piero della Francesca and three of his major works hang in a room of their own, among rooms of prehistoric axes, collections of small boxes, and a couple of dozen other paintings, some of which are quite interesting in themselves but suffer from proximity to Piero. A plump little boy pulls and pulls on his mother's arm, begging to go eat. She's trying to look at the art. He pulls again and she knocks him sharply on the skull with her knuckle and points to a devil in one of the paintings.

Ed and I look first at the *Madonna della Misericordia* – same face as Mary in Monterchi but wearier, tighter. She has gathered many under the protection of her outspread cloak. A standard image in Italian painting, it must have been comforting when the Guelphs and Ghibellines were pouring boiling oil on each other and warring mercenaries ripped around the countryside pillaging and burning. There's still comfort in it.

The plump little boy leans against his mother's leg, pulling her skirt around him. The room empties, except for a man looking earnestly at Piero's *San Giuliano*, with his puzzled – or is it lost – expression.

Ed and I sit down in front of the famous *Resurrection*. Christ, emerging from the tomb, is draped in a chalky pink shroud, while below him, four guards are sleeping. The second one from the left, the security woman tells me, is a self-portrait of Piero. He looks the soundest asleep of all. 'And look,' she points at his throat, '*gozzo*.' I have no idea what that word is but see immediately: goiter. I've always admired Piero's necks on women. Odd to see that his own had an unnatural bulge. When he lived, the local water lacked iodine. He must have been a man of no vanity not to have edited the disfiguring goiter from his portrait. Behind Christ, we see a landscape, sere on the left, and coming into spring on the right. The composition is simple, the power palpable. 'His foot looks as big as yours,' I tell Ed. The body is lovingly painted. A muscular man in his physical glory. I wonder if T. S. Eliot had this image in mind when he wrote the line, 'In the juvenescence of the year came Christ the tiger.' He has raised himself with force from the sepulchre. The pallor of the tomb is not on his flushed cheeks and sensuous lips.

Kenneth Clark's often-cited perception of this painting is close to the heart of its strange emotional magnetism: 'This country God, who rises in the grey light while human beings are still asleep, has been worshiped ever since man first knew that the seed is not dead in the winter earth, but will force its way upwards through an iron crust. Later, He will become a god of rejoicing but His first emergence is painful and involuntary. He seems to be part of the dream which lies so heavily on the sleeping soldiers, and has Himself the doomed and distant gaze of the somnambulist.'

'He emanates the same mystery as his *Madonna del Parto*,' Ed notices. Yes, he's looking at what we can't see.

Driving home, the women along the road are still out, casing cars as they pass. I can read nothing in their eyes. The tragedy, surely there is one, does not show. We turn off to take a shortcut and are relieved not to pass these women again. There are violets, hawthorn, plum trees, and quince to see, spring waterfalls slushing over the rocks, and bare deciduous trees glowing red with buds. They don't erase the brutal fact of women for sale along the road nor do they erase the flip-side connection with the stations of the cross.

Ed zips around curves; we don't pass a car for miles. We're rushing back for the opening of our friend Celia's paintings at a gallery in Cortona. The small room is so packed with people that it's hard to see the bright blue and yellow paintings of flowers. Trays and trays of food go around, wine is flowing, everyone wishes Celia well. Vittorio, her husband, comes over to us with a plate of slivered truffle *crostini*. Ed asks him about the women on the road. 'They're Nigerian. I know you are shocked. They are brought in by the Russian Mafia. They promise them modeling jobs, then this happens.'

'The Russian Mafia in rural Tuscany? You can't be serious,' Ed says. 'Why don't the police round up the women, try to send them home?'

Vittorio shrugs. 'Prostitution is not illegal. Pimping is but it's hard to catch them in the act. They know when the police are coming and scatter.'

'How?'

'Oh, cell phones. Some guy is probably in the village – sees who's heading down the road.'

'How do they have that much business on such a road?'

'I don't know but people say there's plenty.'

Antonio comes over and the subject shifts. I have questions. On the way into town, I saw a scrawled sign on the door to San Filippo announcing the blessing of the eggs from four to five at San Domenico, and five to six at San Filippo. Vittorio explains that Easter Breakfast is the one time a year when Italians abandon their quick espresso habit and prepare a huge, American-style breakfast. The day before, the eggs, as symbols of rebirth, are taken to the church to be blessed. 'Easter week is also when the priest comes by to bless the house. Everyone does a gigantic cleaning for it. He will bless the eggs then, too.'

'We did that in Winona,' Ed remembers. 'After my mother cleaned the house, she sprinkled holy water on the beds to protect us, then the priest came to bless the house.'

'Did you have your house blessed, Antonio?' He lives alone and his girlfriend refuses to stay there because of the '*confusione*.' He just smiles.

I never knew Ed slept in a blessed bed. Maybe that explains him.

★

Easter itself is a peaceful day. In my favorite church, San Cristoforo, a red basket of round buns is passed out to the twenty or so worshipers. Bread of life. The priest blesses and shakes a few drops of holy water over them. One woman brings her own basket of bread for her Easter dinner and asks for blessings on it, too.

Many who shouldered those figures through the town must be groaning under heating pads. We take pots of pink hydrangeas to Donatella and to Anselmo, and see to our embarrassment that they already have several, as well as mounds of chocolate.

Families are gathering around long tables and someone – not I – is bringing out the platter of lamb ringed with rosemary. I'm happy not to have cooked all day, happy not to serve forth, happy not to have so many dirty dishes that they must be taken outside and stacked on the wall. Another time, *va bene*. Tonight, we're alone. Because they are so fresh, we have a bowl of peas with plenty of pepper and a hunk of butter melting into them. A lovely first course. A bottle of clean white wine, veal chops, and a salad of wild greens 'married,' as the Italians say, to our oil and a little fifty-year-old balsamic, so precious that I sprinkle the elixir onto the lettuces with an eye-dropper.

Since Ed is Catholic, I expect him to know everything about the liturgical year. 'What does "Maundy" mean?'

'Um . . . I think mandate comes from the same Latin root.'

'What was the mandate on Thursday?'

'To wash the feet of the poor? Seems like that was it. From Mary Magdalene washing Jesus's feet.'

'Remember that small, intense Piero della Francesca fresco of her with her hair still wet in the Arezzo cathedral? It's as intimate a look at her as his Jesus just rising. Too bad it doesn't hang near his *Resurrection*.'

'Mary Magdalene comes to mind when I think about that music in the procession Friday night.'

'Why?' I'm waiting. Having grown up in a very Polish Catholic church where he served as an altar boy for years, Ed isn't as mystified by rituals as I am.

'Well, the word "maudlin" comes to mind – and "maudlin" comes from "Magdalene."'

'Those cross-bearers from Friday night probably could use some attention to their feet about now.' I think of the displaced women on the road to Sansepolcro. 'Were there the same number of prostitutes as there are stations of the cross?'

Ed shakes his head. 'I'm glad Easter is over. Now it can just be spring.'

FOLLOWING SPRING: THE WATERY VENETO

Infatuated with Italian spring, we follow it north to the Veneto in April. I am returning to Venice, after an absence of twenty-five years. As we drive into the flat, big-sky landscape, I'm reeling through my earlier visits. Slippery, slippery time – the interim slides away; Venice lives close in memory. I am puzzled by the long interval, equally puzzled by the particular allure of Venice. I've read that bees, their stomachs full of nectar, have magnetic forces in their brains which lead them to the hive – I feel that way toward Venice. Flamboyant and decadent, it is still to me a sacred city. I'm a fool for beauty, and its poise on the edge, facing the exotic east, with its back turned to the rest of Europe, adds to the attraction. I had not meant to stay away so long. There's more to the allure – something I've never been able to articulate for myself, something I've never seen or read, out of all the books and images of Venice. What is it?

★

Only a few hours northeast of Cortona we are entering a different spring. People with seasonal allergies must go mad here. If we park the car for an hour, we find it covered with yellow, sticky pollen. Whorls of airy white puffs blow across the windshield and tractors spume dust in the fields. Breezes send clouds of gold dust from the pines' white candles and cones. The new green of leaves and crops seems to reflect in the air, giving it a watery tinge; we are driving through an aquarium light.

Near the port of Chioggia, south of Venice, the land turns marshy. Reedy shores wave and blur into water. I always have loved the smell of marshes. My early summers were spent on the Georgia sea islands, still one of my favorite landscapes. Grasses growing out of the sea. Land that is tidal, the slick creatures of both land and water, the thrill of what looked like a log suddenly coming alive and opening hilarious jaws. A salty, iodine, rotting, fresh smell signaled summer and freedom. Packed in the Oldsmobile with my two sisters, Willie Bell, records, toys, clothes, and my mother (my father was driven separately by an employee so as to avoid our chaos), I leaned out the window like a dog, my hair springing into curls, waiting for the first scent. No one seemed enchanted in the least when I began to quote the Georgia poet Sidney Lanier's 'The Marshes of Glenn,' which we were forced to memorize in endless stanzas in the fifth grade. I imitated the declamatory style of my teacher Miss Lake:

As the marsh-hen secretly builds on the watery sod,
Behold I will build me a nest on the greatness of
    God.

I will fly in the greatness of God as the marsh-hen
    flies
In the freedom that fills all the space 'twixt the marsh
    and the skies:
By so many roots as the marsh-grass sends in the sod
I will heartily lay me a-hold on the greatness of God:
Oh, like to the greatness of God is the greatness
    within
The range of the marshes, the liberal marshes of
    Glenn.

'Can't you make her stop,' my sister said. She was turning down page corners in *Mademoiselle*, already planning
her clothes for college in the fall. Louder, I shouted:

How still the plains of the waters be!
The tide is in his ecstasy.
The tide is at his highest height:
And it is night.

I loved that chopped-off last line. My other sister
remembered that the Marshes of Glenn ran red with blood
in some war. My mother began to sing 'You Are My
Sunshine,' which I hated. I rolled down the window again
and let the smell wash my face until we entered the
sulphur stink of the paper mills.

Marshes, islands, lagoons – the smell of old landscapes
where water will have its way. These marshes, too, probably have run red with blood from time to time. Those
Doges of Venice did not govern with peace in mind.
Chioggia doesn't rate much mention in the guides. We
take to it immediately as a racy, working-class version of
Venice. Like its elegant cousin, Chioggia stands on low
land with canals and medieval rabbit-warren *vicoli*, narrow

streets, leading to arching footbridges. Flag-bright colors of fishing boats repeat in the waters. People crowd the wide main street's cafés and shops. The decline of the birth rate currently experienced in Italy must not apply here. Out for afternoon shopping, many young women push strollers, sometimes with two tiny children in tandem. I hope they rotate who's first in the stroller. I would hate for my first world view to be the back of my little brother's head. Fish restaurants cluster near the harbor. How fresh can fish get? We see a man carrying two buckets, fish on top still flapping their tails. Lines of bright laundry string across canals: yellow-striped towels, turquoise blouse, red pants, flowered sheets, quite colossal bras, and a few sad pairs of graying panties. Through a kitchen window I see a woman moistening her hands with olive oil so working with the pasta will be easier.

After cross-checking the Veneto in several Italian guidebooks, Ed has pinpointed a lauded restaurant with rooms upstairs. We're delaying Venice, saving it for last. The restaurant is in the village of Lorregia, our head-quarters for a couple of days. En route from Chioggia, the brakes start to grate. Not a good sound. At the hotel we ask about an Alfa dealer but it is late in the day. Unfortunately, tomorrow is Sunday. Ed asks if he could call, just in case someone's still there. If we can't take the car until Monday, we'll be stuck and all we can do is eat in the lauded restaurant. 'Bring it over *subito*. I'll take a look at it,' the mechanic responds.

The woman at the desk, one of the owners, becomes concerned. 'How will you return? That's thirteen kilo-meters from here.' Ed asks if there's a place to rent a car if he needs one. 'Closed. They close at five on Saturday. You call me from the mechanic. I'll see.'

Where cars are concerned, my participation in the

equality of women stops. I want a car to turn on, go. I don't like looking under the hood. All that convoluted metal and the battery that could send you over the moon if you touch the wrong plugs. I trail upstairs and Ed takes off.

The room is severely plain but immaculate. Checking into a hotel, sometimes austere as a monk's cell, sometimes grandly luxurious, I always revel in an anonymous sense of freedom, particularly if I am alone. I take off the bed-spread, turn back the sheets, look out the windows, open the drawers and minibar, feel the towels, examine the lotion and shampoo, the glass jar of cotton balls, or what-ever amenities are offered. I'm the opposite of my fastidious aunt Hazel, who travelled with her own pillow and a spray can of Lysol disinfectant. She held it over her head, dousing every available surface, backing out of the room for an hour while all the germs died. I like the leather folders of nice writing paper, the pad by the phone with the pencil just sharpened, the slick magazines about the town, the terrycloth robes. This room, however, has few of these checkpoints to explore. It does have a good shower, and I have a good book.

Where is Ed? An hour goes by, then another. Finally, he comes in and tosses keys on the bed. 'We now have a Fiat Panda until Tuesday morning. The Alfa's brakes need parts and the mechanic will have to find them in Treviso Monday.'

'What was wrong?'

'Nothing drastic. Wear and tear. He can finish early Tuesday morning. You would not believe how nice the signora was. I called the hotel and she came and got me, then she drove me umpteen miles, at least ten, in the other direction where she arranged for me to rent a car from the Fiat dealer. It was in some industrial zone. We'll probably never find it again.'

'How incredible.'

'She drives like a real Italian,' he said with admiration. He opens the window and the earthy aroma of *funghi porcini* sizzling in hot oil causes him to shower quickly and change into his blue shirt. We descend to the dining room. Because of the adventure, we are treated like old friends. Everyone in the family knows about the *problema* with the Alfa. Glasses of *prosecco* are brought to us and everyone agrees that the Alfa is a fine car, that Italian cars are superior in design to any in the world.

'We're totally in your hands,' Ed tells the waiter. 'Bring us your favorite local wines, the specialties of the house.' This is Ed's favorite way to dine, to give the chef the compliment from the outset of selecting our menu. A more trepid diner, I'm not always thrilled when the sliced *lardo*, basically a buttery fat, or sea urchins are presented. I hope we will not be served the *medaglioni d'asino*, which I spied on the menu. Medallions of donkey I can live without.

The waiter invites us to follow him downstairs. Their wine cellar is an arched brick cave filled with racks of wine. He pokes around and pulls out a bottle of Amarone, one of my favorite wines for its dark taste.

The courses start to roll out. Fortunately, we're served pasta with vegetables, ordinary enough but special because the pasta is made here and the vegetables are perfectly cooked. The waiter comes around with *gnocchetti*, little *gnocchi*, also with vegetables, to give us a taste. The provincial dining room fills with local people dressed out of designer shops. The prosperity in the Veneto, even compared with the high standard of living in Tuscany, is simply astonishing. I've never seen a general population so well-off. A movement has been long simmering to separate this area from the rest of Italy. Economically, it is a country apart, light years from Sicily. I wonder how many of these Gucci- and Escada-clad women have ordered the donkey. Roast rabbit, the next course, is cooked in wine and tomatoes, pine nuts, and currants. The slight raisiny taste just matches the wine. The family makes all the desserts and they look tempting but we order a selection of local cheeses. At the next table, one of the lovely couples is dining with their son, perhaps nine or ten. We'd noticed him examining the menu carefully and asking questions of the waiter. The parents looked bored. He ate with gusto, looking at the plates each time the waiter passed their table. His father poured him a half-inch of wine, then added mineral water to the glass. Now we watch him examine the peach bavarian, the strawberry pie on the dessert cart then plop back in his chair and order the cheeses. We're impressed. A natural gourmand.

Since we're near the source, Ed has a glass of *grappa*. How divine to hoist ourselves upstairs to bed.

*

I could move today into the Villa Barbaro, one of Palladio's happiest moments. The garden is bare, mostly just a stretch of lawn, but the house remains felicitous, with its playful Veronese frescoes and intimate rooms. The exterior invites you, unlike some of Palladio's dour houses which seem swamped by architecture with a capital A. This one sings. Scuffing through in the felt slippers provided for visitors, I see that the house is actually still lived in. Two roped-off rooms are filled with family photos and reading lamps beside capacious chairs. Could that be the electric bill on the desk? How odd to vacate on Sunday afternoon, so that we teeming hordes can gaze on their frescoes, admire the view, imagine ourselves penning a note at the gilded secretary.

The Panda seems to know the roads. Somehow we

don't get lost. Bassano, Treviso, Castelfranco. We don't encounter any of those mysterious signs we face so frequently in Tuscany that say *tutte le direzioni* – all directions – and point both right and left. We park outside Asolo and walk in because cars aren't allowed to enter this fantasyland, home of one of my favorite writers. No, not Robert Browning, who immortalized the town in his poem, 'Asolando,' but Freya Stark, who lived here when not on her adventurous travels in Iraq and Persia. What a contrast to her journeys; Asolo makes no demands. I feel that I'm in an older, Italian version of Carmel, California, with many secret gardens, vine-covered gates, and charming houses. A place you could imagine retiring someday, if only you had tons of *lire*. Roses are tumbling in Asolo. Every few steps, new soft fragrances fall in your face from the walls above. I don't look for her house or grave. I am just curious to see where she walked during her many last years after writing her books. Surely she took her tea near the fountain. I'm quite certain she shopped at the paper store in town. I don't emerge until I have bought my next blank book, a yellow one to replace the blue book, where I wrote about our first experiences in Cortona, and a photograph album with a cover of painted wildflowers.

I resist the tiny bottles of lavender, indigo, and green ink sealed with wax, and the rows of expensive pens. The sensuous pleasure of good writing materials is like no other. The attraction links to the excitement of school supplies purchased every year for so long. Few things I've bought exceed the delight of yellow legal pads, spiraled and colored index cards, five-subject notebooks, and leather three-ring binders. And if there's a red satchel with compartments and zippered pockets, so much the better.

The first experience of these joys comes back – the supply cabinet at my father's mill office. He let me take stenographers' pads with a line down the middle, a red pencil that could be sharpened right there in a machine with a dial which rotated to accommodate different pencil sizes. On one of those Saturday mornings when I rode out to the mill with him, I became fascinated with a large gray staple gun. I liked the ka-clink sound it made. My teacher had told our kindergarten class that hair and nails have no feeling, so I put my left thumb in place and pressed hard, sending excruciating bolts of pain through my thin nail. I was stapled. My father said some horrible words and pried out the staple with a screwdriver. The body remembers everything. I still can shudder at the pain. 'See this thumbnail?' I hold it up for Ed.

'Yes − what?'

'Can you see the break in the crescent moon?'

He holds it next to the other one. 'I guess so.' I tell him the story. 'Ouch. You make my knees weak. What made you think of that here?'

'Wanting the lavender ink but being afraid it would leak in the suitcase.'

'Wait a minute. Is that old clunker of a stapler you use at home the same one from your father's office?'

'Of course.'

★

For two easy days we drive about, returning at night to our little outpost of fantastic food. The hallway of the inn is lined with family photographs − men home from war, babies in arms, group portraits. We love this intimate atmosphere and the warmth the family projects as we come and go. Townspeople gather in the bar, banging glasses, watching soccer on TV, exchanging the news about the daughter's first communion and the idiot who backed into the sycamore at the post office. We participate peripherally, briefly, in the ongoing life of this place. Ed tells them we'll be back to try the fall menu someday. As we leave, he looks sorrowfully into the dining room.

★

The *primo* approach to Venice is not Marco Polo airport or the train; having driven around in the Veneto, and stopped in Chioggia, I've absorbed a new sense of this watery location. I'd always thought of Venice as a risen place which not long ago was sinking and might sink again. Wandering in the Veneto, I absorbed the real *geographical* sense, and I'm more awed than ever. The land under Venice is often little more than the sandbars I used to wade to at St Simon's Island. The feat of establishing an empire on this marshy archipelago shows that the settlers were strong on imagination. They wove willow dikes to keep away the sea. What madness! Foundations were built on wooden poles, driven all the way through the water and silty land to the packed clay substrata. The hundreds of tiny islands were later linked by bridges, giving the impression of canals carved out of a single island. Some waterways were filled in, further changing the reality of the actual topography.

Instinct tells me that by learning to 'read' the watery map, I may be able to feel my way toward the source of this place's hold on my imagination. I know already that it's not only Venice's extravagant beauty that pulls me. My clues toward a solution may begin with the realization that Venice's origins are *against all rational thinking*: Build your church – or your insurance company – on a rock.

Ed and I park in a remote garage, leaving most of our luggage in the trunk, and board a boat, which crosses a flat stretch of water and soon enters the Grand Canal. Holy

106

Toledo! Holy of holies! Memory has abstracted the city into watercolor scenes. The reality of the dips of the boat, the working gondolas laden with fruit and cases of *acqua minerale*, the construction barges piled with boards and sacks of concrete, the mind-stopping, stupendous, fairy-tale, solid beauty of the *palazzi* lining the canal and reflecting in the water – I stand at the rail biting hard on the knuckle of my right forefinger, an old habit that returns when I am knocked silent. The beauty does not just pass before your eyes. It ravishes. I begin to feel the elation that a traveller experiences when in the presence of a place supremely itself.

Arriving in Venice seems like the most natural act in the world. Is it this way for everyone? The place is so thoroughly known through film, photographs, calendars, books. Is there another layer to this easy familiarity?

I'm feeling a rush of memories and I want them to end by the time my foot steps out on the *fondamenta*. Venice was 'our' city, my former husband's and mine. Although we went only twice, we'd loved the small flower-filled hotel, where we pulled the mattress off the bed when it squeaked. Our gondolier had a piercingly sweet voice and glided through canals, ducking under bridges. Well, yes, he did sing 'O Sole Mio,' but he also had a good fling with 'Nessun Dorma.' At the early morning market, a vendor built a ziggurat of ripe white peaches. Every fish in the Adriatic seemed to be lined up glassy-eyed on ice, ready for the women with their baskets, and restaurant owners trailed by minions who balanced crates on their shoulders. Because I am cursed with a bird phobia, I hovered under the arcades of the Piazza San Marco while my husband walked among the thousands of pigeons then came back to describe the *piazza* from the perspective I never will see. We found the paper store with blank books bound in vellum and marbled paper. We tried the pasta with squid in its own ink. I loved the cycle of Saint Ursula paintings by Carpaccio. Ursula, lying there in a tall bed, dreaming, while the angel bringing the palm of her martyrdom steps through her threshold. Four years later we returned with our daughter and had the pleasure of being in her happy company on those canals. She wore a straw gondolier hat, ran to pet cats who wouldn't be petted, left her drawstring pocketbook on a *vaporetto* and cried for the loss of a dozen pieces of broken glass she'd collected on the trip. Odd what fragments of memory stay. I don't remember how she liked the lagoon, the bridges, the *piazza*. She loved the hotel tub's brass swan handles and spout. Strange how memory can reach *around* years and reconnect to the place and time where old loves are still intact. The memory rush subsides.

Many high waters have washed through Venice since then. Now I am back. With Ed. A different life. We'll make our own way here. I look over at Ed and have to laugh. He has the deep-space stare. 'Venice,' I say and he nods.

He's already tan, and leaning on the rail in his yellow linen shirt, with the pure glory of Venice racing behind him, I think he looks like someone I'd like to run off with, if I already hadn't. The prospect of days with *him* roving around Venice: *bella, bella*. As we enter the widest part of the Grand Canal, it seems to tilt. Soon we're bumping into the dock. 'Heaven. Unbelievable.'

'Yes, if there's no Venice in the real heaven, I don't want to go there.'

★

The hotel, a former convent tower, faces a harmonious *piazza* which used to be water but somewhere along the way was filled. Tower means romantic and also narrow. The frou-frou furniture and tiny room seem very Venetian to me. Ed looks somewhat like Gulliver in this Lilliputian space.

We've arrived in time for the shadow rounds. An Italian friend in Cortona told us about the Venetian late afternoon 'bar-hopping' custom. Tucked away in the neighborhoods are small bars, often with a counter opening to the street. Neighbors gather for an *ombra*, shadow, a half-glass of wine. The 'shadow' comes from the original gathering place in the shadow of San Marco. People visit, sip, then wander on to the next bar. Often those who join don't know each other outside this custom. 'He's a friend from the shadow rounds,' Venetians say to each other. *Antipasti* are laid out on the counter, savory nibbles somewhat like *tapas*: polenta squares with fish inside, *moleche*, tiny grilled crabs eaten whole, fried anchovies, and various preparations of *baccalà*, dried cod. They visit two or three then go home. The groups keep reconfiguring. We stop at one bar with so many delicious *antipasti* that we decide to stay for dinner in the back room. We try the *sarde in soar*, fresh sardines in a sweet and sour sauce, a dish the old Doges must have enjoyed. Venice has a bad reputation for restaurants but in the neighborhoods, the authentic dishes and the freshest seafood are served in intimate *trattorie*. The classic Venetian repertoire includes calf liver with onions (forget college dining room liver and onions); risotto or pasta with squid in its ink; that great comfort food *risi e bisi*, rice and peas; as well as fish with red radicchio, both grilled; fish soups; various shellfish with pastas; fish, fish, fish. Venice and Sicily, opposite in most ways, share the boon of the sea, and the intricate use of seasoning and spices supplied by the history of domination by many nations.

We leave the map in the room. We just walk. Walk and walk. Away from the main sights, the Venetian neighborhoods are endlessly appealing. We happen upon a *squero*, a yard where gondolas are made and repaired. A man brushes on black paint and I remember that once, before plague and sumptuary laws, gondolas were decorated in many colors. I want Ed to see Carpaccio's nine paintings of the Legend of Saint Ursula. She's sweetly asleep in a four-poster bed, a little dog on the floor, potted plants on the windowsills. The other side of the bed is conspicuously empty. She has, I remember, rejected Conan as her groom in favor of virginity. At her door, the hesitant angel will cross the threshold, touch her shoulder and hand her the palm of martyrdom. Irrationally, I say, 'She's still sleeping, all these years I've been gone.'

In small shops, which make me think of medieval guilds, we see supple cutwork velvet, candied fruit, bracelets of gold chunks, porphyry heads, and colored blown glass. I long to go in the houses, experience from the inside what it's like to have high tide lapping at the lower floor, smell the damp marble, see the rippling shadows of the water on painted ceilings, push back faded brocades to let in the sun.

★

When we find ourselves at the quay where you catch a boat for the islands, we jump on. The ports of call ten or twenty minutes away are remote from Venice in time and space. Poor little reedy islands barely out of the water — this is what supports the splendors of Venice, too. We pass Murano, don't stop at a farm island, and disembark at Torcello.

From the dock we follow a brackish canal to the

remains of a settlement. The deserted town gives me the feeling that all the inhabitants have fled. Malaria did devastate the population but that was centuries ago. The Romanesque-Byzantine church of Santa Fosca was a late-comer to the island in the eleventh century. If I could draw, I would take out my pastel pencils right here and sketch its delicate arched portico. The cathedral, oldest building in the whole Venetian lagoon, was started in 639. From then until the fourteenth century, Torcello thrived. Twenty thousand people lived here, most of them raising sheep and making wool. Not until the early eleventh century were the mosaics laid in the floor of the cathedral. Others later were added to walls, including the standing Madonna holding the Infant, in a field of golden tesserae. Of the thousands and thousands of Madonnas, this is definitely one to see. So is the Last Judgement, with its spooky mosaic skeletons.

After the fourteenth century, Torcello began a long slide into its current decline. I read that sixty people live here but we don't see anyone except at makeshift tents where touristy souvenirs are sold. 'What a great place to make a movie.' Ed is looking at a wild garden filled with statues, the exotic rounded forms of the cathedral, the blond light.

'What kind?'

'One with nothing of modern time in it. We're in a serious warp. But look, that *casa* is being restored. Maybe some of the workers who commute from Mestre to Venice will move here. Instead of breathing factory fumes they could have land. It would be a great place to live.'

'If you had a boat.'

'And a garden, and a wine cellar, and a good library.'

'Next time I'd like to spend the night at the *locanda*. Even the few tourists would take the last boat back to

Venice. Islands at night . . .' He doesn't finish his sentence.

★

Crowded, lively Burano is the polar opposite of Torcello; it's jarring to arrive after the quiet, and then impossible not to love the bright houses along the canals. I find myself taking pictures of a flowery balcony on a purple house, fishing nets draped to dry over the prow of a yellow boat, a woman in a blue-framed window shaking out a red tea towel. All the colors you'd never paint your house look marvelously festive here. It's as if every resident rushed off to a giant paint sale for bargains on pumpkin and lavender. Many awful paintings must have commenced with a day-trip to Burano. The village feels buoyant and playful. We have a picnic on the grass overlooking the water, then board the boat that plies these islands, passing San Michele, the cemetery, on the way back to the landing.

Standing near the prow, I realize I have my face out for the smell of marshes. Across pale green water, Venice, shimmering in diluted sunlight. Lulled by the slap of waves against the hull, I recall the stunning opening of one of my favorite books, Nabokov's *Speak Memory*: 'The cradle rocks above an abyss, and common sense tells us that our existence is but a brief crack of light between two eternities of darkness. Although the two are identical twins, man, as a rule, views the prenatal abyss with more calm than the one he is heading for (at some forty-five hundred heartbeats an hour).' I was rereading him last night and felt the charge of that passage.

Is the passion for seeing what remains of the past a bridge to 'the prenatal abyss'? *All this took place before you.* And look, you can touch so much that preceded you. All the clear markers which ultimately led to you, your brief moment in a crack of light. *I'm floating.* Venice is all alluvial light. *Riding the waters.* I'm mesmerized by the nacreous sky and the marshes and the Venice of. . . I'm searching. Yes, here, ah, yes, the Venice of the slippery pass, the watery link to the preconscious.

My mind comes to rest; this is what I've been trolling these waters to find. The watery city *takes me there* as the cities on land *cannot*, cannot, with their divisible reality of streets under our feet and tires, their exits and entrances so spatially broken. Venice is simultaneous, like all time before we existed. *Because we are swimmers. The slick creatures of land and water.* And the scent of marsh drifts deeply into the medulla, that old hard-pack.

Now, I finally notice: The gondoliers *stand* as they work the water. They cross from one side to the other side. *Death in Venice*, Thomas Mann wrote; so, of course, of course we recognize that 'strange craft . . . with that peculiar blackness which is found elsewhere only in coffins.'

But no, the gondoliers don't look like Charons on the River Styx. Instead, they walk the water, miraculously. The shape of the gondola shares more with the treble clef than with a coffin. The death connection is preconditioning, received knowledge, not experienced knowledge. This water is too glorious, a swabbed silver light streaking rose-gold, tesselate and far, far from death. But now I understand why Shelley, Mann, McCarthy, Ruskin, travel articles, films – all the ways I pre-experienced Venice – never got to the Venice I sensed under my skin. *Death* is what they called the mystery of Venice's allure. For me, they had it backwards. For *birth* we cross through the waters.

From a distance, the gondoliers appear as somnambulists, the black silhouettes of the gondolas propelled across the waters of the unconscious by dreams.

In the early evening, I'm still reflecting. We're having a glass of wine at a bar right on the Grand Canal. Is it always shimmering and clear? Probably it smells like garbage in August. The waiter is solicitous, friendly. 'How can they stay nice when they have to put up with so many tourists?' The American at the next table has banged his glass to get the waiter's attention. His friends are pretending they're going to push each other's chairs into the water. And they're adults.

'Tourists are how they live. They're used to us. Imagine what it's like in July, with crud bobbing in the canals. We'd all be in a mob, sweltering, and oozing garlic sweat.'

Since it's April, the throngs have not yet arrived, but enough of the world's masses are here to make me want to avoid the main sights. They're often the unappealing kind of tourists in caps and shorts, trailing McDonald's junk behind them. I cross my arms and look sullenly at my neighbors, who are having a fine time.

When I turn my chair so that I can face the water directly and watch the gondolas pass, I observe the oddest thing: The faces of the tourists who are being ferried by the *palazzi*, the Ca'd'Oro, the lacy Gothic windows, landings lapped with moss, and the umber and old rose façades reflecting and lifting and breaking in the brushed blue water, the faces have gone blank. Their edges soften. Their eyes are full of beauty and the limpid light is on them. They are changed by what is seeing them. They step out of the gondolas like new beings.

*

All the restaurants we choose are in remote neighborhoods. We get lost and found over and over. After dinner, almost midnight, the *calli* fall silent; our footsteps echo and we find ourselves whispering. Sleeping cats on windowsills and doorsteps don't even look up. Back at the hotel, the desk clerk tells us about Padania, the separatist group dedicated to seceding from Italy. Today they've hijacked a ferry – although they paid the fare! – and loaded a panel truck painted to look like an armored vehicle. They drove across Piazza San Marco, waving guns. They were shortly arrested. '*Carnevale*. They think it's carnival time,' he shrugs. Around four, we awake to the sound of 'Hut, *uno, due, tre, quattro*,' and rhythmic marching. We look out onto the *campo* and see about twenty Padania men in black, goose-stepping around – surreal flashback to the Fascist thirties. They look well-trained to me but Ed says it doesn't take much talent to goose-step. 'I was dreaming', Ed remembers, 'of ice skating down the Grand Canal, doing figure eights in Piazza San Marco, then I was gliding backwards underneath bridges I had to duck under.'

'What do you suppose that means?'

He's falling asleep again. 'Venice on ice. Iced Venus. Venus and Venice. Us in Venice.'

Now I can't sleep so I read about Lord Byron's wild liaisons with Venetian women, his afternoons of study on the island of San Lazzaro, where Armenian scholars still live, and his swims from the Lido to the end of the Grand Canal. Ed has a talent for sleep. When his head touches the pillow, he's gone. I wonder if Lord Byron's back was as sexy as Ed's, if his luminous skin was as healthy and alive to the adoring wife of some Venetian merchant. Way back *in the prenatal abyss* – Byron's actual body in the cold; he shakes water from his eyes and sees the *palazzi* at sunrise, his lame leg trying to work against the tide. *Almost, I can feel the current rush and the strain in his muscles*. Impossible to read – my eyes are still printed with Venice and the wattage of the bedside lamp rivals a nightlight. Nothing is harder to hold than the reality of the past. My daughter's lost red pocketbook full of treasures. My book slides to the floor but Ed doesn't move. Briefly, I contemplate diving into a canal myself. Although I probably would have to have my stomach pumped, it would be something to add to my résumé.

DEEPER INTO THE COUNTRY

Bats are back, swooping erratically above us. They don't seem to fly but to scatter like dark confetti in gusty wind. I used to be afraid one would land in my hair, but, after hundreds of dinners under their flight path, I trust their echolocation. I remember seeing an x-ray of a bat in anatomy class. The bones look like a homunculus hidden inside the leathery body. D. H. Lawrence described a bat as 'a black glove thrown up at the light,/and falling back,' and its wings 'like bits of umbrella,' but I can imagine only the rudimentary trapped human, fated to eat its weight in bugs. Since they share Bramasole with us, somehow folding themselves into cracks between stucco and stone, they now seem like friendly presences.

They may be excited at the energy emanating from a bowl of fava beans and a board holding a wedge of *pecorino* on the top of the wall, our convenient sideboard. If not, they are the only creatures in the Arezzo province not sharing this Tuscan mania.

To start or to finish dinner each night, we are fated to eat *fave*. Anselmo's crop, as predicted, overwhelms us. We give bags of the tender young things to neighbors, friends, anyone who will take them. The local ritual of *pecorino* and *fave* is one of the most loved combinations in Tuscan food. Served as lunch in itself, or an *antipasto*, or in place of dessert, this sacred marriage exists for a short, intense season. The *pecorino* of choice is fresh; these two spring arrivals go naturally together.

Tonight's *pecorino* is special, thanks to our friend Vittorio. He grew up in Cortona and works for a vineyard now, after several years of working in Rome, commuting the long distance so he could continue to live the way he wants. He stops by the house after gathering *funghi porcini* in the mountains. When we're in town, we leave a bag of *fave* on his doorknob. He is president of the local chapter of Slow Food, an international organization devoted to preserving traditional cuisines and dedicated to pure methods of growing and preparing food and wine. Slow Food – as opposed to fast food. Naturally, we have joined. Local meetings consist of eight-course dinners with ten or twelve wines from a particular region. A club after my own heart. At the time of our 'meetings,' other chapters around Italy are meeting, too, and at the end of the evening votes are cast, phoned in, and the best wines are elected.

Late in the afternoon, Vittorio took us far into the hills to meet a friend of his family, a farmer whose name, to our astonishment, is Achille. We waited for him to come in from milking. Outside the farmhouse, a metal bathtub under a cold water faucet was positioned for a perfect view of Cortona in the distance, with orchards sloping down his hills. Half an olive oil can nailed sideways to the wall held soap and a brush. Around the courtyard stood benches made from hollowed-out logs. Achille, around seventy years old, came in carrying a bucket of ewe's milk and a rake, the rake's handle a straight limb smooth from use, the tines strong sticks carved and set into a piece of branch, all finished neatly. He'd *made* his rake. Such a beautiful thing and a symbol of his individuality; rakes don't cost much and he prefers to make his own. Achille is a compact man, grave and slow. His remote tortoise eyes seemed to take the measure of us quickly. Every day he has lived in the sun has added a wrinkle to his face so that now he is completely furrowed and tanned to the color of an old baseball glove. We followed him into a room next to a stall with calves closed inside. His cheeses lined four hanging shelves. Ed noticed jagged tin rounds at intervals along the ropes. Achille smiled quietly and nodded. The *topi*, mice, can't crawl around the tin and eat the cheese.

Grass floated on top of the milk. He took a wad of cotton and covered the mesh of a sieve, then poured the milk through. He took a jug of what must be rennet and splashed in some. I wanted to ask questions but he did not seem cut out for casual conversation. The room smelled like nowhere I've ever been, a powerful, primitive lacteal ripening. Forget European Union rules of pasteurization, this is cheese as it has been made through the eons. He asked us to select a cheese, one with no cracks in the outer layer. He rotated the cheese, looking at me intently (I'm probably as exotic to him as he is to me) and said we should turn it every day. 'Why?' I ventured, although I assumed the ingredients were not yet stable and continued to need mixing.

The straw-colored two-pound round looked like a

little moon. He wrapped it carefully in foil.

Achille's wife came in with another bucket. She wore boots and a housedress, and, like her husband, was deeply sunbaked. They are extremely quiet, I think shy, probably from years of isolation. Right away, she started another batch. She has a wood stove in the courtyard for cooking in hot weather. A battered pasta pot on top attests to frequent use. I imagine her in the evening, after all the chores, bathing in that tub, nothing but silence all around her.

★

Young *fave* do not have to be peeled, just shelled at the table and enjoyed with the *pecorino*. Achille's cheese is smooth and tangy, without the barnyard taste many fresh *pecorini* seem to impart. Ed cuts another piece. I notice he has eaten a quarter of the yellow moon. We walk up on the terraces after dinner, carrying a last glass of wine. The zucchini are starting to bloom. Those audacious flowers deserve a van Gogh or Nolde to capture their melted gold. We linger at the tomatoes, figuring how long until we're coming up with baskets to pull them from the vines. Ed rubs a leaf on his fingers and lets me smell the promise of ripe tomatoes. The chard, more chard than I can imagine for risotto, is ready. We stop at the patch of *fave*. We hardly have made a dent. Something tells me I won't want to see a fava bean for years after this spring.

★

I'm spending the afternoon with Vittorio, roaming around the countryside in his car with all the windows down. Ed is taking a day for writing. We stop to visit a farmer who lives in a house built in the 1400s and still is owned by a count of the same family, whose villa is down the road.

Tommaso is delighted to see Vittorio, who grew up nearby and used to play in the hay barn. He shows us an old painted cart still stored there. These places sequestered from time never become familiar; visiting, we drop behind the years, into a way of life we've imagined but never known.

When I ask about the chapel at the back of the house, Tommaso casually tells us that it has been closed since Napoleon passed by, as though he were saying it's been closed since Wednesday. 'Before,' he says, 'pilgrims used to stop for three days; the count gave them food and lodging.' The way he talks, we think it could be the current count, could be his own extra rooms involved.

Tentatively, I ask if we could see the inside of the chapel. He leads us through his house. I glimpse bare rooms where he and his brother live: iron beds, chests, yellowed crochet-edged linen curtains, remnants of a sister or wife, and a few photographs on the wall. No TV, no technology at all, not even a radio in sight. Austere as monk cells and utterly clean. We're winding around medieval corridors with no light. Tommaso's steps are secure. We follow blindly and finally he turns a key with a loud ka-lunk, ka-lunk and pushes open the door. The first thing I see is a copper bathtub, then some farm equipment and barrels. As my eyes adjust to the gray light falling from a single high round window, I make out frescoes of a saint and of the Madonna. A glaring blank space shows where a painting was removed. 'It's down at the church now. Stop and the priest will show you San Filippio, who used to live happily here.' The chapel is oddly elaborate for a farmhouse of this type. Maybe the count wanted the sweaty pilgrims to stop somewhere well away from his own enclosed park.

Tommaso takes us to the kitchen and pours glasses of *vin santo*, the drink of hospitality in all farms. I've had *vin santo*, which tastes something like sherry, at all hours of the day in various houses. He props himself inside the walk-in fireplace in a chair and he and Vittorio reminisce about telling stories around the fire years ago. Tommaso is the opposite of the solemn Achille. He's lived his life without much of a cruising radius, too, but he's a talker, a story-teller. He stretches out his legs, mimicking how in old times the *contadini* used to toast themselves in winter, while staying close enough to stir the polenta. Looking around the kitchen I see no sign of heat, so I expect they still have this ancestral habit on January nights.

Tommaso shows us his Val di Chiana cows, those white beasts who turn into the famous Florentine beefsteak, grilled with rosemary. He has four grown ones and three calves, who fix great dark eyes at us and stare. Around their necks he has tied red ribbons to protect them from the evil eye. I always wondered why the steak highlights Tuscan menus yet you never see these creatures in fields. They're raised indoors, babied and petted but cruelly chained to the manger. They are immense, growing to three times the size of a normal cow.

Next to the house an enclosed and overgrown flower garden again attests to a long-lost feminine presence. The old roses trained on iron poles still bloom profusely. The yellow rambler with tiny blooms has spilled from its pole and crawled to a fence where it swoops and spreads recklessly.

I'm following warily because of the roaming ducks and chickens. My old bird phobia is a liability not only in *piazze* full of pigeons. If Tommaso suspects that I'm afraid of a chicken, he will think I am nuts. Two white turkeys peck the ground near the barn. They are the ugliest birds on earth.

We drive past the count's villa, a melancholy shuttered

place surrounded by chestnut trees, and stop at the church. Stanislao, the Pole who helped build our long stone wall when we first bought Bramasole, and his wife Reina, live with the priest of this parish, Don Fabio. She cooks and takes care of the house and church. Stanislao works as a mason but does odd jobs for the church property on weekends. Some Saturdays when Stanislao works with Ed at our house, she comes to help me in the garden. Tiny and wiry, she has tremendous energy. The priest is teaching two children their catechism in the garden. Reina takes us in, pausing to show us Don Fabio's study. It could be the study in the paintings of Saint Jerome. An open window throws dusky light onto a desk stacked with leather books, some open, some turned face down. All we need is Saint Jerome's attribute, the sleeping lion. In a corridor we see the dim painting that used to hang in Tommaso's chapel. On a side wall in the church, snapshots of all parishioners who have died are arranged in rows. Vittorio finds many familiar faces from his childhood. We leave Reina to her ironing of the altar linen, leave Don Fabio to his two red-haired charges in the garden.

★

Growing up in a small town, I felt the tight bit in my mouth. I couldn't wait to leave. The pull of cities was strong. I remember, however, a slight pull, too, toward life far in the country.

My boyfriend's grandmother, Mimo, lived near Mystic, a crossroads out in tobacco and cotton country. A porch ran the length of her two-storey house. Her pie safe always was full of lemon and coconut meringue pies. In plain bedrooms her quilts lay folded at the foot of each bed. The porch faced the fields and she sat there in the afternoons shelling butter beans. Occasionally, she picked up a wooden-handled church fan printed with a picture of Jesus and fanned away the flies. I sat in the swing reading *Anna Karenina*. In this memory, I am somehow missing the boyfriend altogether. Through stirred-up field dust, the sunset sky turned lurid and splendid, popsicle orange and grape, with sprays of gold, and cheap-underwear pink. After the wobbling gold blob of sunset, the air over the tobacco turned blue, as though over a lake. We were the solemn witnesses. It could have been Doomsday every afternoon. After that Mimo would go fix herself a tall gin and tonic.

In his book I once loved, *The Mind of the South*, W. J. Cash observed that this air is responsible for Southerners' romanticism – they see through a haze and consequently have a hard time distinguishing reality. Mimo's life appealed to me. She roared in her Buick across rutted roads through crops to check on workers. Long a widow, she ran the farm, put up preserves, birthed calves, quilted and cooked, and always kicked open the screen door when we arrived, throwing open her arms.

Rediscovering deep country life, I wonder now what it would be like to live like Achille and Tommaso. For years I would have thought *What a waste*. I was interested in the dramatic life – maybe someone would throw himself under a train for *me*. I was pretty sure I never would be called on for something that rash.

Now I feel the lure of country dawns, sunsets, the satisfaction of living in a green kingdom of one's own. I feel as well a growing distrust of spending too much of one's life deifying work. Finding that running balance among ambition, solitude, stimulation, adventure – how to do this? I heard Ramsey Clark, then Attorney General, speak when I was in college. All I remember him saying was something like, 'When I die, I want to be so exhausted that you can throw me on the scrap heap.' He wanted to be totally consumed by his life. I was impressed and adopted that as my philosophy, too. As a writer, I also had an inclination toward meditation and reclusiveness, and so have maintained for most of my life a decent balance. The last few years have pulled me too much in the exterior direction. After devoting five years to chairing my department at the university, I resigned from the hot seat and went back to teaching. I saw how a few months later hardly anyone remembered what I thought of as vast changes, how instantaneously time slid over my absence. I was left with the private satisfaction of a job well done. Considering time, stress, and pure hassle, private satisfaction did not seem like enough. I had wanted to rethink the department from the bottom up and was willing to write endless memos, reports, evaluations, and to straggle home at 8 p.m. What is replenishing? What is depleting? What takes? What gives? What wrings you out and, truly, what rinses you with happiness? What comes from my own labor and creativity, regardless of what anyone else thinks of it, stays close to the natural joy we all were born with and carry always. Mystic, Georgia, was not for me. I would have been hell on wheels by thirty. Oddly, oddly, I probably could live a happy, sensuous life there now. Is the sun still blistering the paint on Mimo's house? Do the fields shimmer in the blue heat? Hey, Tommaso, Achille, do you want to die so exhausted you're just ready to be tossed away? *That American, have you ever known a woman afraid of a chicken?*

★

Anselmo takes his time. Even when he had his office covered with photos of broken-down houses, where he hoped someone would invest their souls, he had time to talk. In his transformation to gardener, he lavishes his attention on perfect bamboo tepees for the tomatoes. He brings me roses from his own garden and flats of strawberries. Best of all, he takes us on excursions. When Ed asks him about a cart for hauling the lemon trees into the *limonaia* in winter, he drives us immediately to his neighbor, a blacksmith in Ossaia. The *fabbro* makes a sketch, promises the low cart, which will slide right under the pot, for next week.

Anselmo motions us to follow him. 'What is that flower?' I ask, pointing to a compact bush growing out of a stone wall.

'I've seen that all over the town walls. Looks like the flower on a passion vine,' Ed notices.

Anselmo looks at us incredulously. '*Capperi.*' He pulls off several buds. 'I'll plant them in your wall, but they are bad for the wall. You must control them.' Capers – wild, everywhere. We'd never known.

In his barn, a royal mess, he leads us far in the back where extensive wine-making equipment is covered with dust: barrels, small casks, bottles, and a grand *torchio*, the slatted vat with iron bands and levers where grapes are pressed. Ed is admiring it the way men admire a new car, nodding his head and walking around it. Anselmo explains the mechanism to us. From a shelf he pulls down two bottles of his own *vin santo*. 'Something to drink with *biscotti.*'

His *vin santo* looks slightly murky. I wonder how long it has waited for us on the shelf.

Since we are close to his sister and brother-in-law's house, he wants us to meet them. We pile back in his huge Alfa and he shortly takes a rough turn up into their yard. His sister comes out and greets him as though she hasn't seen him in years. His brother-in-law, thinning pears on one of his acre-long lines of espaliered fruit trees, comes running. We are introduced as '*stranieri*,' foreigners. Out comes the *vin santo* for the foreigners. 'Is this yours?' Ed asks Anselmo, but no, it is the brother-in-law's own. Ed is looking at the orchard. In the distance I see a corrugated roof on poles has been erected over what looks from here like a swimming pool. 'May we look at the fruit trees?' Ed asks.

'*Certo.*' The rows are elegant. The vase-shaped trees are developing vase-shaped pears. They are vigorous, all except for one section, which has a deep hole around it, causing roots to die and leaves to drop. The brother-in-law seems annoyed. He pulls on a nonexistent beard. His mouth curls in scorn.

'What happened here?' Ed asks.

Anselmo shakes one hand slowly in the air, that flinging gesture which means something like Good God Almighty. '*Porca miseria*,' the brother-in-law says, pig misery. He points toward the roofed structure. 'They have discovered a Roman villa, the archeologists, and are making an excavation. They have dug here, and have killed this tree.' Clearly the sacrifice was not justified in his eyes. In Italy, whatever is underground on your property does not belong to you. 'They have killed an olive.' He inclines his chin toward an olive now on a raised mound with a ditch around it. We know that to be a cardinal sin.

'A Roman villa?'

'The whole hill is a museum. There was not only a villa, but a whole town. Everyone knows, but now it is a discovery.' He shrugs. 'If they asked me, I could show them where Hannibal's house is. But they don't ask. Just dig.'

Hannibal's defeat of Flaminio was a few miles away. Ossaia means 'boneyard' and is derived from the stacks of bodies brought here after the battle. He leads us through his vegetable garden and a field to a ruin of a stone house which does look old but not two thousand years old. 'Sì, Hannibal lived here.'

We walk back by the dig. Under a temporary roof, we see a black-and-white mosaic Greek key floor, the geometry of rooms. A large villa stood here, with a view right into the sister and brother-in-law's garden. The dig is inactive at this season.

As we drive away Anselmo tells us they added a room years ago. 'They found a mosaic floor right where they poured the foundation.'

★

We stop once more to talk to a widow who wants him to sell her house. Even though Anselmo has closed his office, he still does a little business. 'Maybe you would like this house. There is everything to restore.' He looks at me in the rearview mirror, almost clipping a bicyclist.

'Not interested.' He pulls inside the gate and stops in the dirt forecourt, scattering chickens. A woman in the old-fashioned black dress comes out, bent as a comma. She is older than Cortona. When we are introduced, she grabs my hand in her dry, hard one and does not let go as we walk around the property. As if anticipating that she soon will enter a silent eternity, she talks nonstop. I can barely look at the adorable bunnies she has scrooched together in a pen. 'She sees something different when she looks at them,' Ed says. 'She sees them roasting in the pan with fennel. She's not focused on their soft ears.' She tours the *orto*, where vegetables are thriving, looks in on two cows, flings open the lower doors of the house. Ah, a completely unrestored house, with the mangers and *cantina* still intact. Wine-making equipment crowds every square centimeter, dozens of rotting straw-covered demi-johns, oak barrels, and bottles. In a small, immaculate room, she shows me a corner table where she still makes pasta when it's hot up in her kitchen. Jars of tomatoes line the shelves. A straight chair with a cowhide seat stands by the door to catch a breeze and her mending and knitting lie in baskets. Since she is crushing my ring into my fingers in her grip, I wish she would let go, and, at the same time, I am flattered by her instant attachment. 'I think she wants us to buy the house,' Ed whispers in English.

'Yes, and it's no later than 1750 in here.'

Upstairs, she opens the rooms where her parents lived until they died. Their iron bed with a white bedspread dips on either side, conjuring the bodies of the two grim-faced sepia photographs framed on the wall. Bed. Chair. *Armadio*. A commode for the *vaso da notte*, the chamber-pot. Her room is the same, with the addition of a lugubrious framed print of Christ, with dead palm branches tucked behind, and a yellowing oval photo of her husband as a young man. Fierce-eyed, tight-lipped, probably in his wedding suit, he stares toward the bed they shared as they grew older and older, older than he could have imagined when the camera caught the hot gleam in his eye. In a water glass floats a set of false teeth with plum-pink gums. His?

Like most Italian kitchens, hers looks and smells recently scrubbed. Even the faucets are polished. Inevitably, she pulls out the *vin santo* and pours, then she brings out *biscotti*. They are stone-hard; perhaps they were made in 1750. She is wonderful to behold. Since she's talking mile-a-minute to Anselmo about going to live with her daughter, and how the place is too much for her, I get a chance to look at her darting eyes full of intelligence, her hair tied under a black scarf.

Her thin body is all force. I feel the indentations in my fingers where she squeezed – at least she had to let go to serve the wine.

She closes the gate behind us and waves until we're gone. Four feet eight inches at most, she's a whirling dervish of energy. I wish I knew her life story. I wish I could watch her make pasta and buttonholes. I wonder what she dreams.

'I hate for her to leave and live in an apartment in Foligno. Who will buy the place?' I ask as we drive away.

'She is asking twice what it's worth. I don't think she wants to sell.'

'I loved it. The manger could be a fabulous living room with doors opening onto a terrace.'

'I like that upstairs loggia,' Ed says.

Anselmo shakes his head. 'You never know what foreigners will like. She'll probably sell to some crazy foreigner.'

★

'Be prepared for a six-hour feast,' our friend Donatella tells us. 'Giusi has set up a kitchen in the whole barn so six cooks can work.' Her sister, Giusi, helps take care of our house when we are not here. The sisters are opposite. Donatella has an angular, dark beauty, somewhat like the Mona Lisa's, and an ironic humor. You can look way into her black eyes. Giusi in America would be Homecoming Queen. She could captain any pep squad. She's pretty, sociable, and upbeat. They are sisters and best friends. Each time we arrive at Bramasole, they've left flowers in the house, and the kitchen stocked with fruit, coffee, bread, and cheese so that we don't need to dash out if we are tired from the flight. Both are excellent cooks, who learned directly from a mother who still makes her own ravioli.

Giusi's two young sons are taking their first communion. This calls for a feast. We have not seen Giusi for weeks because she has been preparing the *festa*. After the service, around eighty people gather at the house in the mountains Giusi and her husband, Dario, share with his parents. Dario's sister and her family live in another house on the property. They are close to self-sufficient for all their food. The family takes care of a large vegetable garden, raises chickens, rabbits, lambs, and geese. The men hunt, keeping a supply of wild boar at the ready.

Everything they produce, and a lot more, goes into the first communion dinner. When we arrive at noon, the party is in full swing. Giusi gives me a tour of the house. For almost two years she has endured an extensive remodeling. She's kept the warm feel of the ancient farmhouse, but has installed lovely bathrooms, stone stairs, and an up-to-the-minute kitchen, which, of course, includes a wood-burning stove for cooking. Every knob and surface gleams. Every window sparkles. Outside, the *prosecco* already is flowing and women are passing trays of *crostini*, Tuscan *antipasti* of rounds of bread spread with various toppings: *porcini* mushrooms, spicy cheese, and chopped, seasoned chicken liver. Under a white tent, they've set a U-shaped table under balloons and twisted colored-paper streamers. The two boys are seated at the head, flanked by their parents. We've peered in the barn where many hands are at work. A table down the center is crowded with fruit tarts, enormous bowls of salad greens. Each woman has on a flowered dress. The barn whirls with color and motion. They're still chopping and peeling, putting the finishing garnishes together. For each plate, spring leeks, carrots, and asparagus are deftly tied in bundles with a blade of chive. I'm surprised to meet Guisi's mother. Young and red-haired, she looks nothing like her daughters. She has made *cappelli del prete*, pasta called priest's hats, for eighty-odd people.

As we soon find out, there are two pastas. Everyone is served a large helping of *tagliatelle* with a rich sauce of *cinghiale*, the wild boar. Many have seconds of this and I'm wiping the edge of the plate with bread for every drop of the delicious sauce. Then comes the priest's hats with four cheeses. And seconds of that. The efficient army of women swoops down and replaces our plates after each course. Someone in the barn is washing dishes like mad. Lamb with the vegetable bundles comes next, their own lamb roasted in the outdoor oven. In the distance we can hear sheep and cows, who don't yet know they will not always dwell in the lush pasture below but will be appearing on these same flowered plates. Two spotted puppies are passed around the table, petted and rocked. In earlier years it would have been babies, but with the Italian birthrate the lowest in Europe, babies are in short supply. A four-year-old flirt in a red dress is making the most of her position. She's practically ambushed by admirers. Toasts begin but the two boys, along with several friends, have absconded from the table. One gift to them was a computer with games so they've run inside to strafe the enemy. New carafes of wine replace the empties immediately. I am through. This is a stupendous groaning board. But Ed keeps eating. A little more lamb? I see him look up and smile, '*Sì*.' And *patate*? Again, '*Sì*.'

Suddenly three men appear, carrying something heavy. People rush forward shouting and snapping pictures. Too large for their ovens, a gigantic thigh of a Val di Chiana cow has been roasted in a hotel oven in town and has just arrived on a tray that could hold a human. Soon platters of beef and more crisp potatoes circulate. I give in and have some. Oh no, it's too good. I can't have more, maybe a taste. Ed is eating like a lord. Two Italian women have asked him if he's in films so he feels particularly expansive. Salad arrives. Then fruit tart, *tiramisu*, and the reemergence of the two boys, galloping out like ponies. They shyly cut a three-tiered cake and offer the first pieces to their parents. The cake has rich layers of lemon filling. Out comes the *grappa* and *vin santo*. I'm astonished. Ed has some of both. He finds himself arm-in-arm with several men, singing a song he's never heard. An accordion starts and the dancing begins. I have never eaten this much at once in my life. Ed has eaten a prodigious amount.

At five, we are the first to leave. Our friends Susan and Cole, who married at our house during the restoration, are arriving in time for dinner. We find out later that most guests stayed until eleven, with the beef making several more appearances.

Our friends have arrived early and are sitting on the terrace. Happy as we are to see them, we barely can walk or speak. Ed describes the meal, ending with, 'I just hope we're around when those boys get married. Imagine what that will be like.' We collapse for two hours then emerge in the sweet time of day to take them around our garden, gathering lettuces, zucchini, onions, and herbs for a simple salad and frittata. For them. We don't want to eat or drink for three days. We sip tepid water while they enjoy a great Brunello.

★

In the morning, we awaken to the grinding noise of a truck coming up the drive. Anselmo is directing as it swings backwards up our lane. We get downstairs in time to watch two men unloading the *torchio*, the great wine-press Anselmo showed us in his barn. '*Un omaggio*,' he says briskly. The gift is left in the middle of the front yard. We thank him profusely, wondering where this huge piece of equipment is going to live. He launches into instructions on the mechanism and then moves into the details of *vin santo*. That we are not here in fall, that we do not yet have many grapes does not seem to matter. When we first saw the house, one room was strung with wires overhead and Anselmo at the time had noted, 'For drying the grapes for *vin santo*.' Susan and Cole, both ardent gardeners, join us and assure us they'd love to come help harvest grapes. Anselmo found this place for us. All along he has helped us with restoration. Now that he is retired, he has transformed two of our terraces into a vegetable paradise. He has taken us on jaunts in his car, introducing us to country people with their own ways. He has watched Ed learn about vines from Beppe and Francesco. I feel a quick shiver in accepting this gift. Now he is passing on the *torchio*, like passing the torch.

*

Dark never turns black-dark. The stars exert their most powerful kilowatts. Also the moon, glassy in old windows, wavering and rising from bottom pane to middle to top is a pleasure for the insomniac to watch. The one nightingale, who must live in the ilex above the house, pierces the quiet with insistent notes. Dawn is the sweetest time on earth. In the last moments of dark, the bird chorale begins. One of us wakes the other. *Listen, they're starting to sing now.* So many, a rising cloud of birdsong, a lift, an ushering-in. Then the sky – no rosy finger of dawn but a suffusion of rose out of indigo, the quietest light on the hills and the rushing songs of the birds still rising over the absolute world unto itself. Moles, voles, porcupines, snakes, foxes, boar, all the creatures burrowed for the night return to day with this music, as we do. The deep freshness of the earth returns to those who sing, to the fusion of colors. As the sun brightens, colors sharpen and separate from each other. But where is the cuckoo at this hour?

Our friends wake to the sound of the bird who sings, 'Wheat, wheat.' Ed listens every day for the bird he says sings, 'When you're a Jet you're a Jet all the way, from your first cigarette. . .' from 'West Side Story'. We take them on a wildflower walk around the land. All spring, I've photographed each flower as I found it. Most amazing have been the wild white and purple orchids. My book with the medieval wildflower cover, bought in Asolo, now bulges with poppies against stone walls, ragged robin, purple lupin, cotton lavender, wild carnations, lilies, dog roses, still unidentified spiky blue flowers. The many yellows are hardest to identify with the wildflower book in hand. There simply are too many that look similar.

Susan and I cut off rose leaves with black spots and some with the dreaded rust. These go in a bag to be destroyed. She shows me how to take cuttings from my favorite pink roses in front of the house, which survived thirty years of neglect and still bloom with a clean, violet fragrance especially strong early in the mornings. We spend hours in the garden and on the terraces picking wildflowers, then down to the *orto* to fill a basket with lettuces for lunch.

At home in California we are so busy we have 8 a.m. phone conversations two or three times a week, shorthand exchanges of vital information about our daughters, both of whom are in graduate school, about her bookstore business, and what we're managing to read. A few days to walk, go to a museum, cook dinner, and sit out under the benign lights of fireflies and the Milky Way, reconnects our friendship. 'Why don't we have more time at home?' we ask each other, but we don't have an answer.

Like the birdsong, like the droves of butterflies and bees, the volunteer flowers in profusion delight me because they come purely as gifts of the land. Just as I'm waxing about the pleasures of rural life to Susan and Cole, an English friend calls and says they've arrived to find two drowned baby boars in their well and they've fished out the rotting, bloated carcasses with a hoe.

At dinner Cole speculates on why we've taken this place so much to heart. 'Is it because it's a return to a simpler time? You get to erase the urban blight from your minds for a few months each year?'

Relaxed and enjoying the evening, with lanterns along the wall, lasagna, and the Vino Nobile they have brought, we agree. By dessert, I retract. 'That's not really it. It's the end of the ugly century here, too.' I flash on the prostitutes along the Piero della Francesca trail. Trucks on the autostrada polluting like mad. Frustrating strikes, which are so frequent there's a space in the newspaper announcing when public services will not be operating. 'The people aren't in a simpler time. Generally, they've just managed the century better than we have in America. Everyday life in Tuscany is good.'

'The everyday interactions with people are drastically different – personal and direct,' Ed says. 'We were too geared toward the long range and the long range is a long shot.'

'There's very little violent crime, people have manners, the food is so much better and we all know the Italians have more fun.' I realize I've said 'manners,' and sounded like my mother. 'I love the courtesy of encounters in the streets, purchases in stores, even the mailman seems pleased to hand me a letter. When strangers are leaving a restaurant they say goodnight to the people around them.'

We tell them about our recent trips into the country-side and the lives we've glimpsed. Our expat friends talk about how much Cortona has changed. But the changes were rapid – and needed – after the war. Now they have slowed. The life of the town is intact, they've taken the right measures to protect the countryside, the cultural life of this tiny town puts to shame most good-sized American cities. I think of the younger generation – Giusi, Donatella, Vittorio, Edo, Chiara, Marco, Antonio, Amalia, Flavia, Niccolò – bringing along all the good traditions. When our adored Rita retired from her *frutta e verdura* last year, a young man took over. Unlike many rural towns, this one hasn't lost its young to the cities. I've said enough and don't say any more.

A group from town walking by the house is singing together. They walk and sing. In my normal life I cannot imagine doing that on a Wednesday night. We listen to the unfamiliar song.

'Like that – Italian life is still sweet.'

'And what's also sweet is this peach parfait,' Ed says. 'It makes my teeth ache.'

★

The past few days have added hundreds of images to my mental archives. Finding the taproots of places far in the country counterweighs the noetic life with a powerful reality. Already I return in imagination to Achille's place in the mountains with joy. Right now he may be soaping his wife's back in the cool night air. Could we have a bathtub outside? And Giusi's long, long feast, over in a day, will stick in time for its intense celebratory generosity. Ed probably will dream of the entrance of the beef leg into the tent, adding the blare of a trumpet. The *signora* sleeping near her framed husband with the shining eyes has spanned the century and still grabs my hand, pulling the new into her world. Anselmo has made his last wine in his barn but has his eye on our grapes. We will make the wine someday. His brother-in-law, on intimate terms with the Romans and Hannibal, has a sense of time that irritates the hell out of him; he wants his pears and olives to live right *now*.

THE ROOT OF PARADISE

Ed heads for the upper terraces early. He wants to cut out a trunk of ivy which is menacing a wall. If he doesn't, tentacles will twist between stones and in two days or twenty years the whole wall will cascade down onto our roses. He pauses to watch our neighbor Placido's fifteen white doves swoop over the valley. Let out twice a day for a few minutes of freedom, they fly in loose formation round and round, then all at once head back to their cage. A movement to his left startles him. From behind the ilex tree, a woman emerges, holding a cloth sack and a stick. The forager!

She is not at all abashed at being caught. '*Buon giorno, signore,*' she greets him. '*Una bella giornata.*' Beautiful day. She waves her stick over the valley.

Ever polite, even to someone who may have helped

herself to our daffodils, Ed introduces himself. 'You're the Swiss professor,' she says.

'Not Swiss, *americano*.'

'Ah, *sì*? I thought you were Swiss,' she says dubiously.

Although the morning is mild, she's wearing two or three layers of sweaters, a scarf knotted at her throat, and rubber boots. She grins, showing gold. 'Letizia Gazzini,' she says in a loud voice. 'I used to live here but many years ago.' She opens her bag. 'I always come back.' She has collected several kinds of greens and a separate plastic bag of snails. She holds up spindly weeds. 'You have the wild leeks, naturally.' She rummages deeper and pulls out more. '*Prenda, prenda,*' take them, take them, she offers.

Ed is totally disarmed. He likes her tanned, creased face and shiny black eyes. He takes the leeks. 'Did you own the house?' He's confused. We'd been told that ancient sisters from Perugia held on to the place, leaving it abandoned for thirty years.

'No, no, *signore*, my husband was the farmer, we lived only in a portion of the house. That part.' She points with her stick. Ed knows all too well; that section was walled off when we bought the house and had to be opened on all three floors. 'Many years of hard labor. Now my husband is dead and I'm left.' She pauses. '*Insomma,*' she concludes, an untranslatable expression, in summary, meaning more closely, what else is there to say.

Ed tells her we'd like to learn more about what's growing on the land. Perhaps she could show us the *mescolanza*, the edible greens. Would she mind?

'Ah, *sì, sì, certo,*' Yes, certainly she will. She waves her stick again and disappears behind the *ginestre*.

★

I yank tender clumps of weeds from the rose bed and dig

out evil, thorny ones. The wheelbarrow fills over and over, and the pile way out on the land grows larger than a haystack. When the terrace brush is cut, other haystacks rise. After the next rain, Ed and Beppe will burn them. Dry weeds create a fire hazard so after every rain in early summer, fires start up all over the valley, ruining the just-washed air. The fires always scare me, even though they stand by with buckets of water in case the wind lifts the fire over to dry grass. This spring an experienced farmer burned to death when the blaze suddenly blew back, catching his clothes on fire.

With my stoop-labor fork I loosen the soil. The beds are ready. Time to plant. We loaded the car with flowers at the nurseries yesterday and the day before. Each time we leave, we're given a gift. The *signora* runs out, '*Un omaggio e grazie.*' She hands me a campanula, or terrace rose, or a fuchsia. Twice we've been given a burgundy red coleus, a plant I don't fancy. They look like what would survive after a nuclear blast. Naturally, they're thriving in their far corner. Sometimes we're asked to choose something we want. After rampaging through, buying dozens of plants, suddenly it's difficult to select the gift. One of these small pots from two years ago has turned into a bush covered with yellow blooms which last for two months.

Many businesses give customers gifts – a T-shirt to celebrate a store's anniversary, beautiful calendars at the new year, and, once, a box of fifteen different pastas when we spent more than 200,000 *lire*, around $120, at a discount store.

I somehow love the gift plants even more than what I've bought. A scented geranium given last year has tripled in size, a dwarf lavender seems especially fragrant. Maybe the gift aspect makes me care for them more carefully, or

141

maybe something given naturally thrives. I'm even growing fond of the coleus.

After working outside all day, the last task remains. We prime the hand pump and trudge out to douse the lavender and new cypress trees with the icy water. Once established, they won't need watering. The walk toward the lake view, formerly a jungle, then a path, now is a lane. Next year, more grapes on the right side (too late for planting grapes now) and a trail of lavender along the left.

Ed has eggplant *parmigiana* in the oven. While I bathed and fell into reading the poems of Horace in the tub, he picked lettuce and set the table outside. Is there anything more splendid than a man who cooks? I bring my new yellow book, where I have begun to list garden ideas. Before we launch into that all-night topic, I read him something amazing I found in Horace:

> . . . In spring the swelling earth aches for seeds of
>   new life.
> Lovely the earth in labor, under a nervous west
>   wind.
> The fields loosen, a mild wetness lies everywhere.
> Confident grows the grass, for the young sun will
>   do no harm.
> The shoots of the vine do not fear a southerly storm
>   arising
> Or icy rain slanting from heaven under a north
>   wind—
> No, bravely they bud now and reveal their leaves.
> So it was since the beginning of the world,
> Here is the brilliant dawning and pitch of these days.

I love the last two lines. Horace could sit at our table, not having to ask that we keep his glass full of the local wine, while he tells us how little has changed and that we need to thin the fruit in the pear trees.

We assess the current state of the land. Right away, we found the good bones. After bringing back what was already here, although smothered by vines and brush, we are starting our more ambitious phase of gardening with the original structure in place. In Renaissance and later formal gardens, a central axis usually boldly joined the architecture of the house with that of the garden. Walkways were like halls, with glimpses into the interior of the garden from the paths. The perpendicular dimensions of our own front garden approximate the size of the house, with the terraces above and below roughly half the width of the front garden. Vestigial formality remains in the long boxwood hedge with five round topiary trees rising at intervals out of the hedge.

It's time to regard the garden long range, feel my way toward a philosophy of gardening. I visualize how it looks from the third-floor windows, what has lasted these first few years, and, primarily, what truly gives me pleasure, rather than simply what will grow. Ed is interested in what brings bees and butterflies. Because lavender is a magnet, especially for white butterflies, we've seen how they put the garden in motion. Motion and music — the bees' humming forms a sleepy background for the birds' twitters, arpeggios, and caws. I like cut flowers in the house every day. We both love the currents of scents swimming through the garden and how they rise to the house early in the morning. The ripe peach colors of the house rhyme with yellow, rose, and apricot flowers.

Because the land is steeply terraced, our garden has distinct parts:

At the side of the house, the shady rectangle we call the

Lime Tree Bower stretches maybe sixty feet, then turns into fruit and olive terraces. We've given every area a name, to save each other the bother of saying, 'You know, beyond the lilac bushes on the way to the view of the lake,' or 'On the east side of the house under the *tigli* trees . . .' We've even named each olive tree. All our family members and friends, favorite writers and places are immortalized with a tree. We haven't yet checked to see which ones passed away in the freeze.

Because of the view over the valley and Apennines, the Lime Tree Bower is our noontime outdoor dining room. The front yard, where we live from breakfast to the last firefly count, leads to stone steps then down into a long garden. On this broadest terrace, called the Rose Walk, we have now planted fifty roses on either side of the lawn. I'm confused to see the volunteer, lush lawn, which thrives with a variety of hearty wild grasses. How do you have a lawn without planting a lawn? The top of the immense Polish wall, which we built in the second year, lines one side of this garden. An original stone wall and the inherited boxwood hedge with its ball topiaries line the other. Iron arches mark either end, one covered with jasmine, the other to be planted with two Mermaids, a climbing rose with a flat yellow bloom.

So a slight geometry is in place. While we were clearing jungle growth from the years of abandonment, we followed the cue of the boxwood and reestablished a well-defined rectangle perpendicular to the house. There, during the wall–building era, we unearthed a portion of a former road, with tightly packed stones laid sideways. We hauled away one level, but the next level still lies beneath the grass. I've read that Roman roadbeds were sometimes twelve feet deep.

To the left, curving stone stairs lead down to the Well

Walk, another swath of front garden where the well and cistern live and where, previously, we had the well-established hedge of lavender, rosemary, and sage. We didn't know to cut back hard in the winter. At a California vineyard with extensive lavender, we saw the gardener cutting it back beyond belief, almost to the ground. Because we'd never trimmed, the freeze killed all but two.

To the right from the Rose Walk is The Lane, with the boxwood and a tall stone wall on either side. The green underfoot seems to be mostly camomile and wild mint, whose oregano-peppermint smell, I'm sure, attracts the black and white snake who has taken up residence under a rock beneath the faucet. The old well and the spring we discovered during our second summer are on The Lane. It ends with a mass of lilac bushes, then, joining the main garden and the driveway, proceeds to what we call the Lake Walk. From there to the end of the property, we have planted the cypresses and lavender. We want to reclaim an overgrown track – medieval, Roman? – which leads eventually into town after joining a Roman road. The immense views are from that far end of the property. Most of the land is given over freely to the olive, fruit, almond, and grape, with a few stretches abandoned to wild broom and rock. Two terraces are for herbs and vegetables, the first upper terrace for *le erbe aromatiche*, and for lettuces, the second for Anselmo's realm, his mega-*orto*, his grand illusion.

★

I have visions for all these areas. Making a sketch persuades us that we know what we're doing. 'Think perennials,' Ed says. 'We can't reinvent the wheel every year – we plant a carload and it doesn't do zip. We need plants that can take care of themselves when they grow up. Remember the summer I spent hours hauling buckets to those thirty olives?' We'd planted on various far terraces, not knowing we'd have no rain that year from May through August. With five acres, quantity and size are whole different issues. We've been slow to adjust our sense of scope. Finally we're getting it – our sense of scale needs to cube itself. 'Think bushes.' He starts a list: hibiscus, forsythia, holly, oleander.

'I don't like oleander. It reminds me of freeways.'

'Scratch oleander, then.'

'What about more roses? We could build a running arch all along the top of the Polish wall.'

When we go inside, an e-mail has arrived from my friend Judy, a rose expert. 'Mermaid alert. Beware of Mermaid. It's liable to grow forty feet and it has hideous hooked thorns.'

Too late. Two innocent Mermaids are ready to go in the ground tomorrow.

★

I'm thinking tonight of Humphrey Repton. He is an ancestor of mine on my father's side. My great-grandmother was Elizabeth Repton Mayes, whose memory is preserved only in my middle name and in a photograph of her cradling my newborn grandfather in her arms. He must have been the ugliest baby born in England at the end of the nineteenth century. He's glaring fiercely at the camera, already full of will. He waves his tight little fists, while she looks lovingly down at him. When he was still a small boy, she died. His father went to America and later sent for his son, who travelled across the Atlantic at nine carrying a small suitcase and a bag of apples. He watched from the railing as his aunt Lily receded on the English shore and finally disappeared. I've remained heartless to this story – impossible that cold, bossy Daddy Jack ever was a vulnerable child travelling alone to a foreign country. Instead, I see him tearing around the deck, terrorizing his fellow-passengers.

Farther back in Elizabeth's line was Humphrey Repton (1752–1818), a garden designer who popularized what we know as the English garden. Since my grandfather was a tyrant, I like knowing earlier men in the lineage loved flowers and trees. Humphrey's father was a tax collector; maybe he had someone to rebel against, too.

Instinctively, my preferences are toward blowsy, abundant, spilling flower beds with everything about to bolt across the grass. I like blue delphinium and foxgloves tall enough to arc and sway in the slightest breeze. There should be plenty of yellow lilies looking back at the sun, and dark gardenia bushes for the evenings, the pure white flowers anticipating the moon. Larkspur, coral bells, love-in-a-mist, strawberry borders, and as many pink roses as possible.

Humphrey wrote five books, plus fifty-seven Red Books, his designs for gardens with transparent overlays showing the after over the before. Even the title of his first book, *Sketches and Hints on Landscape Gardening*, tells me a lot about him. Casual, low-key, inviting. Observations, sketches, and hints, after all, offer a lot of leeway – such a different slant from my grandfather's approach to life, he who went to *the school of hard knocks*, called all my boyfriends 'little two-by-fours,' and thought my writing *with your head in the clouds* was close to a criminal act. Humphrey's English garden style gradually influenced the more rigidly conceived Italian garden design. I'm searching for a blend at Bramasole, along with our own idiosyncratic preferences.

With only a little over an acre of our five devoted to the

frivolity of flowers, I know Humphrey would not devote a Red Book to my garden. But I'll take him along as I plan.

★

During the winter in San Francisco, I began to read about the evolution of the Italian garden. I knew that in ancient times, Pliny wrote about fanciful creatures cut from box-wood, and names spelled out by vines and flowers. His lost garden is thought to be near Città di Castello, just a few miles from Bramasole. During suppers in Pliny's garden, light courses were floated in artificial birds and miniature ships on the surface of a stone pool. As you sat down, a spray of water shot up. His concept of gardens blended sweetly into his version of happiness, a philosophy of *otium*, life spent in elegant, intellectual freedom.

Propped on pillows in bed while wind swirled the trees and scoured the windows with rain and salty mist, I read *Gardens of the Italian Villas* by Marella Agnelli, and *The Italian Renaissance Garden* by Claudia Lazzaro, trying to imagine the decision to build a garden with paths which could be flooded so your guests could drift through the garden in little boats. Some gardens had waterworks which could simulate rain or the wind howling. I was struck with the concept of the garden not only as a setting for the house and a place of pleasure but also a place of surprise and fun – fountains that unexpectedly sprayed you as you passed, and *il giardino segreto*, the secret garden within a garden. Who would not love the idea of a secret garden? I've planted a double circle of tall sunflowers on a high terrace, making a little round room. They're almost knee high. In July, the big flowers and leaves will almost hide the inner circle. I hope someone's children come to visit. As a child, I would have loved that space.

Scherzi d'acqua or *giochi d'acqua*, water jokes, more than any other aspect of the historical garden, reveal a vast cultural space between us and them. They were a staple of Italian gardens. Rounding a bend, your step on a certain stone would set off a shower, suddenly drenching you. Search the literature; these water jokes were enjoyed and expected. No one went home in a huff over her stained blue silk. I don't know of anyone over ten who would like to be drenched on a tour of my garden. But I'm convinced by water; there must be water in the garden, an element of obvious joy, just as flowers are. Water is music and a place for birds to wash, water is movement and a cool spot for toads.

I take statues for granted in the old Italian gardens. They served ideological purposes, reflecting a philosophical stance or interest, such as theater or music, of the owner. But often, I now realize, they were for pure play, as in the grotto pool at the entrance to the Boboli Gardens in Florence, where three marble children swim and duck each other. As a child I loved the mirrored globe on a pedestal in my grandparents' yard. Looking in it, the oak tree above went wonky and my face distorted crazily. Silver shoots of sunlight reflected so brilliantly that I hoped a fire would start.

Of all the gardens I can think of at home, few are playful. I met a woman in Dayton who has bowling balls scattered around her long sloping garden. Otherwise planted with conventional bushes, the balls certainly surprise. 'How did you start collecting bowling balls in the yard?' I asked her.

'I had one. It looked so pretty with the snow on it.' She paused, groping for a reason to state; I realized my mistake in urging her to pin down whimsy with some rational explanation. 'Anyone can plant flowers,' she continued.

Long wicked pause. 'It takes a real gardener to have balls.'

The traditional urge for garden ornaments persists in Tuscany. Olive oil jars, topped with pots of geraniums, decorate country gardens. An iron fence around a house in Camucia is decorated with musical notes. At garden supply departments, statuary is easy to find — David (gross in terra-cotta), Flora, Venus, the four seasons, various nymphs, the Seven Dwarfs. In antique shops, I see sublime travertine fountains with Latin inscriptions and garden ornaments too valuable to be left outside.

The whimsy of the eternal Italian topiary craze, too, seems to come from a great distance. I imagine Ed on a ladder, snipping our ball-shaped topiaries into ships, dragons, the Pope, a deer complete with antlers. One Medici *palazzo* had boxwood in shapes of wolf, dog, ram, hare, elephant, boar, and other creatures. A house in Camucia has topiary squirrels at the entrance. A neighbor's topiary I finally decided is a peacock. Why not a Ferrari, a glass of wine, the 'finger,' or a soccer goal?

While reading about the great old Italian gardens, mentally I wandered through the local gardens of my Cortona neighbors, who emulate on a modest scale many of the traditions of the grand historical gardens — paths of river pebbles; little or no lawn; pots, pots, pots for flowers and lemon trees arranged around the garden; aviaries; box or laurel hedges; and shady arbors for dining outdoors. I've never seen roses bloom the way they do in Tuscany. They tend to be planted along a fence or — oddly — just off to themselves in a row. Flower beds and rolling lawns hardly exist; they require what Tuscans instinctively conserve: water. A small garden may have fifty pots of various sizes as well as a *limonaia* for citrus, geraniums, and hydrangeas. Cortona's park starts with a shady area of benches and bordered flower beds around a playful fountain of nymphs entwined with sea creatures. Beyond that area, the park, called the Parterre, stretches a third of a mile along a wall with long views over Lago Trasimeno and the valley. A gesture toward a formal garden remains in the linden-lined walk which is broad enough for two carriages to pass, though now it is only walkers and joggers. While I haven't seen a hilltown park as lovely as Cortona's, many medieval towns have parks just outside the gates, respites for the citizens from the heated stones and cramped streets.

The Italian concept of severe geometric gardens contradicts all my innate preferences. At heart, theirs is an entirely different design aesthetic. Historically, flowers play a minor role compared to statues, patterns of walkways, fountains, hedges, pergolas, and pavilions.

The Italian garden, Ippolito Pindemonte wrote back in 1792, was 'ruled more by sun and marble than by grass and shade.' Wandering in gardens here, I've felt their austerity, a forlorn quality to the squared-off compartments and the endless boxwood terraces. They seem anti-nature. But, by slow osmosis, I've grown to like the architectural and conceptual sense of space, how often garden layout reproduces the proportions of the house, and the statues, stairways, and balustrades create the sense of outdoor rooms. This *is* the Mediterranean, where people live outside as much as in. In the large gardens, these strict arrangements of nature give way to orchards or woods, the last buffers between the house and wild nature, a fine idea that crosses time and architectural styles. The early garden writers refer to gardening as 'third nature,' first nature being the natural wild, second nature being agricultural cultivation, and third being nature in sync with ideas of beauty and art.

Even though the gardens appear highly artificial to my

eyes, trained by Southern lawns of dogwood, azalea, and camellia, and by casual, low-maintenance California gardens, on reflection, they make sense. Italy, until recently, has been utterly fragmented. The castle, walled village, or villa of necessity had an us-against-the-world stance. Gardens, of course, would be enclosed or controlled or designed to make one forget the danger or chaos just beyond the confines.

★

Over and over, I surrender to the Italian sense of beauty. How to bring the elements I've come to love into my own garden? I want Humphrey's fast and loose arrangements, his rustic sense of comfort and ease. Can I have those along with the Italian geometry and playfulness, those oxymorons that give such a sense of surprise?

Reading about gardens is instructive but frustrating. Photos do not convey depth, and perspective is too limited. Worse, I can't smell the layers of fragrance as my eye follows the paths, can't bend down to rub a furry leaf, or see how a willow in new leaf fractures the light. I was transported only partially by the glossy pages to the grandiose waterworks of the Villa d'Este. The delight and luxury of water spilling from the breasts of women, the mouths of dolphins, the simulated cascades and stepped, downhill courses – the pictures stilled and silenced the gush, splash, and trickle you must bend close to hear.

Two hours in the Roseto Botanico at Cavriglia are worth a whole winter of looking at books. June is an ideal time to see – to smell – the garden of Fondazione Carla Fineschi, the largest private rose garden in the world. I immediately start writing names of roses we like, regardless of the fact that nurseries in our area often don't sell roses with names so we may never find any of these. Every category of rose — Bourbon, Chinese, Damask, Tea, Ramblers, etc. — has its beds and every bush is fully labeled. Ed and I lose each other then meet. Out of the thousands of roses, we hope to identify the two pink ones that belong to the history of our house. We both spot the indecently fragrant Reine des Violettes — similar, but ours are more cupped, like a peony. Maybe the *nonna* who lived at Bramasole never knew the name, or maybe such an old country rose just doesn't make it into the blood-lines. Let's just call it Nonna's Rose. Finally, we wander, watching the gardeners clip the dead, watching other people swooning over the fragrances. Behind the garden a few roses are sold. We buy three called Sally Holmes to sprawl along the driveway, offering white clusters of flat roses among the lavender. I'm not drawn to white roses but why not have a few to catch the moonlight?

★

At Firenze Com'era (Florence as it was), one of my favorite museums for its tranquil convent setting and its lack of other visitors, I'm fascinated by the dozen paintings of Medici villas by the Flemish painter, Justus Utens. These half-moons (painted in 1599 for lunettes in a Medici villa at Artimino) depict bird's-eye views of the houses and gardens as they were originally, a rare glimpse at ideal garden layout of that time. Villa Pratolino shows an elaborate sequence of pools spilling downhill into each other. At Lambrogiana's garden, four grand squares, bordered by pergolas, are subdivided into four others, with square pools at the entrance to each big square. The walled courts of all these villas are oddly empty — perhaps a well, but otherwise lacking ornamentation. If I ever win the lottery, I'd like to create a garden on this scale. Ever since the enormous fun I had reading George Sitwell's (papa of the marvelous eccentric writers Osbert, Sacheverell, and Edith) ruminations on his gardens, which involved the creations of hills and lakes, and other ambitious manipulations of the landscape, I've been in awe of gardeners who think on this scale.

The remnant of the Medici Giardino dei Semplici (garden of simples: medicinal plants) is still open to the public in Florence. Since Cosimo the First had the idea for this garden in 1545, botanists have planted specimen ferns, palms, herbs, flowers, and shrubs, as well as studied healing properties of plants. It's a weedy spot behind imposing gates near San Marco. This morning, it's empty, except for a woman wheeling a baby, and a man with a stringy garden hose drowning plants. At his rate, it will take a month to water the garden, which may be why so much of it droops. I take away no ideas from the garden of simples but it is a shady walk out of the heat of Florence, a glimpse back into the awakening of gardening as a subject of study and importance.

The herb garden at San Pietro in Perugia had me taking notes immediately. The San Pietro complex now shares its deserted, pure courtyards, grounds, and austere monks' cells with a university agriculture department. Guidebooks to Umbria don't even mention this peaceful oasis, with its accompanying book (in Italian) explaining the intricate numerology and plant symbolism of the reconstructed medieval meditation garden, which adjoins a clearly laid-out garden of simples. I found that a sticky weed, *la parietaria*, which sprouts from every crannied wall at our house, has a past. In Latin, it is called *elxine*, and possesses the powers to expel stones from the urinary tract, heal wounds, and calm colic. Local people have told me it's a chief cause of spring allergy, as well. As I dig out its tenacious roots, I'll have more respect for its existence. A pink version of what I know as yellow oxalis in California is called *acetosella*. The low, spreading plant Beppe calls *morroncello* is labeled *pimpinella* (*sanguisorba* in Latin), good for everything from plague to ulcers. *Santoreggia*, savory, which I thought of as an innocent addition to summer soups and salads, turns out to be a powerful aphrodisiac when mixed with honey and pepper. Even the wild melissa appears in new light: Its leaves produce gold dreams. Since I'm not sure I've ever seen gold light in a dream, I'd like to try this tea. How perfectly blue the flower of borage, a bright spot in a herb garden.

★

From my reading, I gleaned an unpleasant insight – how unformed and narrow my views of gardening were! In my new yellow book, I'm starting a list of newly realized possibilities for my more mundane-sized garden, beginning with sketches of pergolas. Anyone looking at them might think they're scaffolding or subway tunnels. Almost everyone with a garden in Tuscany has a pergola, not only because they're practical for grapes. Chestnut, stone, willow, iron, they direct a view, provide a focal point, and protect you from the sun, an easy contrast and defining point. Lunching under dangling bunches of grapes imparts a delicious mood of hedonism, while the splashes of sunlight falling over the table make faces beautiful and seduce everyone to enjoy themselves fully. Why have I never built a woven willow pergola in California? I can superimpose one over my memory of the yard of my house in Palo Alto – there behind the house. I should have taken out that ugly juniper hedge and put up a lovely arbor.

★

I have a practice which must release beneficial rushes of body chemicals, purify the blood, and strengthen the heart. When I can't sleep I imagine holding all the animals I've loved; I revisit my happiest moments; I walk through the streets of Cuzco, San Miguel, Deya, recalling views, windows, faces, sounds. I think of everyone I love unstintingly. To this habit I now can add the revision of the gardens of all the houses I've lived in, budgetary considerations of the time notwithstanding. I'm more accustomed to the revisions of interiors, a large topic among the women of my family, any one of whom might say something like, 'I never should have papered that dining room, especially with those Chinese cranes coming in to land. I always feel like one will plop down into my soup. I should have lacquered the walls *brilliant* yellow and a mirror should go over that sideboard, not those puny sconces . . .' I wonder if they, when insomnia strikes, have practices like mine.

★

Formal squares traditionally organize large Italian gardens. I knew that, of course, but did not know that the square was called a quincunx, for its four trees planted at the corners and one at the central point. Ever since Cicero, many gardens are a series of quincunxes linked by paths. Boxwood was the common border but some quincunxes were edged with sage, rosemary, lavender, or myrtle. Within the quincunxes, gardeners planted lilies, roses, and bulbs such as hyacinth, narcissus, and crocus. Pergola walkways worked as boundaries on the sides of the gardens, offering shaded walks.

Reading garden inventories from hundreds of years ago, I see how many of the plants loved then still are — cyclamen, jasmine, honeysuckle, savory, clematis, anise.

Others have fallen from favor: hyssop, mugwort, rue, tansy, melissa, black cumin, sweet cicely, balsam apple, black bryony, and woodbine. Herbs often were used interchangeably with flowers. The iris and the orange lily (*giglio selvatico*), both of which grow wild at Bramasole, are mentioned frequently, causing me to wonder how long ago they naturalized.

I'm happy that some plants I've chosen are on the lists of common herbs and flowers in Renaissance gardens. Last summer I planted *issopo*, hyssop, as a border. It rewarded me with long-blooming spiky purple flowers and an ambition to spread into a bush. Francesco recognized it as something good to rub on bruises. Another I planted was melissa, which I then found was the same as the wild mints I'd called lemon balm or citronella. It smelled like the oil my mother used to rub on me in the evenings when mosquitoes swarmed and I played late in the alleys and neighbors' back yards. Now I cut branches and lay them under the table when we eat outside at night. Maybe it helps.

Savory, another mint cousin, I planted by accident. At the market I bought a pot of *santoreggia*. 'Use the flowers and the leaves,' was all the seller told me.

'In what?'

She raised both arms, 'In the kitchen, *signora*. *Insalata, zuppa*, everywhere.' By chance I came upon a mention of santoreggia as *satureja hortensis*, the Latin name for savory, and noticed the connection.

Jasmine grows over an arch and along the iron railing on the upstairs terrace. Honeysuckle I also planted early. The scent takes me straight to a white Georgia road in moonlight, when my true love in high school picked a branch and put it in my hair. When we kissed, his mouth was hard and unyielding, then suddenly open and alive.

Honeysuckle doesn't dazzle anyone with its flowers, but I can lean out of my study window, look over cypresses and hills and breathe not only the honeyed fragrance but the sand road cooling off behind Bowen's Mill, the wind in long leaf pine, and Royale Lyme aftershave liberally doused on the cheeks of a shy boy years and miles away. I was not shy; I'd been waiting for him to kiss me for weeks.

Southern scents are powerful. I always keep a gardenia pot going in the shade, a connection to the old giant in my mother's yard, a scent I slipped past when coming home late, the green-black leaves and the gardenias so white they seemed to have a nimbus of light around them. I'd pick one and float it in a water glass by my bed. By the time I woke up late the next morning, the scent had invaded every corner of the hot room. My family's garden in Georgia was nothing special, just nice, though by August almost everything looked exhausted. We had camellias, lilies, azaleas, crape myrtle, larkspur, bachelor's buttons, which we called ragged robin, and a back hedge of bridal bouquet. Inside it I had a hideout and would not answer when my mother called from the back door. Through long swoops of white bloom, I could see her fuming. I liked to spy. My other hideout, strategically located near the front door, was under the porch, behind the blue hydrangeas. I could see the postman's hairy leg and black socks, the skirts of my mother's bridge friends, and sometimes hear bits of forbidden conversation about Lyman Carter 'running around,' or Martha's shock treatments in Asheville.

Here I have pots of pink and white hydrangeas, the blooms as large as a baby's head. Between two of them Ed built a stone bench, an almost hidden vantage point for viewing our garden, though nothing as exciting as who entered and exited my family's home.

We have planted both white and lavender lilac, which has the lovely name *lillà* in Italian.

★

The garden, I begin to see, is a place where I can give memory a location and season in which to remain alive. Ed, too, loves the lilac. They grew all over his hometown in Minnesota and, after the harsh winter, must have been a sweet sight. His neighbor Viola Lapinski, an 'old maid' (he now realizes she was in her thirties), used to bring bunches when she came over on Saturday nights to watch *Gunsmoke* with his family.

I'll have to ask my daughter, whose first word was 'flava,' flower, if she feels a memory imprint from our Somers, N.Y. back yard of maples, which in autumn dropped knee-deep yellow leaves she and the dog burrowed under. Along the boundary wall, I planted my first herb garden and never since have had one so extensive. Digging beside me one day, she found an amethyst medicine bottle which she kept for years. In the front yard, a peony hedge popped up every year. Ashley thought someone with too much lipstick had kissed the crest of each pink globe. What does she remember? Her room in Palo Alto had one sliding glass wall. She stepped outside every day to mock orange, lemon, kumquat, loquat. The inheritance of those light scents must be floating in the canaliculi of her brain. I wish she had the grape arbor to remember. Perhaps building one here will do.

Scents operate like music and poetry, stirring up wordless feelings that rush through the body, not as cognitive thoughts but as a surge of lymphatic tide. Ed walks by the lilac and simultaneously his mother places the vase of ashen lavender blossoms on the coffee table, his father offers a box of toffee to Viola, whose hair is rolled on orange juice cans in preparation for mass tomorrow, Lawrence Welk starts to bounce, and the room is presided over by the shadowy tones of the framed Jesus over the TV, pausing to look out at everyone from the garden of Gethsemane. *His eyes follow you everywhere.*

A garden folds memory into the new as well. I have no history with lavender, pots of lemon trees, balconies of tumbling coral geraniums, double hollyhocks shooting up, tree roses, dahlias – but now I see that when (if) I am ninety, a lavender sachet will return to me the day Beppe planted forty lavenders, will bring back summer after summer of white butterflies and bees around the house, dipping in and out of the lavender haze. Probably nothing will stir the memory of the horrid weed that smells like old fish, or the sticky one that makes me rush inside for the allergy tablets.

★

'If we plant everything you list in your yellow book, we'll live in a botanical garden.'

'Or maybe an Eden.' Ed has told me the etymological root of the word 'paradise' comes from the Greek *paradeisos*, meaning garden or park, and, farther back, from *dhoigho-*, clay or mud wall, and from the Avestan *pairi-daeza*, meaning circumvallation, walled-around. Paradise: a clay-walled garden. Genesis says nothing about wall-building on any of the seven days, but I can imagine a high perimeter of golden bricks thumb-printed by the hand of God. If He has hands, of course. Was the Eden wall covered with Mermaid, a quick-growth rose? Ours seemed to plunge down roots and surge forth the moment we planted them. Surely the wild magenta rugosas behind our house thrived there, the low branches sheltering the serpent. Maybe a new apple is in order on our land. Since ours are gnarly, they tempt no one.

From much-later historical inventories of gardens, I'm intrigued by black bryony – whatever that may be. It sounds like something entwined over the graves of Catherine and Heathcliff. One writer of the time recommends carnations every three and a half feet, the intervals planted with marjoram, lily of the valley, ranunculus, and cat thyme. Thyme and marjoram would add texture and cover bare dirt. 'What about zinnias,' Ed says. 'Old plain zinnias. What *do* you have in store for me in that yellow book of yours?'

'OK, I'll skip the plants. We've got a pergola to build. I'd love at least one statue. And a fountain.'

'Is that *all*? What about a folly? I like the idea of those ornamental hermits you read about, too. And we could build a fake ruin at the end of the Lake Walk. A broken arch, a piece of a door, a tumbled wall.'

'That's a great idea! A place to sit . . .'

He looks stunned. 'No wait, back up. I was kidding. You're not serious, are you?'

SPRING KITCHEN

ANTIPASTI

★

Paolo's Fennel Fritters

Anything Paul Bertolli cooks I will eat. Once he even
served me tendons. 'Whose tendons are these, anyway?' I
asked. He flinched only a little. 'Veal. You'll like them.'
He knows I'm somewhat squeamish and tries to educate
me. When he was chef at Chez Panisse, I was allowed to
assist him in the kitchen a few times. My first assigned task
was to behead a mound of pigeons. Their closed blue eyelids bothered me, but not wanting to be just the lettuce
washer, I began to whack their little heads off. Paul has
Italian parents and deep affinities with Italian life. His

genius is for revealing the essence of whatever he's cooking. His pleasure and integrity are clear to anyone who reads and cooks from his *Chez Panisse Cooking*. Recently he has built an *acetaia*, a barn for the complex process of making balsamic vinegar. He was one of our first guests here and helped us set up our prototype kitchen. When I'm in California, I love to go to his restaurant, Oliveto's in Oakland, especially on nights when he celebrates truffles or *porcini* mushrooms. This is his recipe, just as he handed it to me, for fennel fritters. Select young fennel — older plants are too fibrous.

> 6.5 ounces of wild fennel hearts, cleaned
> 6.5 ounces of tender fronds and leaves
> 1 whole head of garlic, peeled
> 2¾ cups of sturdy bread crumbs from a day-old loaf
> ¾ cup of freshly grated parmigiano reggiano
> 1 whole egg
> ½ t. sea salt
> freshly ground black pepper
> ¾ cup of olive oil

Pare the fennel stalks down to their tender centers and while doing so, separate and retain the leafy fronds. Combine the stalks, fronds, and leaves on a cutting board and chop them coarsely. Place in a bowl, cover with cold water and drain well.

Place the clean fennel in a steamer along with the peeled garlic cloves. Steam over high heat for 12–15 minutes, or until the fennel and garlic are very tender. Cool and transfer to a cutting board. Chop the mixture finely.

Add 1¾ cups of the bread crumbs and the grated parmigiano. Next add the whole egg, the salt and a little freshly ground black pepper. Stir with a fork until the mixture forms a firm mass.

Using two soup spoons, portion the fritters evenly. One by one, toss the fritters into a bowl containing the remaining bread crumbs and form them by hand into small uniform patties.

Warm the olive oil in a large skillet. Test the temperature of the oil by tossing in a crumb. It should sizzle and dance in the pan. Fry the fritters over high heat, turning them with the help of a slotted spoon. Transfer to a platter lined with absorbent paper or towel, then to a service platter. Pass while still warm.

*

Fried Artichokes

As a Southerner, to me 'deep fried' is an enchanting phrase. We never met an artichoke, when I was growing up, except marinated in a jar. Still, this seems like soul food. At the spring markets, vendors sell five sizes. For stuffing with bread, herbs, and tomatoes, I buy the largest ones. For frying or eating raw, the smallest, purple-tinged ones are best. Even with those, trim off any part of the leaf that might be stringy.

Select ten small artichokes. Strip any tough outer leaves and trim off the tips quite close to the heart. Quarter and pat dry with paper towels. Heat safflower, peanut, or sunflower oil. Beat three eggs in a bowl with ¾ cup of water, and quickly dip artichoke pieces in the egg then shake them in a bag of seasoned flour. Brush off excess. Fry in hot oil (350 degrees) until golden. When done, remove to brown paper to drain, then pile on a platter and serve with wedges of lemon. Serves eight as an hors d'oeuvre.

★

Odori

Usually the greengrocer, whether in a shop or outdoor market, will give you a handful of *odori*, literally 'odors, herbs,' aromatic flavors for your pot: a handful of parsley and basil, a couple of stalks of celery, and a carrot or two. If I'm not making a stock or stew, sometimes this little gift wilts in the fridge. One night when the cupboard was bare, Ed minced the *odori* and invented this simple mix for pasta. After that, we spread it on *focaccia*, and also pulled apart the petals of steamed artichokes and stuffed it between the leaves, a fresh alternative to lemon butter or vinaigrette.

Finely chop – almost mince – 2 carrots, 2 stalks of celery, and 3 cloves of garlic. Sauté in 2 T. of olive oil until cooked but still crunchy. Scissor basil and parsley into the mixture, add another 2 T. of olive oil and cook on low flame for 2–3 minutes. Prepare enough spaghetti for two. Drain and mix 2 or 3 T. of the pasta water and a little olive oil into the pasta. Mix 4 T. grated parmigiano *into the* odori. *It should have the texture of pesto. Toss with spaghetti. Serves two.*

★

Risotto Primavera

'The best meal I've ever had,' a friend said, after a simple dinner of *risotto* with spring vegetables. Of course it wasn't, but the effect of a lovely mound of *risotto* in the middle of the plate surrounded by a wreath of colorful and flavorful vegetables inspires effusive declarations. This seems like the heart of spring dining. It could be followed by roast chicken but I like it as a dinner in itself, followed by tossed lettuces with pear slices and gorgonzola. A special local *risotto* is made with nettles. Evil as they are when mature, they're a spring treat when they're very young. Some farmers' markets at home have them occasionally. Chop and quickly blanch them, then stir into the *risotto* at the last minute of cooking.

Prepare and season the vegetables separately. Shell 3 pounds of fresh peas, steam briefly. Clean a large bunch of new carrots and cut into pieces about the same size as the asparagus stems. Steam the carrots until barely done. Break 2 pounds of asparagus stalks just where they naturally snap, and steam or roast. Heat to a boil then turn down to simmer 5½ cups of seasoned stock and ½ cup of white wine. In another pot, sauté 2 cups of arborio rice and a finely chopped onion in a tablespoon of olive oil for a couple of minutes, then gradually ladle in the stock as the rice absorbs the liquid. Keep stirring and ladling in more until the rice is done. Some prefer it almost soupy, but for this dish it is better moist and al dente. Add the juice of a lemon, stir in ½ cup or so of grated parmigiano, and season to taste. Serve the plates with the vegetables surrounding the rice. Serves six.

*

Orecchiette with Greens

Orecchiette, pasta shaped like little ears, work well when served *con quattro formaggi*, with four cheeses: *gorgonzola, parmigiano, pecorino*, and *fontina*. In spring, they are popular with greens.

Sauté 2 bunches of chopped chard with some chopped spring onions and garlic. Cook enough orecchiette *for six. Drain and toss with the greens. If you like anchovies, sauté about 6 fillets, then chop and mix with the greens. Season, then stir in ½ cup of grated* parmigiano, *or serve separately.*

*

Orecchiette with Shrimp

This combination, amusing because of the similar shapes of the pasta and the shrimp, makes a rather substantial course.

Shell enough fava beans for 1 cup. Sauté the beans in a little olive oil until almost done, then add a finely chopped small onion, or a couple of fresh spring onions, to the pan. Cook until onion is soft. Season and purée in food processor. Clean and sauté a pound of shrimp or small prawns in olive oil with 4 cloves of garlic, left whole. Add ¼ cup of white wine, turn heat to high very briefly, then turn off. Discard garlic. Cook pasta for six, drain, toss with almost all the green sauce; stir shrimp into remaining green sauce. Serve pasta on plates, arranging shrimp mixture on top.

SECONDI

*

Spring Veal

This completely simple veal, discovered when I suddenly had no tomatoes for the stew I was about to make, has become a favorite. The lovely, pure lemon flavor intensifies the taste of the tender veal.

Pat dry 3 pounds of veal cubes. Dredge in flour and quickly brown in a heavy pot. Add 1 cup of white wine. With a zester, remove the thin top layer of peel from 2 lemons; add to pot with salt and pepper. Cover and bake at 350 degrees for 40 minutes, or until veal can be pulled apart easily with a fork. Stir, add the juice of the 2 lemons. Add the lemon juice at the end, since it would toughen the veal to add it sooner. Put back in the oven for

5 more minutes. Stir in a handful of chopped parsley. Serves six.

CONTORNI

*

Fava Beans with Potatoes and Artichokes

First and most loved of the spring vegetables are the raw *fave*. Fresh *fave* are nothing like the ones I've found in supermarkets, which must be blanched and very tediously peeled, bean by bean. Although they still can be good, basically a bean that must be peeled is past its prime. Easy to grow, they're hard to find at home, although sometimes farmers' markets will have a bin of just-picked tender green ones. In one Tuscan friend's home, a bowl of raw, unshelled *fave* were brought out with a round of *pecorino*, served with a bottle of wine late in the afternoon. At another friend's house, the *fave e pecorino* ritual was observed at the end of a light dinner, a simultaneous salad and cheese course. Any time seems to be a good time for this sacred combination. The following recipe could accompany a veal chop or a pork tenderloin, but is a happy spring main course, too.

Quarter and steam 6 small artichokes until just tender. Drain and set aside in acidulated water. Peel and quarter a pound of white potatoes (you can use tiny red new potatoes). Steam these, too, until barely done. Shell 2 pounds of fava beans, as fresh as possible; steam until done. Heat 4 T. olive oil in a big sauté pan. Sauté 2 or 3 chopped young spring onions (or a bunch or two of scallions) and 3 or 4 cloves of minced garlic. Add the vegetables, chopped thyme, salt, and pepper. Squeeze the juice of 1 lemon over the vegetables. Gently toss the mixture until nicely blended and hot. Turn out onto a platter. Serves six generously.

Roasted Vegetables, Especially Fennel

The larger your oven, the better to roast a variety of the vegetables-of-the-moment. I've come to prefer oven-roasting to grilling vegetables. The individual flavors are accentuated, while grilling imposes its own smoky taste. Oven-roasted fennel is unbelievably good. I find myself stealing a piece as soon as I turn off the oven.

Generously oil a non-stick cookie pan with sides, or a large baking pan. Arrange halved peppers, quartered onions, separated pieces of fennel, halved zucchini and squash, sliced eggplant, whole heads of garlic, and halved tomatoes. Drizzle with olive oil, sprinkle with chopped thyme, salt and pepper. Slide the pan into the oven and roast at 350 degrees. After about 15 minutes, start testing the squash, zucchini, and tomatoes, removing them to a platter as they are done. Turn the eggplant and peppers. Everything should be done before 30 minutes have passed. Arrange on a platter. The garlic requires hands-on attention. Guests pull off the cloves and squeeze them onto bread.

★

Other Roasted Vegetables

Since my friend Susan Wyler, author of several cook-books, taught me to roast asparagus in the oven, I've never steamed it again. Even burned and crisp, it's delicious. Little string beans also benefit from a run in the oven. Roasting brings out a hidden taste. With about 200 onions growing like mad in the garden, I've taken to roasting them frequently. Balsamic vinegar adds a sweet surprise. Surround a roast chicken with a ring of these onions.

Arrange asparagus spears in a single layer in a pie or cake pan.

Trickle olive oil over them and season with salt and pepper. Roast for 5 minutes — or until barely fork-tender — at 400 degrees.

Steam Blue Lake string beans until almost done. Shake them dry and roast with a sprinkling of olive oil for 5 minutes at 400 degrees.

Arrange almost peeled onions — leave a layer or two of the papery skin — in a non-stick baking dish. Cut a large X-shaped gash in the top. Sprinkle liberally with balsamic vinegar and olive oil. Season with salt and pepper. Roast for 40 minutes at 350 degrees. Check a time or two and add more balsamic and oil if they look dry.

DOLCI

In *primavera*, fruits aren't ripe yet. Most of the *gelato* stands are still closed for cold weather. As in winter, dessert is often chestnuts roasted at the fireplace, a wedge of *gorgonzola*, or *baci*, the chocolate kisses of Perugia, along with a glass of *limoncella* or *amaro*, or, for the stalwart among us, *grappa*. One stand at the Thursday market sells dried fruits. Poached in wine, with a few spirals of lemon zest and spices, and served with *biscotti*, the fruits come to life, good to hold us over until the fruits of summer begin to arrive.

*

Fruits Plumped in Wine

Delicate and light, this homey dessert falls into the comfort food category. Pass *biscotti* for dipping into the sugared wine. Children hate this dessert.

Pour boiling water to cover over a pound of dried fruits — apricots, peaches, cherries, and/or figs — and let them rest for an hour. Bring to a boil 2 cups of red wine, ½ cup sugar, a little nut-meg, and spirals of thin lemon peel. Stir in 1 cup of raisins (a mixture of gold and dark), and the drained fruit. Reduce heat immediately to a simmer. Cook for 10 minutes. Remove the fruit. Boil down the remaining liquid until it thickens and pour over the fruit. Better the next day. Sprinkle each serving with toasted pine nuts.

★

Frozen Sunset

Just a plain ice, but anything with blood oranges seems exotic and primal. Is it the word 'blood' that enters the imagination as a glass of the scarlet juice pours into a glass? Or is it just the jolt of slicing the orange, seeing the two rounds falling open, glistening scarlet, and vinous. The mind is cooled and soothed by the sweet-tart layers of taste in the icy melting of this blood orange sorbet.

Make a sugar syrup by boiling together 1 cup of water and 1 cup of sugar, then simmering it for about 5 minutes, stirring constantly. Add 2 cups of blood orange juice, and the juice of a lemon. Cool in the fridge. When well-chilled, process in an ice cream maker according to manufacturer's instructions. Or you can freeze it in ice trays until slushy, break up the icy mixture, then partially freeze again. Garnish with lemon balm or mint.

★

Ginger Pound Cake

Baking must be a deeply encoded instinct. When it comes to dessert, I find that I often return to something I know from my mother and Willie Bell's kitchen. Ginger has nothing to do with Italy but it has a great deal to do with fruit. My carry-on luggage would puzzle a customs inspector, if one ever bothered to look inside. She might find a bottle of cane syrup – because how can one have biscuits at breakfast without butter and cane syrup – or a bottle of corn syrup for various desserts such as this old favorite.

Sift 3⅓ cups of flour, ½ t. salt, 1 t. baking powder, 1 t. baking soda, 1 t. nutmeg, and 1½ T. ginger. Cream 1 cup of butter and 1 cup of sugar. Separate 4 eggs. Stir beaten yolks into sugar mixture. Beat in 1 cup of light corn syrup, then stir in flour alternately with ½ cup of cream. Beat the 4 whites until they form stiff peaks, then fold egg whites into cake mixture. Pour into a non-stick tube pan that has been lightly buttered for good measure. Bake at 325 degrees for 1 hour. Cool briefly then invert on a plate.

★

Blood Oranges with Vin Santo

If you do not have *vin santo*, substitute brandy. This is a vibrant dessert, especially paired with slivers of Ginger Pound Cake. Later in the season, prepare peaches this way, too, simmering them only five minutes.

Boil 2 cups of water, 1 cup of sugar, 4 T. of vin santo and 3 or 4 cloves. Add sections of 6 peeled blood oranges, then turn heat down and simmer for 10 minutes. Drain and cool. Mix 3 cups of mascarpone with ½ cup of sugar, ½ cup of white wine, and the juice of a lemon. Serve the mascarpone in 6 bowls, topped with the oranges.

CIRCLES ON MY MAP:

MONTE OLIVETO MAGGIORE

A dreamy day to drive. The green landscape smears across the windshield. Flowering chestnut trees begin to droop under the rain. We cross the valley, skirt the hilltown of Sinalunga, and drive toward Monte Oliveto Maggiore, one of the great monasteries of Italy. The greens! Hills look as though footlights angle across them – neon green, poison green, green velvet, Life Saver green. When I was five, I saw an irresistible green moss and jumped on it. I quickly sank into sludge and my father, in a pale linen suit and shouting 'Jesus H. Christ,' had to fish me out. I had jumped through a brilliant, thick algae covering the surface of an open septic tank behind the cotton mill. But this green is innocent; I could jump into it and roll like a horse.

We start to glimpse the wild landscape of eroded *crete*,

clay, which you see in many Sienese paintings. Dramatic and forbidding in late summer, the crevices are still softened by grasses. The monks who chose this spot definitely wanted to leave the world behind for a place of contemplative seclusion. I try to think of travelling here in the 1500s, when twenty miles was the most you could count on covering in a day and the maps that existed rarely showed roads. A curvy one like this must have been a tortuous track susceptible to washout in storms. Italian roads still depend on a directional sense rather than highway numbers. You see signs to specific places rather than 580 East or 880 North, a custom probably connected with early travel. One traveller in the 1500s wrote, 'I have had so little respite that my bottom has been constantly a-fire from the saddle.' Obviously a common problem; earlier, the rigors of the road inspired Cato to give a bit of advice, 'To prevent chafing: When you set out on a journey, keep a small branch of Pontic wormwood under the anus.' The more comfortable Alfa hugs the road nicely and Ed loves the constant downshifting on hills and hairpin loops.

Around a curve, suddenly the red brick complex looms. The moat and stronghold effect of the massive structure remind me that even here in the Middle Ages defense was an issue. Cypresses and chapels and footpaths surround the monastery, which looks like a beautiful prison. At the entrance, a Benedictine monk in an ankle-length white robe that looks unbearably scratchy and hot checks everyone for proper attire. My daughter was turned away last summer by this fashion policeman when she presented herself at the door in a sleeveless Lycra top and a short skirt. The monk wagged his finger in her face and shook his head. Arms may not be exposed. She was furious when she saw men in shorts being admitted but she went back to the car, borrowed her boyfriend's baggy T-shirt and then was allowed to enter. Today, I see him turn away a man in short shorts. If the Benedictines must wear those wooly robes, I suppose flesh has to be a philosophical concept. At least today proves it's not a misogynistic one. He scans my mid-calf-length skirt and yellow sweater and nods me in.

Once inside the fifteenth-century cloister, the impression of a fortress dissolves into the serene quiet of a light-drenched courtyard with pots of geraniums. Somewhere in the complex, monks labor over the restoration of old books, or engage in concocting Flora di Monte Oliveto, a herbal liqueur used as a curative. Their other main product is honey. I would like to see them in their robes, opening the hives, an act unchanged since medieval times.

Behind the bordering carved arcades, the Sodoma and Signorelli (a Cortona boy) frescoes of the life and miracles of San Benedetto − holy inspiration for this order − line the inside walls.

During these years of transforming the house, we become obsessed at different times over aspects of construction. For a while, wherever we were we noticed drainpipes, how they were attached, where they leaked, whether they were copper or tin. When we had a humidity problem on a wall, we found ourselves spotting areas of mildew and rippled paint on cathedral and museum walls, ignoring the art and architecture while trying to pinpoint the source of the problem.

Today, we're riveted by the Signorelli fresco of a falling wall. 'Walls fall,' in the immortal words of Primo Bianchi when our Lime Tree Bower wall careened into the road below. Falling stone is a particular nightmare of ours. In the background of the fresco, a monk loses his footing when a wall starts to slide, and he tumbles through scaffolding. A little devil hovers above him. Was there a red devil hovering in the linden trees over our wall? In the middle distance, three monks are carrying the lifeless body, and in the foreground the monk is miraculously revived by a blessing from Benedetto. As in other frescoes, this event does not seem to qualify as a major miracle. After all, the monk probably was just knocked out. Benedetto must have been loved and revered, so much so that everything he did seemed miraculous. If I had not bought the guidebook in the monastery shop, I would have no idea of all that is going on in these paintings.

I love the sense of time found in many frescoes: The whole sequence of a narrative is composed as one painting, with past to present depicted from small to large or left to right; the viewer first perceives the whole simultaneously happening event, then 'reads' the progression. Time collapses, as it so often does in memory. The painter, seeking to tell a story, is bound by the Alpha-Omega concept of time, but the structured composition of the whole fresco runs back to an earlier intuition: All time is eternally present.

In the next fresco, four monks cannot move a large stone. Look closer – there's a devil in the stone. The monks have long iron poles exactly like ours and have wedged them under the stone, but the evil force keeps it immovable until Benedetto makes the sign of the cross over it. We have confronted many such stones, without the help of divine intervention. Now I'm understanding his sainthood. The power to lift stones surely qualifies him.

Off to the side in another Signorelli, a woman in blue is three-quarters turned away from the viewer. She's as lovely as the famous Vermeer painting of the woman pouring from a pitcher at a window. Two monks, against the rules of their order, are having a fine meal in a house outside the monastery. They're focused on a laden table, which is served by two women and a boy carefully holding a bowl. The woman in blue pours wine from a pitcher into a glass and you almost can hear it splash. Her hair is caught up in a cap which pushes out her ear. The long line of her neck and the faint indentation of her backbone through her dress give you the muscular sensation of her body in the act of pouring. Everything about her feels intent on what she's doing. The other woman in sea-foam green has rushed over from the fireplace, skirts in motion, carrying aloft what looks suspiciously like a *torta della nonna*. For all her delicate, almond-eyed beauty, she has exceptionally large hands and feet. Perhaps an assistant stepped in and painted them while Signorelli himself went out for a pitcher of cool wine. These women flanking the fresco are two of the most arresting images in the whole cycle. Just out the window, it's later. The two well-fed monks have been found out by Benedetto. They're on their knees begging forgiveness, with the taste of the wine and *torta* still lingering in their mouths.

During the decoration of Monte Oliveto, which he began in 1495, Signorelli left after painting six frescoes, and the Benedetto cycle became Sodoma's project in 1505. Il Sodoma, what a name. He was born Giovanni Antonio Bazzi. The monks called him 'Il Mattaccio,' which means idiot or madman. On the way over, I pulled Vasari's *Lives of the Artists* out of our travel books in a box on the back seat of the car and read aloud to Ed, 'His manner of life was licentious and dishonorable, and he always had boys and beardless youths about him, of whom he was inordinately fond. This earned him the name of Sodoma; but instead of feeling shame he gloried in it, writing stanzas and verses on it, and singing them to the accompaniment of the lute. He loved to fill his house with all manner of curious animals; badgers, squirrels, apes, catamounts, dwarf asses, Barbary racehorses, Elba ponies, jackdaws, bantams, turtle-doves ... so that his house resembled a veritable Noah's ark.'

'Maybe his nickname comes from his love of beasts instead of what we assume – bestial,' Ed muses. 'I saw somewhere that he also had three wives and fathered thirty children. That seems impossible.'

'He thought of nothing but pleasure ...' Vasari continues. There's where he's wrong. I've seen his frescoes all over Tuscany. He thought a great deal about working at his art. Oddly, I think of Warhol, who seems decadent and frivolous, tossing off his art. A visit to the Warhol Museum in Pittsburgh cures that impression. He worked like a demon, amassing an immense body of varied, imaginative, playful, and seriously iconographic work.

It's easy to see where Sodoma stepped in because his menagerie starts to appear on the walls – ravens, swans, badgers, an anteater, various dogs, and what I take to be an ermine. His seven dancing women represent the temptations of the flesh, which Benedetto was able to resist. He has a whole fresco devoted to the saint's temptation, in which he restores himself by stripping off his robe and throwing himself onto a bush of thorns – probably more effective than a cold shower. He peers down from a balcony, directing the departure of his monks with a mule; obviously he's orchestrating their escape from the seductive women. This is one of the most beautiful frescoes, with the lovely flowing dresses of the women contrasting with the cumbersome robes of the monks, and the two groups divided by a doorway through which we see a distant curving road leading to a lake. I can't help but think that the rowdy Sodoma took special pleasure in creating gorgeous women for the monks to pass every day. When Sodoma painted them, the viewers experienced even more tension because the lovely women were nude. Someone later dressed them, cutting down on the perpetuation of temptation.

One of Sodoma's great moments is easy to miss. In an archway, Ed happened on his Christ bound to a pillar, with rope-burns swelling on his arms and criss-crossed blood marks of flagellation on his torso. Like Piero della Francesca's Christ in *Resurrection*, Sodoma renders him not as slender and pathetic but as a virile, big guy with powerful muscles. Nearby, Sodoma's own self-portrait appears in the fresco of one of Benedetto's first miracles, the mending of a broken tray, again a homely little act accomplished through prayer. Posed as a courtier, Sodoma looks straight out at the viewer with a direct, bemused gaze. At his feet are two badgers and a bird. He's full of life. I'll bet he was a handful for the Benedictines.

Although no one seems to follow the Sodoma trail, as they do the Piero della Francesca route, we could. In the time-stopped town of Trequanda, in a church with a checkerboard façade, SS. Pietro e Andrea, he's left a fresco. In the Pinacoteca and in Sant'Agostino in Siena, I've come upon paintings and enamels. His San Sebastiano in the Pitti Palace in Florence again shows his luminous talent for the glories of the male body: the delight in shoulder and stomach muscles, the filmy scarf around the genitals looped just so to suggest what is covered. I hardly notice poor Sebastiano's upturned face imploring an angel, or the arrow piercing his neck.

We take a stone stairway up to see the library. On the way, we pass a door marked 'Clausura,' behind which monks are cloistered, then we pass the door to the monks' dining room, which is open for a deliveryman to wheel in cases of water. The enormous U-arrangement of tables is covered in white cloths. Flowers, water and wine bottles, and a delicious smell drifting from the kitchen tell us that monks don't have to creep outside the walls for a good meal anymore. The room looks inviting and the lectern suggests that they will hear a reading while they eat in silence. I would love to join them.

Despite fellow-tourists here, it's easy to absorb the isolation of this place, the silence that exists in the closed parts and in the courtyard when the last visitor departs. The men are left to commune with time. I leave feeling that I have read a complex biography, and I have. The scenes from the lives of the holy are everywhere in Italian painting. Each panel or fresco is a chapter. 'Put the action into scene,' my fiction colleagues tell their writing students. Sodoma and Signorelli were particularly good at that.

I collect more images to conjure in nights of insomnia: The pink pate of the monk who nodded to me in the corridor; the fir and spice smell of the frankincense and myrrh in the chapel; an African child staring at the only fresco with a black person in it; a bold intarsia cat on a lectern, a wild-looking thing with eyes fixed on what must be a mouse; a monk singing in the cypress lane. He could be good Benedetto, walking out to help plague victims, or maybe he's just going out to check the hives, to see if the bees have awakened to spring.

BAGNO VIGNONI AND PIENZA

Ed is limping from a stone bruise. He leapt when his hoe suddenly disturbed a snake. His foot came down on a jagged rock. 'What kind?' I asked.

'A very snaky-looking snake. Scared hell out of me. We were eye-to-eye.' He's rubbing his foot with lotion.

'Let's go take the cure. We can be there by four.'

'Then we can go on to Pienza for dinner. I'd like to drive up to Montechiello, too. We've never been there.'

Bagno Vignoni, the tiny hilltop town near San Quirico d'Orcia, and within sight of the castle on top of Rocca d'Orcia, is built around a large thermal pool where the Medicis used to soak themselves. Where the central *piazza* is located in most towns, the pool (no longer used) reflects tumbling plumbago, tawny stone houses and stone arcades. Not much is going on in Bagno Vignoni. Right behind the village, a hot stream runs downhill, through a travertine ditch. On either side you can sit down and soak your feet, just as Lorenzo il Magnifico did in 1490.

When I first started spending summers here, I read in an Italian newspaper a heated debate over whether or not health insurance should continue to cover yearly sojourns to spas and thermal springs, a practice many Italians take as a birthright. I had been to Chianciano Terme and had seen people clutching their livers while sipping small glasses of water. They otherwise looked tan and fit. I glimpsed tanks where various body parts or the whole *corpo* could be immersed for the absorption of the healing properties of local waters. I've heard workers at our house discuss the merits of various waters as though they were discussing wine. Italians are great connoisseurs of the plainest elixir of all. I see them at various roadside springs filling demi-johns. Water is not just water; it has properties.

My grandmother used to take the sulphur waters for a week at White Springs, Florida, down near the Sewanee River. I was deeply bored and considered her a holdover from Victorian times. I only accompanied her so that I could swim in the cold black springs, emerging from the water smelling something like an old Easter egg. She waved from the third latticed balcony around the spring, a small paper cup of the odorous water in her other hand.

I did not expect to be drawn into this passion. Then I went to Bagno Vignoni. I converted. Ed's stone bruise takes us now but we must go at least once a year.

'Her dogs are barking,' my aunt would say when we saw a woman whose feet had swollen over the edges of her pumps. After a few weeks of hauling stone, erecting trellises, and navigating stony streets, my dogs, too, are barking. We like to arrive very early, before anyone has revealed their work-torn, ailing, sometimes frightening feet. We're late today. I take off my sandals, and slowly lower my own miserable feet into the running water. Ed plunges his to the bottom. Then we notice a man with a red, red nose paring his yellow-talon toenails into the water. He must not have cut them for months. We stare as his big toenail, like a curl of wax, falls into the water. We move upstream from him.

At fifty-two degrees Celsius, the shock of hot water on a hot day is intense. Ed's size twelves magnify through the water next to my long rabbit feet. Sometimes the water feels merely warm. Rubbing my heels against the smooth travertine streambed, I concentrate on the invisible but potent minerals which are starting to soothe blisters, relax tendons, muscles, even purify nails and skin. Ed says his purple bruise is fading, fading. The water starts to feel as though it's swirling *through* my feet. When I close my eyes, only my feet seem to exist.

After twenty minutes, I'm back in my sandals, toes glowing lobster-red. Ed slides on his espadrilles under water and squishes out. Cured.

This is the strange part. Walking back into town for a strawberry *gelato*, not only do I feel a surge of euphoria, my feet feel as if they could levitate. Everyday Italian life continues to astound me. What *is* in these Italian waters?

★

We reach Montecchiello by a white road that climbs through fields of purple lupin scattered with the last poppies. The walled town is mysteriously empty. Finally we figure this out: Everyone has simply closed shop and gone home to watch the big soccer match, which we hear blaring from every window. As we wander, we encounter a man peeing outside the closed public w.c. on the edge of town. Much of the castle wall is intact. Inside, the streets are so clean they're like swabbed decks.

'It's tarted up,' a friend had warned us. 'I've never seen so many geraniums in my life.' True, they're on every stoop, step, and sill. The effect is stunning against the immaculate shuttered houses and the pencils of sunlight falling into medieval lanes. It's one of hundreds of such hilltowns but one we'd never visited. We'll have to come back to find the fabric shop I read is here and, since the church is locked, to see the Lorenzetti Madonna. Even the priest probably is riveted to a small ball being kicked around a TV screen.

Down, down from Montecchiello, leaving it to its rioting geraniums, through the wildflower meadows, vineyards, passing abandoned and forlorn farmhouses on hills, through the mellow early evening and pig smells, toward Pienza, the first Renaissance town.

Pienza doesn't look like other towns. A pope with the splendid name of Enea Silvio Piccolomini built it in honor of his own birthplace. He must have knocked down most of the medieval buildings to put up his ultramodern Renaissance town because it's a harmonious whole.

There's a story about Rossellino, the architect, that stakes the heart of anyone involved in restoration or building. The architect overspent outrageously and concealed it from the Pope. When the excess finally was revealed, the Pope told him he was right to have hidden the sums because never would the pontiff have authorized such expenditures and never would he have had as his monument such a glorious town. He rewarded the architect with gold and a fancy cape. Perhaps our first builder had heard that story!

The *piazza*, bordered by the cathedral and several palaces for bishops, canons, and the Pope, is staggeringly, astonishingly beautiful. Pienza is glorious in all its parts, from the felicitous residential street along the ramparts, to the iron flagholders and cunning rings fashioned in animal shapes, where horses used to be secured while their owners did their business in town. Today no horses, and no cars either, which contributes to the silent and unified feeling of the town. We wander the *vicoli*, the narrow streets, with evocative names: Vicolo Cieco (blind), Via della Fortuna, Via delle Serve Smarrite (the lost servants), Via dell'Amore, Via del Balzello (the heavy tax or, in dialect, the man who looks at women), Via del Bacio (the kiss), Via Buia (dark).

The back end of Rossellino's airy cathedral is sinking, the porous limestone soil beneath it giving way a little every year. An ominous crack that looks as if it has been repaired with a staple gun runs down the wall and continues across the floor. I visit my favorite painting here, the martyred virgin Agata, who refused the attentions of Quintino and paid by having her breasts torn off. She comes down through history holding her severed breasts on a platter, which I originally took for a serving of fried eggs. Women who fear for their own breasts invoke her, and she is the patron saint of bell makers, too. Perhaps in a painting somewhere, the dome-shaped breasts were mistaken for little bells.

I once read in a book about the medieval pilgrimage routes that all the towns along the way were crowded with souvenir shops. So, Pienza's plethora of stores selling ceramics to us on our various pilgrimages has a precedent. This area is famous for its *pecorino*. The street leading into the *centro* is lined with so many tempting shops selling the round cheeses wrapped in leaves or ashes that the pungent smell follows us down the street. We buy an aged *pecorino* (*stagionato*) and taste a semi-aged one (*semi-stagionato*). Honey and herbs also are specialties. Some are homeopathic — we see a honey for the liver and one for the respiratory system. One shop has pots of *ruta*, rue, which I'll add to my herb garden.

I'm drawn by all these food shops and also repelled. Pienza has rather too many; I'd like to see the shoe repair and the grocery store back on the main street. What remains of the ancient craft of *ferro battuto*, wrought iron, is an upscale shop selling lamps and tables and a few antique gates and andirons to the tourists down from Bologna or Milano for the weekend. And to us, of course. We look at their hanging iron lanterns with glass globes that end in a rounded teardrop, reproductions of old ones still on some streets of Siena and Arezzo. We need a light outside by the *limonaia* and one for overhead in a bedroom. They have them. I also buy an old iron that opens up to hold hot coals. The worn wooden handle tells me somebody pushed this five pounder over many a work shirt and apron.

Just outside the main gate we find a *trattoria* with a terrace. I'm thrilled anytime to see fried zucchini blossoms. We fall onto pork tenderloin grilled with rosemary, roasted potatoes with lots of pepper, and a salad of young arugula barely touched with good oil.

Around the cathedral *piazza*, the dignified pale stone buildings have travertine extensions around the bases. They serve as benches and over the years have been polished smooth by the bottoms that rested there while viewing the great well and the Pope's magnificent *piazza*. Over one is inscribed 'canton de'bravi,' corner of the good. Do we qualify? We're feeling dreamy after dinner, the travertine still warm from the sun. We watch a small girl in a white sailor dress chasing a kitten. The full moon is poised over Piccolomini's perfect *piazza*. 'Amazing what a little egomania and a lot of gold can do,' Ed says.

'Perhaps he even ordered the full moon to drift overhead every night.'

Another soccer match blares from the TV in the bar, so the women and babies are outside, the men inside. In a *piazza* just off the main one, another TV has been set up outdoors beside a Renaissance well and all the neighbors have brought out their chairs into the early evening to cheer and shout for Italy. The blue light of the screen reflects on the semicircle of rapt faces. Arm-in-arm we walk the rampart road. For the second time today, I'm astounded by everyday life in Italy. Ed holds out his foot and says he feels no pain at all.

A LOOP AROUND LAGO TRASIMENO

With our mad lists of things to do for the house, usually we have a goal, a time limit, a schedule. A sudden 'Stop!' or 'Let's turn up that road' comes too late. But the land-scape around Lago Trasimeno invites you to meander, not to care if the destination you sought turns into another destination. So near, so far from the important towns of Perugia and Assisi and the great Tuscan ones nearby, the lake country is quiet and verdant, with fields of sunflowers and corn around the water. The lake, fifty-four kilometers around, is the largest body of water on the Italian penin-sula and its three green islands – Maggiore, Minore, and Polvese – emphasize its size. Little blue and white ferries ply the islands. The lake looks vast. Tumultuous skies cast dramatic moving shadows on water that is dazzling blue on clear middays and often icy silver when the sun rises or sets. Sometimes the lake surface reflects a gaudy, smeared orange and chrome sunset and the surrounding hills go dark purple. I've never seen a more changeable landscape. I've heard that World War II pilots mistook it for a landing field and the lake bottom is littered with crashed planes. The foothills of the Apennines scroll along the horizon, and towers, ruins, and walled towns perch on many hilltops.

I still can't resist the magnetic pull of abandoned farmhouses. Every few miles Ed pulls over, and we step through briars, mentally restoring and moving into the mellow house which often has no roof. In the larger villages, such as Castiglione del Lago, Città della Pieve, and especially in Passignano, which is right on the lake, there are a few other travellers but no one is pouring off buses or streaming through the streets with the kind of determination I often have. Around here, travellers are more inclined to sit on a lakeside patio eating roasted red pepper pizza, or to stroll along a wall under a Renaissance gate, or to drive through the fresh countryside with the windows down, perhaps turning up the tape of Pavarotti singing break-your-heart arias to maximum volume.

The serene villages with panoramas of blue water contradict everything we know about the history of this area. Only the oldest story is romantic: The demigod Trasimeno went to the interior of Italy on a hunting expedition. When he reached the lake, he glimpsed the water nymph Agilla and fell in love. Naturally he dove in after her and naturally, being half mortal, he drowned. The lake was given his name. After that, recorded history lists battle after battle: sackings followed by lootings, castles rebuilt only to be seized, burned, and reoccupied. Mercenaries and warring dukes and foreign kings and the town on the next hill all made constant raids on each settlement, with the castles, so charming today, acting as local bomb shelter equivalents. Their airy positions *were* chosen for the view – but what they looked out for was the next army of marauders. What exactly was at stake? Inland water is a valuable resource, especially in a dry climate. The castles and unwalled towns were therefore of interest in themselves. A glance at the map will make clear the larger significance of this area. Situated right at the heart of Italy, Trasimeno was the crux of many migrations and passages. Commanders of this area determined to a large extent who passed into the north or south. Many of the well-trod pilgrim routes to Rome edged the lake, following ancient routes south.

All that destruction, in a nice irony, left a bucolic legacy.

I love Castiglione del Lago, a walled town almost surrounded by water. On sultry summer days during siesta, we often bring lawn chairs and books to one of the lake beaches. We can cross the prickly grass to a bar for ice cream, walk along the beach, or just sink into midsummer torpor with the lulling sound of Italian sunbathers in the background. I've been in the water once. It was room temperature with a silty bottom. I had to wade forever to get to water deep enough to swim, while little finny creatures brushed my legs.

The local storybook castle, Lion's Castle, has catwalks along the crenelated top and a narrow stone corridor perhaps two blocks long with cut-out windows for defense. Looking forward or backward seems like walking into a mirror. At the tea and coffee store, the owner also stocks local honeys. I've been wanting to try the chestnut honey, very dark, and *tigli* honey from the flowering linden trees. I was curious about the tisanes, homeopathic infusions made from various flowers and herbs, with cures attached to each. She told us that the honey, too, had specific benefits. It didn't sound very homeopathic to me, but she said the sure cure for migraines is acacia honey mixed with *grappa*. I'd always associated *grappa*, that strongest of grape distillations, with *getting* headaches.

After a morning at the lake and a walk, we drive just to the edge of town to the Cantina Sociale, where local farmers sell their grapes. Red wine, produced from these grapes, can be quite good. We could back up our car and lift out a demijohn, which would be filled exactly the way a car is filled with gas. The pump registers the liters and the charge is about a dollar a liter. Bottled wine is more — two to five dollars. Their reds and whites, under the Colli del Trasimeno and Duca di Corgna — one of those old warriors — labels, are DOC (*denominazione di origine controllata*), certifying that the region's wine meets standards that merit this government designation.

We began my favorite topic of discussion — where we will eat lunch. Since most of the towns around the lake are mentioned not at all in guides, we walk around, examining the posted menus, checking out the ambiance of each of the restaurants. Food is robust and traditional in the whole Trasimeno area, nothing vaguely trendy, though pasta sauces made with rabbit or wild boar still seem exotic to us. During cool weather, *ribollita*, a soup so thick your spoon can stand up in the bowl, is my favorite. Most of the special dishes are fish of the lake — carp, shad, perch, *frittura* (a fried mix of tiny lake fish that look like the minnows that swarmed around my legs in the lake), and *tegamaccio*, the local fish soup that varies with the catch. Yellow eels are plentiful here and are often prepared in a sauce for pasta (*spaghetti al ragù d'anguilla*). A highly regarded fish, *lasca* (the European equivalent bears the unappetizing name of *roach*), has disappeared from the lake.

We decide to circumnavigate the lake, turning off on whatever roads lure us, to take the ferry to Isola Maggiore, and to drive to Panicale, Paciano, and Città della Pieve, slightly off the loop. Since distances are very short, it's easy to return home at the end of a day's travelling. It's just as easy, however, to stop for the night along the way. Passignano, the main resort on the lake, looks like a good choice for a night, as does Isola Maggiore. Like the restaurants, hotels in this area are not elaborate but are pleasant and comfortable, with the additional virtue of being inexpensive.

Before setting off, we stop at the *forno* and pick up two kinds of *torte al testo* (crispy, flat bread cooked on a hot iron in a wood oven), one with *pancetta* and the other with *parmigiano*. The cases also display *serpentoni*, almond pastries formed in the shape of a serpent.

Tuoro is our first pause. We want to get a closer look at the marshes along that edge of the lake. And, of course, we know about the famous battle site. A man pulling his fishing nets off his flat-prowed boat points out where Flaminio bivouacked for the night while Hannibal waited for dawn to attack him with his melting pot army of Numidians, Berbers, Libyans, Gascons, Iberians, and other dissidents he picked up along his way. Hannibal was down to one elephant by then, after his famous crossing of the Alps with thirty-nine. He also had lost an eye but still was in complete control of his 40,000 men. He outsmarted Flaminio and on a foggy morning drove the Romans right into the lake. Fifteen thousand Romans died, to fifteen hundred of Hannibal's men. Besides Ossaia (boneyard), where Anselmo lives, Sanguineto (bloodied) also recalls that day. An ugly modern bust of Hannibal at Tuoro commemorates his feat.

When I was a college sophomore, I was amazed that my

Modern History course began with the year 1500; 1500 seemed beyond the bend of time. When I started travelling to Italy, finally it began to make sense in a real way, not an abstract way, that 1500 is quite recent. It's still hard to imagine Hannibal duking it out with the Romans, here where the tranquil view looks unchanged from long before that era. Just beyond the marshy edge, poles are stuck in the water, with nets attached, a method that could go back to prehistory.

A four-lane highway runs along the Tuoro/Magione side of the lake. We stick to our good map and stay off the busy *raccordo*; the small roads are fun to drive. Along the way, we watch for the thin yellow signs, pointing the way to a thirteenth-century church, a *fortezza*, Roman gates, or a tower. It's fun to stop, too, at the '*vendita diretta*' signs posted near the farms or estates that sell their wine or oil or honey directly to you. Out of Tuoro, intriguing roads lead to Vernazzano's leaning tower, to Mariotella, a medieval fortified *casa*, and to Bastia Corgna, a larger abandoned castle from 1300.

Castel Rigone occupies one of the prime positions above the lake. Substantial sections of the old walls of the town still exist. In the early sixteenth century, a fine small church was built because of local miracles associated with a painting of the Virgin Mary. Inside the plain, pure gray stone church remain wonderful frescoes, including an Assumption by Battista Caporali.

We wind downhill to Passignano, a peaceful resort of oleander-lined streets with a medieval section of town and many cafés and hotels along the lake. Two shops spill out onto the grounds with extensive selections of the hand-painted majolica from nearby Deruta; their prices are lower than Deruta's. How can they stand to take all those mugs, pitchers, candlesticks, and platters inside every night? I find the cheerfully designed espresso cups, plates, and pasta bowls irresistible, even if they are a nuisance to lug to San Francisco. Our china at Bramasole is going to be a wild mixture. Butter dishes, *parmigiano* servers, teapots – thank the gods for bubble wrap; I'm well into Christmas. Ed strolls next door for espresso. He can take only so much. I store the bags in the car and see him heading toward a *rosticceria* and pizza shop, headquarters for potato pizza, which is much better than it sounds. The onion pizza is a close second, with onions cooked slowly, almost caramelized.

No need to plan the hour to go to Isola Maggiore and Polvese; ferry service from Passignano, or from Castiglione del Lago or Tuoro, is so frequent that you can jump on often. Twenty minutes over the water and we step out on strange territory – no cars. Because Maggiore seems so completely severed from time, we decide to spend the night at the island's one inn. We feel the special isolation of the place after the last ferry has departed and the island returns to the fishing village it always has been. A solitary walk down the main street at midnight can make you feel as though you've been stuck into a time capsule. About sixty people live here now; the high point of the island's population was six hundred during the sixteenth century. The one-street village is lined with golden stone houses, with olive groves rising behind. Occasionally, you see a woman in a doorway, catching the light for her lace-making. Large, hooped nets, called *tofi*, dry in the sun. Shaped like cornucopias, the nets are for catching eels. We walk all the way around the island (about a mile), passing a spot where San Francesco landed in 1211. San Francesco was everywhere in Tuscany and Umbria, somewhat like George Washington–slept–here in the United States. Three open churches remain on the island. Right on the main street, Buon Gesù has the feel of many Mexican churches, with naively executed frescoes. The spontaneity makes you aware of the hand of the maker. The other two churches are from the twelfth century: San Salvatore and San Michele at the top of the island, a hot uphill climb through olive groves.

I ask the church caretaker at San Michele about the strange castle on a tip of the island. We'd skirted it on our walk and had tried to see inside, but the shutters were so long closed that ivy has grown over them, splitting the wood and twining into the stone walls – surely Sleeping Beauty is dreaming in an upstairs room. Situated on a curve of the island periphery, it has 300-degree views across the water. The caretaker tells us the castle, abandoned for years, used to be a monastery. 'Any chance of seeing the inside?' I ask without much hope. But as so often happens in Italy, yes, her friend is the caretaker and, yes, she will show it to us. She will be passing the church in an hour, come back then. We go down to the village again and buy a guidebook to the island. The castle, we read, was built at the end of the nineteenth century onto a 1328 monastery and church of San Francesco. A marquis built this folly for his wife, Isabella. The family restored the church, built the boat landing, and imported an Irish woman to teach the villagers the art of lace making. By the 1960s, however, this late fiefdom was abandoned, its luxurious furnishings sold.

The caretaker turns an immense iron key and leads us into the castle's church, totally dark except for her flash-light. We make out a blue vaulted interior with gold stars. Chairs, pieces of the altar, and choir screens lie in heaps. Soon we are turning in corridors and following her light through darker and darker rooms. In some she suddenly flings open a window, letting in the stunning blue view, and we see damask walls hanging in strips, opulent painted borders and mouldings. In a courtyard, we glimpse what must have been the monastery cloister with its great stone well. I lose count of the rooms. We see in the circle of her light the ruined game room and theater, with painted scenery and velvet curtains piled on the floor, a castle for generations of mice. It is astonishing how quickly ruin has again overtaken the place. Will anyone awaken the princess? The caretaker says someone from Rome plans to restore it someday. Let's hope he has a boatload of lire.

★

Continuing around the lake, we zigzag among clusters of enchanting stops. I especially like peaceful Monte del Lago, a castle town with impressive walls and gate right above the lake. The hotel there serves an amazing *carpa regina in porchetta*, carp paired with herbs and bits of roast pork, and *zzurlingo al sugo di lago*. *Zzurlingo* is a dialect word for a thin flat pasta, here served with a rich, fish-based sauce. Their *filetti di persico con salsa della casa*, delicate perch with a herb sauce, is also wonderful with a glass of spritzy white wine. Monte del Lago has wide-angle views of the lake. From the ramparts on cloudy days the gray water near shore stretches to apple green, aqua, lapis blue. No one is about except for a three-legged cat sleeping on a wall.

Equally serene are Antria, a toy walled village, and Montecolognola, with a double-gated entrance. These places rearrange my sense of time. The unchanging places continue to soak in the sun as they always have. The strange gate at Montecolognola accommodates a roaring Moto Guzzi (*why* don't they require mufflers?) as well as a cart pulled by oxen in earlier times.

A larger, less appealing town, Magione sits under a very

tall tower encased in what looks like permanent scaffolding. The Knights of Malta also left a marvelous fortification from the time of the Crusades at Magione but it's privately owned now and hard to see because of the trees. Right outside Magione, however, I glimpsed another *Cantina Sociale* and found their DOC wines as good as their neighbor's across the lake. The *cantina* stands next door to a large wrought-iron works. *Ferro battuto* is the ancient craft of the area. Cortona, like many towns, has torch and banner holders, rings to tie horses, fanlights, and lanterns. Except for a few masters, the craft is dying. Here, however, is a large-scale operation. They still make traditional iron lanterns with clear globes, fireplace and grilling tools, and andirons, as well as tables, beds, and other large pieces. Their warehouse attests to the fact that they deal in quantity, unlike the scattered one-man forges we've used in our restoration. One of my favorite things about Italy is that even in such a large place, they will do anything to please you. I didn't like the flower on the fire screen. 'Is it possible to have it without the flower?' Marco considers. Come with me, he motions. We go into the immense workroom with smouldering fires and pits of paint and stacks of iron parts. With a torch and a touch-up, he has removed the flower in ten minutes. Can we have the andirons without the curve? Yes, next week. I remember the abandoned slab of travertine at the house and ask if they can make a table base. Of course. He takes us into his house and shows us the table he has designed for his family. His wife offers us a Coke, and we sit out on his patio while he sketches a table base he thinks we would like. We do. Expecting him to say six weeks, I ask how soon we can have it. 'Would next Tuesday be all right?'

Nearby is Rocca Baglioni, with a double tower, and

Zocco, an abandoned castle on a prominent knoll over-looking the lake. In the fishing village of San Feliciano, we find the Fishing Museum, where we learn perhaps more than we want to know about the history of local fishing.

Although it sounds as if we're zooming through Umbria, these are short distances, a few miles between stops. We then drop down to the area just south of the lake, in search of the Santuario di Mongiovino. As we arrive, mass blares from the bell tower and the doors fly open, releasing dozens of children and nuns into a fore-court of tumbling ancient buildings; only the church is intact. Its almost square structure is unique among churches I've seen. When we walk around back to examine the building, we find several mobile units, hous-ing for the Benedictines. Up the hill we come to Mongiovino Vecchio, a military stronghold in ages past and now inhabited by a few families. Not that we see anyone. Many of the castle towns have a day-after-judgement-day stillness. We do see wash flapping on a line and from a high stone window we hear the unmistakable sound of Jimi Hendrix. We sit in the grass by a fallen wall and eat the hot grapes we've left on the back seat of the car.

We are looking for the Torre d'Orlando, a castle with a tower built in 917. The detailed map pinpoints it on a squiggly road between Paciano and Panicale. We drive up slopes of olive trees to Paciano and walk through the medieval gates into a town totally closed down for siesta. A pile of ginger cats sleeping in a doorway does not even look up. At a lookout point over the valley, someone planted a flourishing circle of lavender around two facing benches and we sit down to enjoy the secret garden. Bees and yellow and blue butterflies flash and buzz – the only activity in town. After a light morning rain, the fragrance seems to rise in waves. Paciano, we read, has a museum and two churches built around 1000, as well as several fifteenth-century churches with frescoes and carved doors. All closed, of course.

We can't even find an espresso in the eerie quiet, so we drive on, turning left when we probably should have turned right to find the elusive tower. The road opens up at every curve to another broad valley view of the Umbrian countryside. All the traffic we meet is a flock of sheep in the road, madly munching grass and wild arugula on the shoulder, while a frustrated spaniel tries to herd them up the hill. We turn off the car and listen to their bells.

Soon we come to Panicale, home of Boldrino, a famous mercenary and one of the chief troublemakers of the four-teenth century. Several towns paid him a regular salary just to guarantee he wouldn't turn on them. Despite his pillaging and murders, he is commemorated by a plaque. Could it be that the Mafia is a descendant of these medieval mercenaries? Panicale has much more attractive features than the memory of this bad boy. The impressive gate leads to a fountain in the central *piazza*, which once was a well cleverly designed to catch rainwater in the Middle Ages. Like many towns in Italy, Panicale has a Church of the Virgin of the Snows, commemorating a rare snowfall on August 5, 552. Though Masolino was born here, only one of his paintings is on view, an Annunciation in San Michele. The branching streets invite roaming and the distant views of the lake from this high position can't help but remind you of paintings. Perugino's *Martyrdom of Saint Sebastian*, in the church of San Sebastiano, shows, through the arches in the back-ground, the unchanged Umbrian landscape.

Two other Peruginos hang in the same church, his

Madonna and Child and *The Virgin in Glory*. The artist is buried about two miles away, near Fontignano, where he succumbed to the plague. The Church of the Annunciation there contains his (modern) tomb and a fresco. He lies just down the road from where he was born Pietro Vannucci.

Città della Pieve is one of my favorite towns. This lively and odd little city, the last stop on our tour of the lake country, seems like a wonderful place to live. We sit down at a *caffè* to take in the daily rhythms of the place. Large groups of men play cards under an arbor, a girl shouts up to a man in the most picturesque jail, monks stride along with shopping baskets, rainbow banners flap above the *piazza*. After all the pale, lovely limestone of Umbrian villages, this one comes as a shock: It's all red brick. With the tile roofs and the human scale of the architecture, Città della Pieve seems especially warm and amiable. The red brick isn't the only quirk. The 'narrowest street in Italy,' Via Baciadonna, *is* narrow enough for two people to lean out their windows and kiss. The central *piazza*, irregularly shaped, forms a rough triangle with the cathedral as hypotenuse. The cathedral was built over ancient temple foundations; it, too, has its idiosyncrasy. The dark interior is wildly painted with *faux* marble: spiraled columns, bars, panels, circles in all the colors and patterns marble can have and then some. Elaborate painted frames surround the elaborate actual frames of paintings. Of the many paintings here, Perugino's *The Baptism* and *Mary in Glory* are the most arresting. To see them, we dropped *lire* in the *luce* box; the lights then came on briefly.

I knew about the Peruginos in Città della Pieve. I didn't know about the stunning object across the street in the Palazzo della Corgna: a rare, tall Etruscan obelisk from the eighth century BC. There are Etruscan sarcophagi as well.

The town's other local artistic highlight, undoubtedly, is Perugino's *Adoration of the Magi* in the Oratorio di Santa Maria dei Bianchi, next to the church of that name. Restored in 1984, the painting is truly splendid. How did he get those colors, dusky lavender, saffron, almond green, sea blues, and that luminous, sourceless light? Because it is the sole painting in the room, and because we are about to leave this idyllic town, I linger over each detail, an angel in the upper right, a shepherd, a white dog in motion, feathery trees, horses, and there, in the background, the landscape Perugino knew best – the gentle hills sloping down to the waters of Lago Trasimeno.

FROM A YELLOW BOOK:
THINKING OF TRAVEL

I took my first trip alone at age six. I begged to be allowed to go to Vidalia to visit my favorite aunt and my blind grandmother. My mother drove me twenty miles to Abbeville to catch the train. As we pulled up, the train started to chug away. I don't know why this would have been at night, but in my memory the lighted train is bright. My mother leaps out of the car, calling 'Stop, stop!' and somehow the train stops, I am shoved aboard, and we are moving, my mother's blue Oldsmobile scratching off, her arm waving out the window.

The car is empty except for me. I have my round blue overnight bag and a Bobbsey Twins book to read. I would soon be at Aunt Mary's. Tomorrow my grandmother will make biscuits and I'll watch her groping hands do the work of both eyes and hands. She will complain of her liver and sinus headaches without stopping. I will count the diseases to see how many she can have. She's up to seventeen. She'll let me use the green-handled circle to cut the soft dough rounds. I'll play in the damp caves behind their house, make horses and birds with the mucky red clay. The train! Zipping through the dark, all the way – seventy miles – to Vidalia, I am leaving my wicker carriage of dolls, my black cocker spaniel, Tish. Will the conductor tell me when to get off? My mother asked him.

I curl against the window, feeling the clacking metallic noises of the tracks in my shoulder, watching for the lighted windows of farmhouses. *Who lives there?* I wonder about *them*, about the life inside the houses way in the country.

I can almost inhabit the hard little body, almost feel my forehead against the glass. All the mysteries and allures of travel were there at the outset, even the long fascination with the life in a place, that common mystery I recognized years later in one of the last haikus of Basho, written at the end of the seventeenth century:

Deep autumn,
My neighbor, how
Does he live, I wonder?

At the end of his life he was still wondering what I began to wonder at the beginning of mine, and still wonder.

Even earlier, at four or five, I pinched my friend Jane Walker's arm hard and asked her, 'How can you *be* and not be me,' a precocious stab at the metaphysical. It's a lifetime quest, finding out who 'the other' is, and how life is lived outside your own thin skin.

Setting off to see another country, I set off to see what

is more grandly other — whole cultures, geographies, languages. Who am I in the new place? And who are they who live there?

If you settle in, even for two weeks, live in a house not a hotel, and you buy figs and soap at the local places, sit in cafés and restaurants, go to a local concert or church service, you cannot help but open to the resonance of a place and the deeper you go, the stranger the people become because they're like you and they're not. In Pienza, I was struck on that hot night, when I saw the TV dragged out into the *piazza* so the neighborhood could watch the soccer match together. That's not going to happen in Pacific Heights, where I live. Even the smallest things reveal that it's a new world.

I was on a travel-writing panel at the San Francisco Book Fair. One of our topics was 'Now that the world is the same everywhere, how do you find a place to write about? And then how do you write about it in a way that distinguishes it from other places?'

There's a short answer to the first: It isn't. To the second, I always think of what Gerard Manley Hopkins advised: Look long enough at an object until it begins to look back at you. It can be dangerous to travel. A strong reflecting light is cast back on 'real life,' sometimes a disquieting experience. Sometimes you go to the far interior and who knows what you might find there?

I read a lot of travel narratives and newspaper and magazine travel pieces that stop with observation. They tell you where to sleep, where to eat well, and what not to miss. Those articles can become fictions, idylls. An article about a German town that goes on about the colorful characters, the beer and hand-painted toys draws you. Three pages later in the news section there's a huge article on a Neo-Nazi movement shadowing the same town.

The *Gemütlichkeit* dissolves. You turn back to the travel article, puzzled. When I've written travel articles, a few times I have been told not to mention poverty or unpleasantness. Well, fair enough. It's a rainy Sunday morning and the reader wants to dream awhile, having waded through the harsh stories of women on death row and starvation in the Sudan.

But the passionate traveller looks for something. What? Something must change you, some ineffable something – or nothing happens. 'Change me,' Ed writes in a poem. 'Change me into something I am.' Change – the transforming experience – is part of the quest in travelling.

Often we take America with us. How can we not, being thoroughly products of our culture? We see what we know how to see. Powerful built-in genetic strands that go back to Stone Age territorial instincts make us secretly believe the Danes or Hungarians go home and speak English at night. How much is that in dollars? What are these terrible breakfasts? Where's real coffee? More harrowingly, we are wary everywhere of being robbed and mugged. We fear the violence of America everywhere.

We're not alone in carrying our own country before us. The desire for the familiar is a powerful drive. I've seen the Japanese lined up in Perugia for a table at the Asian restaurant. With all the glories of Italian food right there, they opt for some peculiar version of the food of their homeland and then most likely think it's terrible. It's totally natural, even inevitable, to compare the Via Veneto with Main Street. Unfortunately, if extreme, this acts as a preventative to experience; what we know is simply confirmed. Another Japanese poet wrote: Ride naked on a naked horse. But we are profoundly displaced when we travel and denial of that displacement sets in quickly. If only we could recognize this – suspend the rush to judgement and compartmentalizing. Travel can reinforce the primitive urge to bring the new into the circle of the known.

I went to Pasadena – the word sets me dreaming, Pasadena – and walking around on a perfect day, I saw Starbucks, Banana Republic, the Gap, Williams Sonoma, Il Fornaio – all the high-end chains with identical merchandise in dozens of other cities. Where am I? Nothing happened to me. And yet, surely if I'd stayed longer than a day, there are layers of Pasadena. Pasadena must be unlike everywhere else. In America, with franchises and TV pouring their solvents over us by the second, you have to look longer and harder.

In Italy, it's easier. Each town, city, *borgo*, or *fattoria* is intensely itself. It has its own particular fountain of dolphins entwined with nymphs, its stone chapel with an Annunciation painting, its Etruscan obelisk, its families with names on the pews since 1500.

A writer told me, 'Beware of the exotic; it is so easily available.' And here across the waters, the exotic is more available. We see but we don't see the gorgeous man in the Armani suit taking his espresso in the bar, glancing at *La Repubblica*. In Italy, there's the concept of *la bella figura*, cutting a beautiful figure. The gorgeous man in Armani might live in a depressing back room of a store. At least he can dress well and go out into the *piazza* in a cloud of divine cologne.

★

When I first started writing poetry, I kept what I called an Image Bank, a photo album I stuffed with museum postcards of paintings, photos, typed lists of words I liked, anything that struck me as correlative with the writing process. My way shifted over the years. Although I still keep several kinds of notebooks, the images became more internal. Travelling, living in Italy, I'm especially aware of *storing* what I experience and see. If I ever end up rocking on the porch of a dogtrot house in the backwoods of Georgia, I aim to have plenty to visualize. Landscapes, fine meals, solitary walks – yes, I run my mind over those, but it is the lives of people I return to with the most feeling. A hand pulls back a lace curtain. A face appears in the window. Down-turned mouth, gelid eyes naked with disappointment stare out and catch mine. We look at each other for a moment and the curtain drops. *Hello, good-bye.* At 7 a.m., Niccolò, the handsome owner of the tobacco shop, is rinsing the stones around his entrance, sweeping and singing to himself. *Remember him, his hair still wet from the shower, his tune, his sudden smile – who he is on his own.* These glimpses make me understand that hard line of Wallace Stevens: 'Beauty is momentary in the mind but in the flesh it is immortal.'

It is a miracle to see Pompeii, Machu Picchu, Mont-Saint-Michel. It is also a miracle to wander into Cortona, see the young couple at their fruit and vegetable shop. She arranges a pyramid of lemons in a patch of sunlight. She wipes each leaf with a rag so that it gleams. She's fresh-faced and young in her pink-striped apron, probably trying hard to look like a proprietor. Her long and delicate neck gives her the air of having just landed after flight. He looks like the flute player on the wall of an Etruscan tomb – curly black hair, cherubic face. He sets out the baskets of peas he has picked this morning in his mother's garden, then halves a watermelon and tips it up in the window so anyone can see how ripe and delicious it is. She places her sign above the cash register – all the vegetables for minestrone can be ordered a day in advance and prepared by her at home. Each customer is lavishly greeted. If you want three pears, each one is selected and held out for your inspection. I have entered for a moment daily life in a place I don't know, and the red pear held out to me in a work-hardened hand will come back in memory over and over. *Immortal*.

AP

'The Arezzo market is this weekend.'

Ed is mincing parsley, basil, carrots, and celery for his special version of what to do with *odori* – that bunch of flavors tossed in your bag at the *frutta e verdura*. Do I see him wince? Or is that a reaction to the onions he has chopped? 'Do you want to go?' he asks.

'Well, yes, don't you?'

'Sure, if you do.' He rolls the blade of the *mezzaluna* over the celery.

'We always find something fantastic.' Is he thinking of the time he carried the cherry cabinet over his head through the crowd for half a mile? I glance at the cabinet hanging on the kitchen wall, its glass doors left open and the espresso cups from all over Italy lining the shelves. Many were given to us by our friend Elizabeth when she moved back to America; others we picked up in our own wanderings. Friends who've visited have added a few. Odd, many things we've acquired here have accumulated meaning quickly, as though they were long-treasured heirlooms. This confuses me. I thought objects gathered symbolic value only through time, or, if at the outset, by being significant gifts: my father's gold cuff links, my grandmother's silver syrup pitcher, the lapis ring made from an old earring.

Looking around this house, many 'new' things are just as close to me, closer. 'Remember, we found the angel painting,' I offer. Over our bed this eighteenth-century angel now presides, a lovely blond presence whose face I've come to love. She's wearing boots, and her brocade skirts part to show a triangular panel of lace. Who knew angels wore lace? She's androgynous, with her or his pert face staring off into the mirror on the opposite side of the room. In the reflection, I get to see the face twice.

Ed scrapes the minced *odori* into the sauté pan. The sizzle sends up a quick scent of earth and rain. Carrots add that underground smell, while celery, which does not seem as though it would grow underground, always gives over a misty, crisp essence.

'The last time we went we found those chains. Do you want *bruschette* or just the fresh bread?' he asks.

Those chains, I know, weighed about twenty pounds. Unfortunately, we found them early in the day, before the three gold-leaf angel wings, the Neapolitan *putto*, cherub, with the missing leg, and the yards and yards of silk brocade that once covered an altar. The hand-forged chains, made of lovely iron circles, once held pots of *ribollita* and polenta over the fire. Ours now hang on either side of our fireplace. 'They're favorites of ours. *Bruschette*.'

The antique market in Arezzo takes place the first week-end of the month. Except in August, when the heat becomes too formidable, I'm there. The market sprawls all over and around the Piazza Grande, and spills up to the Duomo, covers the *piazza* in front of the church of Piero della Francesca's great fresco cycle, then trails out into side streets. On tables, sidewalks, and streets, fabulous furniture, art, and tawdry junk are displayed. With around eighty shops, on any old weekday, Arezzo is a center for antiques. Behind the fair booths, the regular shops line the streets. Some haul their own furniture out onto the sidewalk for the market. You could find anything there — a fancy cradle, a nineteenth-century still life large enough to cover a wall, embroidered postcards from World War I, garden urns, entire choir stalls. Last year, I began to see World War II ribbons, PW shirts, German war memorabilia, and stiffened uniforms. I even saw a yellow star arm badge with JUDE stitched across it for thirteen dollars. I touched the crosshatch threads around the edges. Someone wore it. It seemed immoral to buy it or to leave it there, an object among objects. Garish glassware and Venetian goblets are abundantly displayed, without ever getting smashed by jostling crowds. There is a buyer, it seems, for everything, no matter how fabulous, dinky, or hideous.

★

I collected as a child. Uncle Wilfred saved his Anthony and Cleopatra cigar boxes for me and I left them open in the sun until most of the pungent smell baked away. I kept arrowheads I found in one; buttons, beads, and pretty rocks in others. In shoe boxes, I saved paper dolls with costumes from around the world, postcards, seashells, and tightly folded triangular notes tossed to me in school by Johnny, Jeff, and Monroe. My oddest collection was brochures. I constantly wrote letters to small towns all over America, addressed to The Chamber of Commerce, saying 'Please send me information about your town,' and letters and brochures arrived, with news of the Pioneer Museum, the Future Farmers of America, the recreational opportunities afforded by an artificial lake, the opening of a tire factory. The longing to *go* seized me early. I no longer remember why, but I wanted to live in Cherry, Nebraska.

Opening a box, spreading out the slipper shells, angel wings, jingles, sand dollars, and scallops, I opened also the memory of a place, a string of moments. When I arranged the shells on the floor, a little beach sand sifted out. As I listened to the conch, the whoosh of my own inner ear brought back the wash of coquina shells against my ankles at Fernandina. I made spirals of the pastel colors and barnacle browns, rubbed the dawn-colored pearly insides with my thumb.

I remember my collections so vividly that I think I should be able to go to my closet and take down a box, spend this rainy afternoon playing with the blond Dutch girl paper doll, with her flowered pinafore and wooden shoes, the Polish twins with their black rick-rack skirts, their ribbons and aprons.

Collecting, like writing, is an *aide-memoire*. An ancient relative bored me wildly with her souvenir silver spoons. 'Now, this one I got on a vacation to the Smokies in 1950 . . .' But memory *can* make you live twice. As words fall onto paper, I can again marry the cat to the dog.

Memory, the graduation pearls unstrung, rolling out of reach on the church floor, the choir screeching 'Jerusalem.'

Memory, they all rise, young again, able to see without looking. They're clamoring for the wishbone, asking what's for dessert. Close the box, close the album, hang the old lace curtain in the south window where it catches the soft billowing breeze, a breeze for a spirit to ride.

★

As an adult, I have few collections. I started to buy old bells once, but forgot them after a while. I have a number of Mexican *ex-votos* painted on tin and have accumulated many antique carved or clay hands and feet, and dolls' arms and legs, a collection I never planned and didn't even notice until someone remarked that there were quite a few body parts around my house. My collection must be expanding to other body parts because, at the Arezzo market, I've also bought three bisque saints' heads, two bald, one with a golden wig and painted glass eyes. When I find early studio photographs of Italians, I buy them. I'm filling one wall of my study with these portraits, for many of whom I've invented life stories. My real passion at the Arezzo market was never planned, either, but springs from an old source.

I go not only for the chance to find furniture for the many bare spots at Bramasole and to discover treasures, but to see the people, to stop for *gelato*, to wander invisibly at this immense market, which retains the atmosphere of a medieval fair. At 1 p.m., the dealers cover their tables with tarps or newspaper and go off to lunch, or they simply set up lawn chairs and a table, complete with tablecloth, right there for family and friends, and bring out cut-up roast chickens, containers of pasta, and loaves of bread. People jam the bars, ordering little sandwiches, slices of pizza, or, in the upscale *gastronomia*, sausage and asparagus *torte*.

Gilded church candlesticks, olive oil jars, stone cherubs

– out of all this, what draws me to the vendors of old linens? 'This time,' I tell Ed, 'I'm not even going to stop. We'll look at iron gates, marble sinks from crumbled monasteries, and crested family silver. I certainly don't need any more pillowcases or . . .'

At first, I succeed. With so much to look at, I can become saturated. Ed is glancing at andirons and a mirror. I spot some painted tin *ex-votos*. He likes looking at the hand-wrought iron tools, locks, and keys, but after two hours, he gets this set half-smile on his face.

He has an effective way of speeding me along in department stores at home. Other men sit in the comfortable chairs put there for waiting men, but Ed stands, and when I linger at the blouse rack, fingering the silk and examining the buttons, he begins to talk aloud to a mannequin. He gestures and smiles, walks around her. 'Love that suit,' he marvels. 'You look fabulous.' People stare, the sales staff looks nervous.

Here, he wanders off for coffee or a paper. He comes back to find me sorting through white piles of linen. I can't tell whether he looks astonished or distressed. I wonder if he thinks to himself, *Oh no, an hour in the rag pile*.

In a heap marked 5,000 *lire*, I turn up a stash of fine hand towels embroidered *AP*.

★

At home in California and here in Italy, slowly I have amassed a collection of old damask, linen, and cotton house linens, some with monograms, some not. 'Why would you want someone else's initials?' a friend asked me as she shook out her napkin at dinner. 'I find that a bit creepy.'

'These are my friend Kate's grandmother Beck's

napkins,' I answer, aware that nothing has been explained. When Kate had to empty her mother's house, she passed on a stash of linens to me. She wasn't interested in ironing them. They are enormous, with *CBC* scrolled in the center, the hump of thread as thick as a child's little finger. 'I have a thing for old linens.' Understatement. Spirals and history spinning out from that flip remark.

I do not mention my mother, that I still have in my trunk her monogrammed sheets I slept on as a child. I remember clearly my white spool bed, the sensation of slipping into chilly, fine cotton sheets, with the scalloped pink edge, and, right in the center, my mother's curvaceous initials, *FMD*, delicate as bird bones. For her room, she had blue sheets with blue monograms, and every other week, white with blue monograms. I have some of those, too, worn to a softness but still good. When she has a house, I intend to give them to my daughter. Dozens of plain towels, sheets, napkins, and pillowcases have passed through my household without a trace, but the hand towels my mother had monogrammed before my marriage are still in service, though the initial K is gone now from my name. When she gave them to me, I was shocked to see my own initials changed: *FKM*. I traced the new initial with my finger; K, the letter still carried forward on unused silver napkin rings, silver shot cups, a bread tray, a pepper grinder.

Monograms in my family were not limited to cloth. Baby rattles, silver cups, shoehorns, dresser silver, and the backs of flatware were subjected to this mania. The urge to monogram always seems mysterious to me, and never more mysterious than when I was ten and found my baby dresses. I loved to plunder, as my mother called it. 'Plunder and strew! Plunder and strew! You strew faster than I can pick up.' Her language was, otherwise, not archaic. I was looking in the hall chest at my father's high school report cards, the deed to the house, a beaded purse with a slippery silver mirror inside, which my mother carried when she was in her belle-hood and did the Charleston, back when a pink feather boa hung in her closet. I was searching for secrets. My hands riffled through the bolts of material that might someday be made into skirts or bathrobes, through the stored-away plastic bags holding my mother's cashmere sweaters, washed and hidden in cedar to protect them from moths. Then I pulled out a flattened stack of blue batiste infant gowns and held one up. There, over where the heart would have been, I saw the monogram: MMF.

A child had died? A secret child? I ran to my mother's room.

She was propped in her canopied bed, reading a fashion magazine. 'Oh, those were yours, if you had been a boy. M for Uncle Mark, F for Franklin, Big Daddy's name.' Her father, the puffy-cheeked man in the photograph, with her pouting in white flounces on his knee, died when I was three. I would have been a Mark and Franklin, not Frances, not Elizabeth. And the inevitable deduction: They had Mark in mind, not me.

'Why did you have them monogrammed before you knew?'

'I don't remember. We thought you would be a boy.' Her hair is caught in silver clamps to set the waves. I could almost see this brat. His ears stick out and he has scabs on his stupid bony knees. He looks out with my blue eyes.

Little wheels of logic spin. 'Where are the dresses with FEM?'

'There aren't any.'

It didn't take long for me to figure that, after two girls, they desperately wanted a boy and that the monogramming was an act of superstition and determination, an attempt to bend the will of fate. Years later, my mother told me that my father disappeared and 'went on a tear' for two days when I was born. Odd, my father was wild about me, and when he said, 'All my boys are girls,' I never picked up any tone of regret.

And is it odd, too, that when I think to myself about a sheet or shirt that is monogrammed, I think of it as a *mark*?

My mother monogrammed *AMY* on the batiste dress of one of my dolls. Amy, a name I loved from *Little Women*, though the name I secretly desired for myself was Renée. That was the one time I ever saw Mother at needlework. Usually, we took a hatbox full of my father's handkerchiefs and shirts, or pillowcases and my mother's silk slips, to Alice's, a woman who lived in a narrow house with a chinaberry tree out front. I climbed around in the tree, where once I saw a swarm of bees, or sat in the porch swing with her dog, Chap, who had swollen ticks on his ears. Sometimes I waited at Alice's table eating saltines and watching my mother and Alice, who was tall and angular, with enormous hands that looked as though they should be kneading great piles of dough – how did she manage to thread the thinnest of needles? She had bright pink gums that came far down to short teeth. She was brown and lived in 'colored town.' That she and my mother were friends may not have occurred to either of them. They gossiped and drank coffee, which Alice made in a blue and white speckled tin pot.

My mother pushed out her bottom lip when she concentrated. They carefully cut around printed initials, pinned tissue paper patterns to cloth, and ironed the indigo script indelibly onto the shirt pocket or sheet, leaving behind the outlined initials and the smell of scorched paper. Mother would then leave the imprinted linens for

Alice. The preferred thread was silky white, limp figure-eight loops held together in the center with a gold and black label. A few weeks later, Alice walked the mile to our house and she and Mother would spread Alice's handwork across the bed, remarking on how nicely everything came out.

★

The June market in Arezzo is even larger than the ones in April and May. I find the torso of a saint, lost from the whole carved wood body. I find a gold-leaf wooden cross and a beautiful studio portrait of a young woman, circa 1910. She is poised on the edge of a chair but radiates an inner calm. Several women gather around a stand hung with filmy lace and linen curtains. The woman in charge has starched and ironed for days. She has a heap of my favorite square pillowcases edged in handmade lace and secured by mother-of-pearl buttons on the back. I have these yard-square pillows in all the bedrooms – such pretty substitutes for headboards we don't have, and comfortable for reading, too. Most are too busy with lace inserts to bother with monograms but here's *RNP* in white swirls. At home in California, I have a handkerchief-linen pillowcase with the same initials. It belonged to my friend Josephine's aunt, who lived in a splendid house in Palm Beach. Josephine gave me, too, Aunt Regina's pale, pale pink linen sheets with labyrinthine cutwork above and below her initials. Josephine had them for fifty years, her aunt for thirty or forty; they are perfect. Why do monogrammed things last, while others are discarded? I have brought the sheets to Italy because in summer heat, nothing is as cool as linen sheets. At the market, I have acquired several more. I also love the heavy white sheets edged in webs of white crochet, and the plain, uneven cotton ones, heavy as a sail. When washed and hung out-side to dry, they do not need ironing, just a smoothing with my own flat hand as I fold them.

Sleeping on linen or the dense cotton spoils me. Occasionally, I'll find a bedspread, white cotton, of course, with the raised matelassé design and swags of handwork along the edge. They're short for contemporary beds but I bought one anyway and let my pillowcases show. I fall asleep thinking of the ancient villas and farms in the deep country where these sheets were used for birth, death, love, and ordinary exhausted sleep after a day of digging fields. They have been washed in stone troughs, flapped in spring winds, and have been hurriedly brought in when rain started across the hills. The ornate *D M* or S L C were worked by firelight for a bride. Perhaps some were 'too good' and were saved (for what?) in the *armadio* shelves with aromatic bay leaves and lavender to keep them fragrant.

All the linen stands at the market have rolls of lace, petticoats, christening dresses, blouses, and nightgowns. I'm not tempted. Once in France I found a long-sleeved gown, buttoned to the neck for modesty or warmth, embroidered in red with my daughter Ashley's initials. That *is* a bit weird, to wear someone else's gown, a French someone with your own monogram. She thanked me but somehow the gown ended up in the trunk with other vintage linens. Maybe the family mania has trailed out in her generation, or has taken another turn. Her art projects have involved damask napkins with her writing on them, and drifting rooms made of gauze with poems painted on the hanging panels.

My sister located a place in Florence that still does hand monogramming. They have a book of styles, some plain, some as ornate as a Baroque ceiling. She took them a pile of linen napkins for her new daughter-in-law and three months later they arrived in Atlanta. At markets, I have been accumulating for my daughter beautiful linen towels with circles for monograms woven into the design. My daughter, who does not yet own an iron. I hope she likes them.

★

When they are almost dry – slightly damp but warm from the sun – I take the six hand towels I bought at the market off the line. Just as I thought, they have come out of the wash white as salt. I hold the monogram to the sun, *A P*. These hand-hemmed linen towels, I notice, have a tab for hanging on a hook. I've never seen that before. Last summer when I travelled to the south of Italy, I saw the grave of one Assunta Primavera in the cemetery near Tricarico. Fresh yellow gladiolus and pink plastic flowers adorned her stone, along with her photo taken in middle age. Rather than an ethereal someone about to be assumed into heaven in spring, as her name suggested to me, she looked hearty and present. She pulled her black hair into a loose bun and her face was lighted by a wide smile. She looked like someone who could take the head off a chicken, no problem, or assist in birthing a breached baby. It seemed impossible that she could be lying under the stone. Surely she was off in some kitchen, the flavorful scent of her *tortellini in brodo* floating up the stairwell.

My hand towels could not have been hers, but her strong face immediately came to me when I saw the initials. And so it is with all these linens. I like to open the lid of my *cassone*, take out a stack, and imagine the dazzling aunt's Palm Beach cocktail parties, jazz on the record player, the champagne, the tiny napkins passed around, the trays of canapés – what did they eat at fancy soirées in the twenties? – the Atlantic Ocean waves spuming over the breakwater. I imagine Assunta's stone house, the walnut sleigh bed where the young husband lay naked, wanting his back rubbed, and later where the old husband snored while she lay awake, wondering if her son would return from the front in Russia, if unweaned lamb would be good for the *festa*, if the cold had killed her fava beans. AP, embroidered by her mother, given on her name day.

I imagine, too, the white nightgowns I did not buy at the market but looked at with amazement. They were as big as tents, all three of them monogrammed with suitably huge letters: TCC. A mound of flesh slept in those. TCC had to roll out of bed, her pink feet cold on the tiles, twins screaming at once in the night, this swift white messenger flying through the dark hall to comfort them.

The monogram is territorial. This is indubitably *mine*, it says. Under that, the monogram is a fixative of memory. The silver cup always goes back to the moment of the baby's christening. The dozen linen napkins for the bride usher in all the Thanksgiving dinners gathering in the future even now toward her table.

Ubi sunt is carved on ancient stones, short for that most haunting of questions, *Ubi sunt qui ante nos fuerunt*, Where are those who lived before us? Naming is deeply instinctive, a motion against the swallowing up by time of everything that exists. At eighteen, about to go to college, I was given a large supply of green bath towels, hand towels, and washcloths, all duly monogrammed. Green was not a color I liked, but those towels went off to college with me, lasted for years, and, even now, two live in the trunk of my car. Decades later, thanks to Aunt Emmy's graduation gift, I wipe off the car seat where Coca-Cola has spilled, my hand around the balled-up initials of a very distant college freshman who dried her hair with this. *A fleeting touch of wet hair, no, a spilled drink.*

Carolyn, Assunta, Mary, Flavia, Donatella, Altrude, Frankye, Luisa, Barbara, Kate, Almeda, Dorothea, Anne, Rena, Robin, Nancy, Susan, Giusi, Patrizia — we're all having dinner at my house.

BREATHING ART

Across the *piazza*, three boys bounce a soccer ball against the side wall of the Orvieto cathedral. The sun strikes the great, gilded façade of that stupendous, dazzling, arrogant building. I'm just basking in the reflected light, sipping a mid-afternoon cappuccino. This month we're free to roam. Primo restored the fallen wall and even improved it with two stone pillars for plants. He and his men 'repointed' the stone walls of the *cantina*, too, closing all the crevices where dust and mice might come in. The planned projects start in July.

Although Cortona is only an hour away, Orvieto seems far. My California sense of distance mysteriously expands here. Sixty or eighty miles usually seem like nothing, but within each kilometer in Tuscany and beyond, something to discover, study, eat, or drink is a potential distraction from the goal. California, at 160,000 square miles, is somehow smaller than Tuscany at 9,000 square miles.

Inside the cathedral, I've already seen the stop-in-your-tracks Signorelli fresco of Judgement Day – when skeletons just raised from the dead are caught by the artist as they are about to, and just as they have, melded back into their restored bodies – bodies at their prime of health. I was happy – the reality of seeing what cannot be seen, and also the activation of the phrase, *the resurrection of the body and the life everlasting*: Something known, hoped for, or disbelieved – but unimagined really – suddenly given full verisimilitude.

I looked up until my neck hurt. When I turned away to explore the rest of the cathedral, I passed a woman praying. Her market basket propped beside her was stuffed with vegetables. She'd slipped out of her shoes and was cooling her feet on the tiles. A little girl nearby braided her friend's hair. Their dolls sat upright on a bench. A young priest idly turned the pages of a magazine at a table laden with Catholic family publications.

They are knowing that splendid place through their pores, knowing so intimately and thoroughly that they do not have to know at all.

I, too, recall every inch of the unadorned Central Methodist Church in Fitzgerald, Georgia. I can still see the worn-down claret carpet, a glassy white light, still feel my fascination with the wooden holders for tiny cups of Welch's grape juice, which would magically and creepily turn into the blood of Jesus as it passed through my mouth.

Sitting under the grand Mediterranean sun, poised at the solstice, I say inadequately, 'Life would be different if you grew up bouncing your ball against the wall of the Orvieto cathedral.' But Ed is trying to parse some *La*

Repubblica article on the latest political imbroglio and so I spoon the foamy milk from my cup. What if the resurrection of the flesh had been painted above the heads of our white-robed choir belting out 'I come to the garden alone while the dew is still on the roses . . .' I would be seven, thirty-seven, seventy-seven — all stages of life, staring at that vision. If I turn my mind's eye around the interior of my hometown church, I see no art at all.

★

When I was growing up, a college textbook of my mother's from Georgia State College for Women stood in the living room bookshelf: *Art in Everyday Life*. I remember grainy photos of bowls of fruit on tables. They must have been suggested arrangements for still-life paintings. As a seven-year-old, I had no consciousness that included an act such as painting. I thought the pictures had to do with table settings because I did see my mother endlessly lavishing her attention on tablecloths and polished silver and flower arrangements.

Art meant the English hunting scene over the sofa, the pink ballet dancers in my bedroom, and the oil portrait of me that scared me with its likeness and crude vivacity. There I sat, caught in the hated blue dress with scalloped collar, my thin lips parted to show teeny teeth, the two incisors pointed like an animal's. A woman in town held after-school art classes on her front porch on Wednesday. I dutifully cast plaster-of-Paris shepherdesses and clowns. The next week, after they hardened, and if the teacher's children and dogs had not knocked off the lamb or the big nose, I painted them with brilliant enamel colors that somehow soaked in and mottled disappointingly.

When I went to college in Virginia, many of my classmates were incredibly sophisticated compared to my backwoods upbringing. They chatted knowledgeably about Cubism and Expressionism and the New York School. Soon I was soaking in the pleasures of the National Gallery with them and making further forays to the Museum of Modern Art. I ran up bookstore bills for art books, which enraged my grandfather, who believed in the Public Library, at most. Lautrec, Dufy, Nolde, Manet – it was exactly like falling in love. My connection with art became intense. So it has stayed.

★

Watching the downshifting of light on the façade at Orvieto, I begin to breath slowly, taking in the shouts of the boys, the man at the next table completing a cross-word puzzle, two nuns in long white habits, the angled shadow of the cathedral crossing the *piazza* like the blade of a sundial. I feel a grinding shift occurring in the tectonic plates in my brain. In Italy, it would be curious *not* to be intimate with art. You grow up here surrounded by beauty, thinking beauty is natural.

Art always has been *outside*, something I appreciated, loved, sought, but something not exactly natural. American towns often are void of art and are often actively ugly. In schools, art is usually a luxury which falls with no thud when the budget ax swings. Art, music, poetry – natural pleasures we were born to love – are expendables, fancy extras, so very non-binary. The unnaturalness comes, too, from the hushed atmosphere of museums, where most of us experience art. In Italy, so much art is in churches. Italians are only slightly less sociable in church than they are in the *piazza*. Art and the mass come not from on high, but with a familial attitude.

Cortona has an art gallery with its door opening onto Piazza Signorelli – his bust, perched high, overlooks the scene. The show changes every week, with the work ranging from excellent to ludicrous. But there it is, integral, right along with clothing and tobacco and flower shops. The artist sits with the show, thereby meeting directly with those who stop to look. In summer, the nearby Bar Signorelli serves at outdoor tables, and the artist can take a *caffè* when no one is about. Down the street, changing exhibitions of photographs are shown in a *palazzo*, which is also open to anyone interested who walks in off the street. Caffè degli Artisti's walls provide a casual exhibition place for young artists.

These galleries are light-years from the closed, cool exhibition spaces of Soho, Chelsea, and San Francisco, where just looking often makes you feel like an intruder. Country/city difference, of course, but in small country towns at home I don't ever see a vibrant art gallery as a vigorous part of the main street. A forbidding atmosphere is sad. Such a generalization – and isn't it true?

Cortona's signs say Città d'Arte, city of art, and it always has been. Cortona was one of the twelve original Etruscan cities and, since the seventeenth century, the town has had an active Etruscan museum. Their showpiece was found in a ditch in the nineteenth century – a heavy bronze chandelier intricately molded into shapes of crouching, erotically depicted figures. A few years ago, archeologists discovered important new tombs, and the museum now has a large recumbent animal figure and an ever-expanding exhibit of exquisite gold jewelry, carvings, and pots. A stone worker last year found a bronze tablet incised with Etruscan writing.

I have acquired, not by discovery but by gift, a piece of ancient art, an Etruscan foot. The touch of the maker is solidly in the folded-over slab of clay at the heel. I feel the indentations for the toenails, the long bone of the big toe, the knob of anklebone. Broken off before mid-calf, the ankle is hollow except for some ancient dirt caked inside. The foot reminds me of all the centuries of people who have walked over our land. Many, many people have these bits. In our neighbors' houses I have seen a Roman votive and an Etruscan glass vial, a marble head, a carved medieval door. The Italians take such ancient objects casually. Many a garage is a former house chapel, painted with frescoes which the owner keeps quiet about, not wanting the *Belle Arti* committee to make them give up their precious garage, home of that most precious *macchina*.

Even in Italian museums, most guards are dying to talk. I remember the guard in Siracusa giving a spontaneous talk on Caravaggio's *Burial of Santa Lucia*. In dank stone corridors in winter they're usually huddled with other guards around the pitiful space heaters, but, even then, a question will break one of them from the circle of warmth into a conversation about the restorations in progress or a disputed attribution.

*

Cimabue, it is said, discovered the young Giotto drawing a sheep on a stone at Vicchio, where Giotto tended flocks. Surely this is apocryphal but it points to an amazing moment in history when shepherds – and apprentices and clerks and noblemen's boys – took up the brush or the chisel all over Italy. The middle class was on the rise. The Tuscan vernacular began to be used in literary works. The painters' subjects were mainly religious; commissions for churches were pouring like *vino da tavola*. And while the subject might be assigned – the Annunciation, for sure, or the life of a saint – the painters began to bring to their 'sermons' in the art of fresco a sweet domestic air and a sense of *campanilismo*, a word that has to do with the sense of community of those who live within the sound of the local parish bell, the *campanile*.

One senses this new feel of the familiar starting in the thirteenth century when Duccio (1278–1318) allowed the flicker of emotion to haunt the face of the Madonna as Christ is removed from the cross, thereby cracking into the static, iconographic, and formalized painting style dominated by the influence of Byzantine mosaics. One probably could trace this new, more expressive, approach month by month. Imagine hanging around those workshops, when new techniques passed from mouth to mouth, village to village. From here, it's hard to gauge the surprise of Duccio's contemporaries. Giotto (1267–1337) codified the new approach in painting and Nicola Pisano (1258?–1284), and later his son, Giovanni (1265–1314), in sculpture. Then the names unroll: Masaccio (1401–1428?), Fra Filippo Lippi (1406–1469), Fra Angelico (14??–1455), Andrea Mantegna (1430–1506), Domenico Ghirlandaio (1449–1494), etc., etc.

When art historians discuss this spreading realism in Italian art, they often speak in terms of the new emotion and perspective, but those are only a part of what happened: When the silly little dog wandered into the foreground of a painting, the imagined wag of its tail caused painting and sculpture to enter the imagination of the viewer at a more direct level. In 1430, when Donatello's David in a jaunty hat jutted out his bronze hip, the fluid sensuality of his pubescent body was lost on no one.

Artists were commissioned to paint churches, chapels, grain markets, banks, cloisters, city halls, lay confraternity halls, bedrooms, cemetery memorials, and standards borne through the streets. Sculptors glorified the rich with statues and local *piazze* with playful and joyous fountains.

The people began to breathe the art every day. *Art in Everyday Life*. Not only a superhuman act to worship. Not only a bowl of fruit on the table.

There must be 10,000 Annunciations. The angel is witnessing the laser beam of the Holy Ghost angling toward a startled (who wouldn't be?) Mary. There's no mistaking the message. But the local resident – her basket of vegetables wedged next to her while she prays for her son off at war against the Guelphs – stares at the lake in the background where her husband fishes, the line of hills as familiar to her as the curves of her own hips.

In Crivelli's (1435?–1495) version of the Annunciation, the Virgin herself is the main focus. The impregnating light beam from heaven, so much like an airplane's contrails, illuminates her crossed hands and wide forehead. But our visitor with the basket of vegetables looks for a long time. What is that outside the Virgin's door? An apple and a squash, plain as day. And over her head on a shelf, her six white pasta dishes. A cheese box. A bottle of oil – extra virgin, no doubt – and a candlestick. From her window upstairs, hangs a wooden cage with a songbird. An Oriental rug drapes over a stone railing, with a house plant airing on top of it. We are suddenly at home.

All over Italy, they are kneeling or cooling their feet on the church tiles. In a side panel, a horse has skidded into a ravine, a man falls from a ladder, a stone wall collapses on a monk. The baby Jesus looks just like the neighbor's baby, born with no sign of a father. Ugly little *bambino* with a stranglehold on a bird. Or there, Saint Jerome, major man, in his study with the shadowy figure of his companion, a lion. And there's his bath towel dangling from a nail, a note tacked to his desk, a small cat. *My house is your house.*

*

A grand Cortona *palazzo* has been divided into thirteen apartments. Behind the Renaissance façade, the medieval house remains. Cutting and pasting those winding corridors and rooms, joined without hallways, into apartments must have been an architect's nightmare. We're having dinner in Celia and Vittorio's kitchen. Formerly, it must have been a sitting room. Vittorio and Celia have found beneath the whitewash a two-hundred-year old garden scene on all four walls. The *trompe l'oeil* iron fence separates the viewer from the flowers and distant hills. We admire the view as we are dipping fennel slices into Vittorio's parents' olive oil. 'Oh, all the flats in this building have frescoes in every room,' he tells us, 'but most people never have bothered to uncover them.' He shows us the other rooms, the tantalizing glimpses of melon and aquamarine colors where they have not yet restored the frescoes. How can they bear not to see? I think I'd be up all night, sponging water and rubbing a toothbrush over the powdery whitewash. When we uncovered a fresco in our dining room we thought it was close to a miracle. A fresco! Since then we've learned that almost anytime you start scrubbing in Cortona, you discover a fresco.

Antonio, who also lives in this *palazzo*, stops in for a glass of wine. He takes us to the mysterious apartment where he grew up. We enter a large room, then another. His dead mother's paintings — portraits and landscapes — cover the walls. Her piano, her furniture, her photographs on the mantel, remain. There is a photo of four-year-old Antonio on Santa's knee. Someone years ago has made a few swipes low on the wall, enough to reveal that something chestnut brown and green lies underneath, but what? I think I see the quick curve of a horse's haunch. This room obviously is unused. We go down a squirrely, low corridor into a vast room under the eaves, with a painterly view of the *piazza* far below. Antonio takes me into a side room stuffed with his paintings. The main room has a long table covered with sketches and squeezed tubes of paint. Two cats fly around the room and then curl together in a mammoth fireplace, where people have warmed themselves since the 1500s. Along the way, who took the brush to these walls and what was painted? And who grew weary of them, decided white was better, and simply wiped them out? Antonio sits by the drafty fireplace with his wild cats, sipping coffee and drawing, walking to the windows to look down at the *piazza*.

He has other rooms we do not see, rooms he has closed. Under paint and smoke, I imagine other garden scenes, Annunciations, mythological trysts, Europas, distant castles, scenes from the lives of saints. But Antonio is showing me the decorative border he has designed for someone's house, a restored house with newly plastered walls, where he will stencil acanthus leaves in gold bounded by lines of Pompeian red. In a hundred years, a woman will wake up one morning, her eye traveling along the top of her bedroom wall, and she will think *no*, she will think *flowers, I would like to see flowers* and Antonio's work will be covered by a border of roses.

I ask Antonio if he and his friend Flavia will paint a border in the bathroom we are about to remodel. I love the stylized, running Etruscan wave. He sketches a few. We decide on milky blue, bordered with two lines in apricot.

The next day, I find myself in the art supply store staring at the pristine watercolor paper, tubes with delicious names, thick sketch pads and trays of colored pencils. When my daughter was small, she and I used to set up a table in the back yard and paint all morning. She had a vigorous sense of color and, even then, thought big. She painted huge purple elephants with backgrounds of wildly splotched colors and princesses in swirling pink. Her boxy houses, with the spoked sun above, always had people in the yard and cats in the windows. And what's that off to the side? A yellow convertible. My watercolors were rolled up and hidden under the bed. The still life of a blue bowl of oranges was born dead. The fragile coral bells against a stone wall conveyed no sense of textural contrast. The immense pleasure of sitting in the sun watching my daughter, thinning carmine to pale pink and dipping in the fine tip, creating something where there was nothing – she had the flow of freedom. I was not spontaneously *good* enough.

In the art shop, I reach for the chalk pastels, the stack of handmade paper. The inkling I began to have in Orvieto slips into consciousness. I'm going to draw the *pleasure* of wild purple orchids springing up every day, the outrageous *upupa*, hoopoe, who lands in my hazelnut tree every morning, and the lines of the hills I can see from my study, how they lap into each other like pleats in a green velvet skirt. I've been breathing these images. And if I could *deeply* breathe art, I would try to paint the *feeling* of all the birds singing every morning splurging all their megahertz on the dawn.

I have always loved that collision point of nature with the desire to create art. For me the form is words. How to pull the scent of wet mock orange through the walls of the house? Through the ink in the pen, through the keys of the computer? The dark when the birds begin – their songs so tangled together that no one can be separated – so impurely accessible to music, art, words. Song like a *riffle*, a sandbar just under water, sunlight pushed by the tide. How do they know and why do they sing? How to say that although everything is at stake when experiencing or making art, that it is at the same time a birthright joy. How to paint or write the everyday rising green burst of birdsong? The levitation, the silverpoint thread drawn along the black hills, slow melting of rose, opalescent blue, and the pulse of the birds still rising?

I am lying half-awake, wondering if I've died and this is what was promised. The ache in my hind end from digging out stones from the flower beds yesterday reminds me that I am still mortal and that the earth simply has returned to aurous colors; to diffusion, then to the birds scattering from their conjoined song and into their own jactations from tree to tree. I long for the creation.

This is every day, how art slips in and out.

MAD JULY: THE HUMMING URN

Thirty-one straight days of house guests. A seventh set threatens to arrive. When Primo Bianchi stops by and announces that he is ready to begin work, we call these acquaintances, having earlier warned them that we might not be able to put them up because of the restoration project. 'We'd love to see the work-in-progress,' my former colleague says. 'We'll stay out of the way.' I rarely see him in San Francisco and can't remember whatever conversation we had at the book signing of a mutual friend, which has now led to him and his girlfriend visiting us.

'I'm afraid it's really not going to work. They're ripping out two bathrooms. I think you'd be more comfortable at a hotel.'

Silence from across the Atlantic. Then, 'Don't you have three bathrooms?'

'Yes — but you'd have to go through our bedroom to get to the other one.' Momentarily nonplussed, he agrees that I can arrange a hotel for them.

★

When I was in college, I used to imagine a yellow house on a shady street. The indefinite location could have been Princeton, Gainesville, Palo Alto, Evanston, San Luis Obispo, Boulder, Chapel Hill — some college town where bicycles were preferred, tomatoes were grown in the back yard, and one's friends dropped in without calling. My writing desk would face a window upstairs where I could keep watch over the children playing, could run down to check on the roast. I imagined extra rooms with blue toile wallpaper, a dormer room with spool beds for children, and a dining room with a wall of French doors. Friends could stay as long as they liked, their children blending with mine at the great round table. This fantasy alternated with another of living alone in a fabulous city, Paris, San Francisco, or Rome, where I would wear a tight black knit dress, sandals, and sunglasses, smoke thin cigars in a café, while writing poems in a leather book.

Through the years, fragments of those dreams actually came true. But never until now have I had more than one guest room. With three extra bedrooms, my dream of the bounteous table and the open door have become reality.

Revolving door is more like it. Dreams sometimes need revision. During the visits of six sets of house guests, I have needed a conveyer belt from town to send out bread and meat. I strip off the sheets, and the washing machine lunges and churns for hours. I have lapsed into a set menu for lunch: *caprese* (mozzarella, basil, tomato salad), *focaccia*, various kinds of salami and ham, green salad, cheeses, and fruit. 'Again?' Ed asks.

236

'Yes! They don't know we've had it four days running. We are definitely going out tonight.'

I'm ready to draw maps to the antique shops of Monte San Savino or the Etruscan tomb near Perugia, but often they say, 'We just want to stay here. Those four days in Rome were exhausting . . .'

At what point did I flip from *Excited to see you* to *How long, oh lord, how long will you be staying?* It must have been around day ten. For Ed, around day five; he is more solitary than I. He must have his private hours of writing and working on the land. Too much socializing throws the circuit breaker and he comes down with a migraine. By the third onslaught of guests, we were growing tired of the sound of our own voices. By the fourth, we switched to automatic pilot, almost pointing instead of speaking. 'Bus is leaving for Siena,' I whispered at their door. Feeble humor. We agreed to leave by eight to avoid the heat. Ed filled up the car so we could get an early start. We're showered and ready by 7:30, plates of melon on the table, the Moka hissing on the stove. They're still sleeping at 9:30. If we're out by 10, we'll arrive with an hour or so before the town closes for the afternoon. Our guests will be sorely annoyed at this retro custom. The rhythm of the Italian day seems impossible to grasp. 'We're on vacation; we don't want a schedule. Let's play it by ear,' he says. 'Yes,' she agrees, 'and besides a lot of places stay open during siesta.' No they don't, I think, but don't say anything.

When they left, I couldn't even say hello to the neighbor's gray cat, who sometimes comes by for a bowl of milk.

'Would ten days be too long?'

'The friends we're travelling with have heard so much about you. Would it be all right if the six of us stopped by for lunch?'

'My son's roommate and his cousin will be passing your way and we thought you might enjoy meeting a couple of kids on their first trip to Italy.'

My mouth has a hard time forming the word 'no' but I'm learning. 'I'm working on a project,' I say, only to hear, 'Well, don't worry about us. We won't disturb you a bit. You just do your writing and we'll go off on day trips.' If I say how sorry I am but we have a full house on the dates they propose, the reply often is, 'Just tell us when and we'll plan our vacation around you.'

★

Primo, welcome. You don't know how welcome. We've wanted to remodel the two original bathrooms ever since we first saw them. Because they worked, other more crucial projects came first. We ignored the chipped porcelain sinks and the funky showers that sprayed all over the floor, simply added brass towel racks and antique mirrors from the Arezzo market and turned our energy and cash over to central heating and unraveling electrical wires. Unlike those monster jobs, changing the bathrooms offers instant pleasure.

While our first guests slathered suntan oil on each other's backs, we dashed out to order toilets and lights. During the next guests' stay, we were looking at tile. Time to choose; the order needed to go. Karen and Michael waved from the upstairs terrace, where I left a bowl of fruit and a pitcher of cinnamon iced tea to hold them until we returned.

Selecting tiles in Italy would be daunting even for my two sisters, who can spend entire days examining fabrics or lamps or wallpaper. The attractive showrooms of building suppliers are backed with dusty warehouses. If you don't see what you want up front in the model bathrooms with the space-capsule showers and gadget-laden whirlpool tubs, you're turned loose in the *magazzino* to fend for yourself among racks, stacks, and boxes of pavers in shades of rose-honey, elegant limestone squares, the thousand versions of hand-painted blue and white birds and flowers, slick primary colors, and – oh, no! – the pink and blue butterfly we are about to exorcise from the house. I found immediately that I prefer tiles with the touch of the maker on them, the rougher surface, and the traditional designs. The range of marble and natural stone tiles also is staggering. For the first time ever, I thought I could not choose. When we built the first bath, I knew what I wanted – large marble squares – and, fortunately, didn't even look further.

Finally, we narrowed our choices and decided to come back in a few days. Back at Bramasole, Karen and Michael were glowing and spotless in new linen bought for their trip. Ed and I were grimy from the warehouses and my dust allergy started acting up. But – lunch in a few minutes! And in the afternoon, the Etruscan museum, the churches of upper Cortona, the monastery where St Francis's narrow bed is still on view.

'*La dolce vita*,' they say, leaning back for a sip of *grappa* in the long evenings, as I'm glancing in the kitchen at the stacks of pots. 'Umm, think I'll go up; it's just so relaxing here. You two are so lucky – all day with nothing to do but enjoy all this beauty.' The lovely guests trail upstairs, forgetting to notice that Ed and I are rolling up our sleeves for a bout with grease and suds. Over our heads, as we scrape and sweep, their bed bangs rhythmically against the wall.

★

By the time they leave, we've changed our minds about

the tile. At last we can just look for a whole morning, without thinking of rushing home to feed ravenous guests. For the original bathroom of the house, called '*il brutto*,' the ugly, by my daughter, we select a rosy natural stone with the same stone in cream for the border. For the nightmare butterfly bath, we decide on a handmade Sicilian tile in a blue and yellow design on white.

The yellow house fantasy is still real. I love having friends and family here. In a foreign country, we see each other in an unfamiliar perspective, which can heighten and enrich the closeness we already have. Good friends jump right in and love walking to the market for strawberries. They come home with ideas for dinner and we have great times frying zucchini blossoms and making watermelon *sorbetto*. They're ready to search for a Roman road we've heard about, to start the coffee, or even to weed the asparagus bed. The bad guest could be anywhere; the good guest seems to know that places are unique unto themselves and gives over to the new heartbeat, letting the place have its way with them.

Now Toni and Shotsy arrive from San Francisco with a list of places they want to see; some are new to us. They're delighted on their first evening when the fireflies crowd the lane. Even a walk into town with them brings new adventures. We're walking past San Francesco, a church perpetually closed for restoration. Shotsy sees a priest at the side door and asks him if we can peep inside. He seems happy that we're interested. A grape-juice birthmark covers half his face. His eyes are direct and he moves his head from side to side as he walks, his black robe catching dust rolls. We spend an hour on a tour inside the vaulted, gloomy church which was re-dressed from its original spare architecture into a Baroque interior. The priest then takes us into a room with closed cupboards. He wants to show us something special, but first he shows us the skulls of several Roman martyrs, eleven or twelve years old. The shelves are full of various hanks of hair and pieces of bone. He reverently takes out a bit of cloth. 'The last sash of Santa Margherita, a rare and precious relic.' Then he shows us a piece of one of San Francesco's garments. This church, named for him, was built by his friend Brother Elias, about whom little is known except that he was a sometime hermit in the hills above our house. The priest shakes our hands and tells us, 'I'll probably go to hell but all of you will go to heaven.'

Near Piazza San Cristoforo, a man picking cherries in a tree calls '*Buon giorno*,' and throws down samples for us to try. All this and it's not even ten o'clock yet. They take off for the day and come home with stories to tell. We're sorry when they go.

My two sisters came with me for two weeks early last summer, when Ed was finishing his spring quarter of teaching. Because our mother has been in a nursing home for many, many years, most of our visits revolve around her dips into illness, her emergencies, or just the painful regular visits to her. For the first time in too long, we talked about everything but Mother. We travelled all over Tuscany, cooked pasta, and worked in the garden.

Our aunt Hazel had died recently and left us each a little inheritance. We decided to splurge. After all, we never expected this little windfall. I certainly didn't. Any selfish act when I was a child was corrected with, 'You don't want to grow up to be like Hazel do you?' When my grandmother died, Hazel was too upset to go to the funeral. When we filed into my grandparents' house afterwards, we found that she'd loaded her car with all Mother Mayes's best things. Because of another painful memory I wouldn't write about, I had not spoken to Hazel since college.

My sisters and I ate in the best restaurants, ending each meal, with 'Thank you, Hazel. We enjoyed that so much.' We began to feel rather friendly toward her. We bought shoes and trays and scarves, saying, 'Hazel, that was so sweet of you,' as we walked out of each shop. As much as I disliked her, I found that her last act toward me stirred up a memory-belief that runs strong in my family, the old impulse, *Blood is thicker than water*, and a late forgiving began to form.

We found ourselves one day in the deep recesses of a medieval building in Florence, being shown rooms of designer bags and jewelry. My sisters were thrilled at the prices and began selecting – gold bracelets, wallets, summer handbags. It suddenly occurred to me that this was stolen merchandise but I couldn't say anything because the *signora* who took us there from her shop understood just enough English. I hoped they'd finish before the *carabinieri* burst in. We left with Gucci and Chanel, the real thing my sisters knew. 'We're lucky we weren't arrested,' I told them in the taxi. Oddly enough, they paid by personal check and no one ever cashed them. Just one comment catapulted us back to familiar ground. At breakfast in the hotel courtyard with a splashing fountain, we were served perfect cantaloupe. Which one of us said, 'Mother would have loved this'? A deep relief to reconnect on a new basis. Now when we send each other unexpected gifts, we enclose a card, *Love, Hazel*.

★

Bathrooms. The Romans loved them. Their bathing pools with black-and-white mosaic dolphins and stylized sea creatures never have been improved upon. Their fanciful designs influenced the original designers of bathroom decor at Bramasole not at all. Early in this adventure, we realized that not only were the old ones ugly, but our sewage treatment facility – one cement tank – was inadequate when several people were staying in the house. Noxious odors and scorpions crept up the drains. We read books on home water supplies, on waste management in the country, made photocopies of septic tank diagrams. After a few hours of digging behind the house, Primo revealed that the shower emptied right into the tank, an environmental no-no. More digging revealed that all three showers and sinks dumped gallons and gallons of clear water right in, forcing the waste out before the biological action of purification could happen. We are polluting our own land. Or so we think, with our book knowledge. 'That's the way it's done,' plumbers assured us. 'Your system is good.' We don't think so. We have insisted to Primo that we want a better plan. We want the showers and sinks routed out of the septic system. We want long pipes to exit the septic tank, with rock-filled pits along the way for further filtering.

*

When Primo and the men arrive, we go out and discuss the plan of attack with them. Ed and I have spent ten-hour days decalcifying tile floors, ten-hour days stripping doors, but facing your true love over an open septic tank may be one of those true tests. Primo wants to explain the compartments. How they purify waste and where it exits. 'This tank is OK,' he insists. 'I need to make another section on the inside. See, *acqua nera* in,' he points to a pipe from the bathroom. He scrapes sand off the septic tank lid and pries it up. I gasp and step back. This is too much. I would like to be anywhere but here. Unfazed, he points, '*acqua chiara* out.' Black water in, clear water out. It all looks *nera*. Primo leaps about with the alacrity of a cat on a dining room table. Ed has stepped back, clapped his hand over his nose. 'There, then there, then out. All clear.' Suddenly Primo makes a little gagging sound as he slides the top back in place and jumps aside. We all start to laugh and run.

Because our steep hill makes the delivery of a huge tank impossible without a crane to hoist it over the wall, Primo suggests two septic tanks, keeping the old one behind the house and installing a new one in the Lime Tree Bower. He shakes his head and shrugs. 'Big enough for an apartment building. A hospital. Call the honey wagon; ask him to come today.'

He takes off for supplies. The men head upstairs. The minute bath goes first and demolition is fast. Franco and Emilio – how do they both work in there? – cart bucket after bucket of tile. How it didn't crush his Ape, I don't know, but Primo inched up the boxwood lane and across the front terrace with a giant cement septic tank, which must be buried. The old toilet is loaded in the Ape. Zeno, a Pole, starts digging a trench and Ed hauls stones out to our pile, with which by now we could build a small house.

The honey wagon honks in the road below. I look out the window and see a man waving and a tractor pulling a rusty tank. Ed runs out. The driver throws a rope to him and Ed hauls up the hose. Secondo comes up, leaving his tractor heaving in the road. He has cottonball hair and a pouncing step. He greets Ed like an old friend. After my brief view into the bowels, so to speak, of the system, I don't even want to watch. I hear suction and slushing. In a short time, I hear Ed in the shower. He's laughing. 'What's funny?'

'That was unbelievable. It's just – you know, I never saw myself that way. Running all over the place helping clean shit out of a tank. The system is empty and rinsed. I really liked Secondo – he wanted to see the olives and told me he'd send his son to plow our terraces.'

★

Even though I have trouble writing, studying Italian, or reading when guests are here, I have no problems at all when work is going on. Primo's men work; so do I. Ed, too. He is up two hours before the workers arrive, writing, as he prefers, in the dim light. In the series of poems he's working on, each one begins and ends with an Italian word, often a word that has an English meaning as well, such as *ago*, needle, and *dove*, where. One of his pleasures in learning Italian has been its invasion into his writing. He spends hours poring over etymologies.

I start every day with a walk into town. My ritual is to have my cappuccino in a bar where *Wonder Woman* blares away in dubbed Italian. She's hilarious, and an excellent companion to the news. Yesterday's headline was 'Lizard Found in Frozen Spinach.' A very short man with a head shaped like a schnauzer's comes in the bar every morning. Instead of asking for a *caffè macchiato*, an espresso 'stained' with milk, he always says, '*Macchiame, Maria*,' stain me, Maria. She doesn't blink.

When the men arrive at eight, Ed is through writing for the day. He emerges in shorts and boots, wanting to attack the brush on the top terrace, but he heads instead to the vegetable garden to hack out weeds. Suddenly, the *orto* is ours. Anselmo is in the hospital with pneumonia, odd for July. He calls on his *telefonino* to tell us to water in the mornings, to dig all the potatoes and let them dry for two days in a single layer before we store them in the dark.

When we take him some flowers, we find him in a depressing ward with seven other men in iron beds. He's in a robe, sitting on the side of his bed. Usually full of opinions and jokes, he suddenly looks frail and vulnerable, his bare round belly poking out under the sash. He asks everything about the *orto*. How many melons? Have we picked the zucchini every day? We know he thinks we don't water or cut lettuce properly. We put the yellow begonia we've brought by the bed. As we leave, we hear him on the telephone, 'Listen, that apartment on the road to Dogana, I can get you in by next week . . .'

Primo's men are *muratori*, stonemasons. We're surprised that they actually lay the pipes. We expected that job to fall to the plumbers. For the installation of the wiring and lights, Mario and Ettore, plumber/electricians step in. They're now-you-see-them-now-you-don't men – incredibly efficient and fast. Mario shouts; Ettore is silent. They run, they're sleight-of-hand, they're *bravissimi*.

'*Squilla il telefono*,' Mario calls out the window. He has the loudest voice in the universe. *Squillare* – to ring, and the squeal in the sound of the telephone always grates. Paolo has bad news. 'The tile from Sicily – such a beautiful selection, truly the sales representative was pleased that someone had the refinement to select this tile – unfortunately this tile has met with an accident in the form of a wreck of the transport truck and the truck has run into the sea. The driver is not injured but the tile . . .'

For a minute, I don't take this in. 'You mean my tile is in the water?'

'*Sì, mi dispiace; è vero.*' He's sorry but it's true. This is so unbelievable that we both laugh. Little fish nosing the boxes? The truck overturned, lodged in sand. 'We must begin again. And soon the August holiday arrives. No one will be making tile.'

Very close friends are arriving. Inopportune timing, but they're welcome anytime. We hope they won't mind a bit of chaos. We dash to Paolo's and wait while he shouts into the phone about the tile. You'd think he was talking to Mars. He slams it down. 'They don't promise but they'll try to get it here on time.'

'If it's not here in two weeks, we won't be able to finish the project.'

'*Boh*,' Paolo goes through several what–can–you–do gestures. 'Sicilians,' he explains.

Fortunately, the men have not yet started demolishing the butterfly bath. As compensation, Paolo shows us his truck, which is loaded with the fixtures we ordered for both baths and boxes of faucets. We take off to shop for food. We want to make duck breast ravioli with olive sauce for Sheila and Rob, our friends from Washington.

When we get home, we find them waiting, six bottles of Brunello lined up on the wall as a welcome home for us, and right in the middle of the front yard, two toilets, two sinks, a tub, a shower basin, and a four-foot stack of boxes. The scarred tub from *il brutto* has been brought outside and someone has put a large box turtle inside it. He climbs the slope then slides down again, frantic claws dragging the porcelain. I know just how he feels. From around the corner in the Lime Tree Bower, we hear the unmistakable sound of shovels striking rock and the voices of Franco and Emilio starting their litany of Madonna curses. It looks as if they're digging a grave for a behemoth. They're up to their waists. Zeno's trench has miles to go. Ed places the turtle in the strawberry patch, Sheila and I shell peas, Rob puts on a Righteous Brothers CD and turns up the volume of 'Unchained Melody.' The men fire up their portable gas to heat the pasta they've brought for lunch. Zeno turns the hose on his filthy legs. I'm completely happy. We're sitting on the stone wall in the sun. Our neighbor Placido calls up from the road,

'Edward, Frances, I have a new name for your house. You should change to Villa delle Farfalle [House of the Butterflies] because it is a miracle there are so many all over the lavender. They are like confetti – there's a big party going on every day.' Wasps have taken up residence in the old terra-cotta urn next to me. It's missing a handle, cemented in ages past to the wall so the wind does not blow it over. The busy wasps exit from a small opening like helicopters angling off a pad. Rob pops the cork of a Brunello. I hear the urn humming. Rob pours, telling us about circling Rome twice on the ring road. Ed the poet speaks truly in my ear: *Don't you love it – this urn is like our house.* He cups my hand around the side and I feel the buzz.

*

Cynthia, an English friend who has lived in Tuscany for forty years, has invited us for dinner the night Sheila and Rob, our last house guests of the summer, have departed. Right now, I'm facing the arrival of my former colleague at the hotel next week. Our house is so full of construction dust today that we found it between our toes and on our eyelids. No sign of the tile's arrival, but otherwise the project is going without a hitch.

We find other *stranieri*, all English friends, at the table. When Ed mentions that we haven't had anyone over because we've had nonstop people at the house, the conversation erupts. 'Guests come in two sizes: excellent and terrible. Most are the latter. Do you know that expression about house guests, like fish, are good for three days? It exists in every language, the remote Pacific islands, Siberia, everywhere.' Max always has guests.

Cynthia happens to be serving a large fish decorated all over with sliced olives arranged like scales. 'Do you know

248

my stepbrother arrived with two children with colds – and he had car trouble. He hoisted his dirty suitcase onto the white bedspread and began tossing their underwear into a pile. Mind you, I haven't even seen him in fifteen years. He stayed ten days – never brought home a flower, a bottle of wine, or a hunk of cheese, and never even wrote a thank-you. He left a hundred thousand *lire* note [about sixty dollars] inside the fridge with a note saying 'for food.' Is that not the limit? No one can top that.' Her eyes flash. 'And I was afraid I'd misjudged the poor boy all those years.' She lops off the fish's head and pushes it aside.

Her friend Quinton, a mystery writer, pours the wine. 'I never have guests. Too disrupting.'

'Isn't it just?' Peter agrees. 'Some friends were arriving by train and I popped down to meet the 1:05 from Florence. They didn't get off. I waited until the 2:14. I gave up. Finally, around 4, quite hot and miffed, they called from the station.'

'One guest came bearing all the tiny jam jars, plastic shower caps, and shoeshine cloths from hotels along her way and presented them to me as a gift. Some of the jam jars had been opened and had a touch of butter stuck to the lid,' I tell them.

'That's rather sweet,' Cynthia says.

'Rubbish,' Quinton laughs. 'These people never would behave this way at home.'

'She kept the nice soaps for herself,' I add.

'Something cuts loose when people travel to a foreign country,' Ed says. 'The words, "*We're going to be in Italy . . .*" ' release them. It's as if we're bonded by being miraculously in this alien place at the same time.'

Quinton agrees. 'We man the campfire and they're the wanderers in the lonely outback who arrive safely.'

'The concept that we have work in progress doesn't

stick. If you are in Italy, you are on vacation. Period.' Peter glances at his watch. 'Actually, an old friend is arriving tomorrow.'

★

Our neighbor Placido comes over to ask if we want town water. We could split the cost of bringing a connection from Torreone. His water supply by midsummer is low and he has just put in a new lawn he doesn't want to lose. We'd investigated bringing town water here when we bought the house and found it to be outrageously expensive. Anselmo had a new well dug for us, a 300-foot-deep well he guarantees never will go dry. But Placido has a friend; the cost we were quoted is now quartered. It seems a neighborly thing to do, and if there's a severe drought, we'd be protected. Why not? We can just have the line brought in, cap it, and leave it until we need it. Fortuitous that we have a trench in progress.

The next thing we know, we are in the middle of an immense project adjacent to our other immense project. A gargantuan yellow backhoe digs a ditch from Torreone, a kilometer away, all the way to our house. All day it scrapes and dumps dirt into the road. Shirtless men lay tubing and shout. Heat is on us like the hot breath of a dog who has run all the way home. The men here are hauling rubble, digging, chiseling into rock. We flash on the layers they jimmied out from the living room floor two years ago; but here they're hitting the solid rock of the mountain. The hole for the new tank could accommodate a Fiat 500. They loop the tank with ropes and the four men edge the tank near the hole, then lower it in a controlled fall. After that, the tubes connect quickly. The men all join into Zeno's trench digging. They're at the melting point. Septic and water pipes are laid running out from the house. The electricians connect tubes for wires, in case we ever want electricity farther out. Other tubes are installed for a gas line so we can move the enormous green tank out of the *limonaia* and reclaim space for the lemons.

On the third day of digging along the road, the back-hoe reaches us, claws out a path up the hill, and the water line, too, is laid in the trench. We just stand and watch with awe. Did we ever imagine we'd dig a half-mile ditch?

This is Anselmo's first day back. He's pale under his red beret and gingerly climbs the steps to the garden terraces. He surveys the havoc we've caused in his garden. We have not directed the sprawling of the melon vines; they're tangled. We have not removed the proper lateral branches of the tomatoes. Obviously, the carrots have not been watered enough because the ground is hard as bone, stunting their growth. I'm the good student, nodding and asking questions. We've come to see that he's always right. He pokes at the weeds around the artichoke plants, clips the blue thistles of those that went to seed. He agrees with Primo – we're foolish to install another entire septic system, and of course the drainage should have been elsewhere.

Nine men are working here. Our tutor, Amalia, comes out for our Italian lesson because we can't get away to go into Cortona. We're gratified when she leans over the upstairs terrace and listens to the workers talking. 'I don't know how you do this. I can't understand half of what they're saying. Do you realize that you've got four dialects going on down there.' Meanwhile, plaster is drying in the little bath. Recessed lighting and the tub are in place. Primo's tiler arrives tomorrow.

★

In July, the garden looks glorious. Everything we planted

becomes its ideal self. Vita Sackville-West spoke of her garden in 'full foison.' This one, too, is abundant, outpouring. Only the dahlias languish. Powdery mildew spots the leaves and the flowers rot before they open. Everything else has spread or sprung and blooms outrageously. From the upstairs windows, I look out and think of Humphrey Repton, who might approve of this Italian marriage to a basic English scheme. Even the spilling pots of geraniums on all the walls have a Humphrey touch. In the corner of each one I planted a morning glory seed. The vines fall down the wall, twine around the outdoor lights or crawl along the stones. They open their pure pink faces to the morning sun. I have found an old stone statue of a woman holding a sheaf of wheat. She stands among hydrangea pots, a nod to the Italian tradition of garden ornaments. Not only has Egisto, master *fabbro* at Ossaia, repaired the house's original gate, he is making iron arches for a pergola of grape vines at the entrance to the Lake Walk. We're still looking for our water inspiration – a small pond, a fountain? At an antique warehouse in Umbria, I sighted a rusted, curvy iron bench shoved up against a fence with some equally rusted iron gates and beds. When we asked the price, the store owner was clearly dumbfounded; he never expected to sell that wreck. We wove back through the mountains with the bench tied to the top of the car. With my arm outside the window, I held on to a leg: at least if it started to slip, we could stop.

Anselmo's lemon pots in the garden are purely Italian. He has shaped them to bamboo supporting cages. 'Pick them, pick them,' he urges. I wait, loving the look of the yellow fruit dangling among the leaves. After their initial spurts, the two Mermaids calmed down and sent out a few creamy yellow flat roses. Each Sally Holmes rose we planted among the lavender, cheerleader that she is, gives us white pompom armfuls constantly. They've choked out the decadent lilac-colored rose, a weak sister anyway. Ed comes across a photo of the wild garden taken when we bought the house, and another from a couple of summers later, when it was nothing but a blank stretch of dirt bordered by the boxwood hedge. If I could have had a glimpse then of what we could do, my nights of wide-eyed anxiety would have been fewer. I love the garden transformation as much as the restoration of the house. This green and blooming swath is where the house combines sweetly with nature. Beyond it, the cultivation of olives, grapes, cypresses, and lavender creates a lighter link with nature, before the natural scrub and broom, the wild asparagus and roses. I love the space for these levels of connection, these cruxes between home and the wider world. 'Every olive has its own story,' Anselmo tells us.

'The roses do, too. They're speaking to me all the time,' I joke.

But he does not care about the roses. '*Mah*,' he replies and turns back to the *orto*.

★

The five-inch-square stones look as though they always belonged to *il brutto*. Gone is the floor of black and dun concrete squares. The sink was set into the stone wall. The hollow above it testified to the height of the first owner. Even I, at 5'4", had to stoop a little to see in the mirror. Primo raised and arched the hollow, and I found an old foxed mirror that perfectly fit the space. Just that one change made the cramped sense of cat-inside-a-dollhouse disappear. Antonio arrives with his partner, Flavia. Making frames is the bread and butter of their shop but they love most the decorative finishes and designs. They have made a mock-up of the blue Etruscan wave which will run around the wall. We sit outside drinking tea and experimenting with paints for the exact milky blue, the exact rosy color for the border. Flavia should be painted, with her expressive brown eyes and almond skin. She ties her long hair up and covers it with a scarf, looking more and more like the Madonna about to mount a donkey for the long journey. Still, a strand escapes and trails through the blue paint. Antonio looks nothing like a Joseph. Too full of fun and irony. After a heated discussion about proportion, they make a plastic stencil for the wave. The painting goes quickly. They draw the border lines in pencil then paint them freehand. We've kept the original wooden window with a wide sill where thrushes hatched in June. We've kept the hip-bath–sized tub, although the original had to be replaced. 'Who would buy one of those?' Paolo asked dismissively, when we asked if they still were made. 'I would,' I answered. 'It seems to belong in the house.'

Antonio comes to get me every few minutes. 'Do you like it? Do you completely like it?' He lights a cigarette and Flavia and I both fan smoke from our faces with excessive gestures, which prompts him to rub it out in a paint can.

'Yes, will you paint something in every room in the house?'

Going upstairs, I open the door just to look. 'Dear Ashley,' I write. '*Il brutto* has become *il carino*, the darling. The tiniest bathroom possible but equipped with mimosa bath salts, the thickest American towels, tuberose soap, and a deserted bird nest on the windowsill. When will you come bathe here?' She is so slender she can slip into the basin half of the tiny tub.

While Antonio is here, I sketch a shelf I would like in

the kitchen, one running the width of the room above the brick ledge, where I prop all the serving platters I've collected. A second row, then I can just grab one for whatever I'm about to serve. He takes a measurement; we walk around the house until I identify the exact stain color I'd like. '*Ecco fatto*,' he says, it's done.

★

What's not done, as July comes to a close, is the butterfly bath. The tile is on its way but will not arrive until after Primo's men are on August holiday. Since we must leave at the end of August, we store the fixtures in the *limonaia* and make room for the boxes of tiles. '*Pazienza, signora*,' Primo says, patience. 'Next year, another new set of problems.' Zeno covers the trench. Tools are cleaned and loaded into the Ape. My colleague does not arrive, explaining he'll come back when he can stay with us. Anselmo hangs braids of onions and garlic in the cantina. Antonio installs the beautiful shelf – some things happen like magic. I lower my tired frame into the new tub, baptizing myself in the cold water that will run out through tubes and rocks and sand, harmlessly, harmlessly, onto the land.

LOST IN TRANSLATION

At an early stage in the human embryo, traces of gill slits appear near the throat, faint reminders that once we were finny and swam freely through the streams and seas. Often I feel in myself another vestigial trait – being locked in one language. Multilingual friends assure me that a new personality emerges when one acquires a new language. This is something to look forward to. I would like a personality that includes flowing hair to toss at appropriate syntactical pauses, perhaps those tinted Italian glasses, which manage to look sexy *and* intellectual. I'd like for my natural reserve to fall away when fluency allows me all the gestures and rhythms of Italian. Meanwhile, I can say, 'Have you washed yourself well?' and 'Sir, you have insulted me! I demand satisfaction'; 'Sooner or later I am going to have a nervous breakdown'; 'Catherine, have you been to see if the barometer has fallen?'; 'Where we come from, we don't have a party when someone dies,' and many other useful sentences my textbooks have taught me. These phrases are not the pertinent rejoinders when Primo Bianchi discusses with us the intricacies of a *fossa biologica*, a biological pit, otherwise known as a septic tank.

Twice a week for two hours, I report to a white room in a *palazzo* in Cortona. I go with anticipation and dread. En route, I pass Caruso, the mynah bird who lives in a cage outside an antique shop. '*Ciao*,' the bird says, and I hear the exact, chomped-on inflection of the local *ciao*. Even the bird has a better ear than I. Amalia is waiting, a pile of photocopied exercises for me to complete in front of her. She plans to make clear to me, finally, the differences among the simple past, the imperfect, and the past definite. I think it goes like this: I shopped; I shopped and continue to shop; and I've shopped until I've dropped. The room's three enormous windows overlook the rooftops of Cortona. We sit at a long table, facing a blackboard. Nothing distracts from the intense study of Italian. We begin with conversation. At half her normal speed, she speaks clearly of a Benigni film, a politician on trial, a local custom. We discuss where we have been, and what we have done since the last lesson.

I am halting, I am corrected frequently, I do not hear the difference in the way she says *oggi*, today, and the way I say it. Because the ceilings are so high, everything we say echoes slightly, amplifying the trauma. With verbs, I hear my own blunders as soon as I make them. Odd – sometimes I understand almost everything she says. We discuss the death penalty, ravioli, or the Mafia. I congratulate myself on a clever question – maybe she can see that I'm not as stupid as I must sound. Other times I feel that my brain is a big potato *gnocco* or a ball of *mozzarella di bufala*, and I'm not hearing half. Worse, I sometimes tune out. She could be speaking double Dutch. I want to cry or run out of the room.

Still, taking on a new language is enormous fun. While waiting for a transaction at the bank or sitting in front of the gas station while the car is washed, I take out my list of past participles. During the afternoon *riposo*, I sometimes close the shutters and listen to conversation tapes. Mine focus on cooking. In the heat, with the cicadas clacking outside, I lie back and hear blow-by-blow instructions on how to make rice fritters and cherry soup. Listening is a thrill because I start to think that I spoke Italian in another life; way inside, I know this language. In his fine World War II novel, *The Gallery*, John Horne Burns was on to something when he said, 'Italian can soon be understood because it sounds like what it's saying. Italian is a language as natural as the human breath. . . It keeps in motion by its own inherent drive. . . It's full of bubble-like laughter. Yet it's capable of power and bitterness. It has nouns that tick off a personality as neatly as a wisecrack. It's a language in which the voice runs to all levels. You all but sing, and you work off your passion with your hands.'

One of those evocative nouns fascinates us. *Galleggiante*. We love the sound – a mixture of 'gallant,' 'gigantic,' and 'elegant.' Ed says, 'You're looking so, how shall I say it, so *galleggiante* this evening.' I say, 'I love Parma. It's *galleggiante*.' We admire the antique iron bench we have bought; truly *galleggiante* in the garden. The real *galleggiante* first entered our vocabularies more practically. When the toilet kept running water, Ed stood on a ladder and looked inside the tank. Lifting the floating ball made the noise stop. There's no way to look up 'floating ball inside toilet' in the dictionary so he went to the building supply store for the thingamajig and endured the charade of gestures and sketches. 'Ah,' the clerk caught on. 'You want a *galleggiante*.' Yes, we did.

★

Because I'm learning Italian while living here, I conduct my education in public. In a bar, I once asked for a grenade (*granata*) instead of a lemon slush (*granita*). I have commented on the beauty of a basket of fish (*pesce*) when admiring gloriously ripe peaches (*pesche*). Imagine pointing to a black cabbage (*cavolo nero*) and asking for a black horse (*cavallo nero*). Tiny but huge differences. The worst was at a funeral when I spoke of the deceased not as a *scapolo*, bachelor, as I meant, but as a *sbaglio*, a mistake.

That was early. Now that I have more understanding of Italian, I have greater occasions to make a bigger fool of myself. I know more and am likely to launch into a description of a trip to a balsamic vinegar maker and forget once again that complicated questions will follow, and I'll need to pull out of my head verbs in tenses that I haven't yet faced. Could I pass it all off as a kind of new dialect? Today, I was telling Matteo at the *frutta e verdura* that overnight something has eaten the young melons and corn in the garden. Perhaps a wild boar or a porcupine – I know both of those – and then, uh oh, I finally see it coming; I want to say 'gnawed the stalk to topple the corn.'

Gnawed – 'ate' won't do. The word for 'stalk' – no, not a glimmer. Topple – forget it. The closest I can come is 'cut' and that's not right. All the synonyms I do know will not convey the sense of something gnawing the stalk to topple the corn. I think for a moment of pantomiming the whole scene with a stalk of celery for the corn and me as the porcupine, but a sense of propriety – thank god – saves me.

But this is good, isn't it? Knowing enough that precision is developing? I'm saved because three other people in the shop have joined the conversation, each with an opinion as to the real culprit's identity. Hedgehogs and nutrias are discussed, but the consensus is porcupine, with one man holding out for wild boar because the tomatoes are untouched. If it were a porcupine, obviously the tomatoes would have been mangled, too. I buy my peaches, never having made *that* mistake again, and leave the shop, realizing I have understood everything, even though I was blocked by my own vocabulary.

At times I am not translating; *arancia* is *arancia* and I'm just listening, the image of an orange flashing in my mind, not the word. This is a mystery to me, those moments when the English melts between the Italian and the meaning. I happily make my way around town, having little conversations in the shops. An Italian tourist asks me, *me!*, for directions and I answer with full confidence. Although I may have sent him to the wrong church, I have faith that he will like it just as well.

Old World–cultured Europeans and the upheaved millions who have migrated in the last half century represent opposite means, but the end is the same – they move among languages – while most of us who were culturally isolated on the great landmass of North America speak English at best. Already, we are a growing minority. Generations hence, our descendants will say to their children, 'Once there were people who spoke only one language,' and the children will be amazed. But I have become determined to survive with the fittest.

Having made many blunders and gone home fuming, I've had altogether too much time to analyze my problems. I've come to know why I have made learning

Italian more difficult than it had to be, perhaps why all the languages I've studied have been so elusive.

I have the habit of wrenching everything into English. Although we have the same structures — all languages basically have the same parts of speech — there is no way to proceed *rationally* with the obliteration of the Italian pronoun, the foregrounding of the verb, and the genders of nouns. The idiosyncrasies of idioms, just as irrational, are immediate to me because they work with metaphors. I love the graphic figurative image *acqua in bocca* (water in the mouth), which means 'I won't tell anyone.' Something between us two is something for *quattr'occhi*, four eyes. 'I feel oppressed' or 'depressed' translates as *sotto una cappa di piombo*, under a hood of lead. Not only is an image conjured, but *piombo*, sounds oppressive, like three low notes plucked on the bass. All the connotations of the English 'rolling in money' are not at all the same as the Italian 'swimming in gold.'

Sound unwittingly often translates meaning where it shouldn't. *Stinco*, a savory cut of meat, and also a thin loaf of bread, sounds unappetizing even when you know *stinco* means shin-bone. And how *foreign* the saying, '*Non è uno stinco di santo,*' He's not the shin-bone of a saint; he's no saint. *Bar* conjures solitary figures hunched over mixed drinks, or more sophisticated scenes, not the Italian version, which is centered on coffee and quick bites. Most certainly, an Italian 'bar' is not a 'pub.'

The common word *più*, more, is hard for an English-speaking person to say without suspecting a bad smell. So I purse my lips and say we're eating tonight at Amico Più, a *trattoria* on the edge of the valley, where to the satisfaction of my inner ear, the odor of pigs sometimes wafts from farms across the grassy outdoor dining area from nearby farms.

'Your friend certainly is handsome but he's so cruel to his dog,' my friend Deb said about stop-traffic good-looking Silvano. 'He kept telling the poor thing to die.' Silvano was trying to talk to her, and his *pastore tedesco*, German shepherd, pestered him to throw a stick over and over. '*Dai, Ugo, dai*,' he told the dog as he threw the stick yet again. *Dai* sounds like 'die,' but he simply meant 'give' – *basta*, enough, give it up, Hugo.

I know well from French, that if one is hungry or thirsty, you *have* hunger, you *have* thirst. This is imprinted on my mind from my first trip to France. I went to a restaurant alone and was seated by a door where blasts of cold air blew in my face. I asked the waiter for another table, explaining that I was cold. Back in the hotel, I realized I had not said *j'ai froid* but instead had said *je suis fraise*, I am strawberry. The waiter graciously had directed me to a cozy table near the fireplace.

Strange that a cat purrs differently in Italian; a cat 'makes the purrs.' *Ha sonno?*, You have sleepy?, now comes naturally. Some things may never. If I forget and take to the literal, I'm often left with 'Now I must to go myself of it,' for 'Now I must leave.' Or 'I myself was forgotten of this,' for 'I had forgotten this.' Translation is approximation; the original doesn't say that at all.

Mark Twain, who obviously had an ear for language, had fun with a literal translation of his own speech, given to the Press Club in Vienna:

> *I am indeed the truest friend of the German language – and not only now, but from long since – yes, before twenty years already. . . I would only some changes effect. I would only the language method – the luxurious, elaborate construction compress, the eternal parenthesis suppress, do away with, annihilate; the introduction of*

more than thirteen subjects in one sentence forbid; the verb so far to the front pull that one it without a telescope discover can. With one word, my gentlemen, I would your beloved language simplify so that, my gentlemen, when you her for prayer need, One her yonder-up understands. . .

. . . I might gladly the separable verb also a little bit reform. I might none do let what Schiller did: he has the whole history of the Thirty Years' War between the two members of a separate verb in-pushed. That has even Germany itself aroused, and one has Schiller the permission refused the History of the Hundred Years' War to compose — God be it thanked! After all these reforms established be will, will the German language the noblest and the prettiest on the world be.

I've had the late realization that English is a spoken language, whereas Italian is sung. An opera teacher at Spoleto told me she has her American students listen in class to someone speaking ordinary Italian while following the tones with their own voices la, la, la-ing. Then she has them perform the same exercise with someone speaking English. The English voice-graph modulates gently and regularly up and down while the Italian zips dramatically around. I knew this instinctively. When people are walking toward me, long before I can hear words, I can tell if they are speaking English, German, or Italian. I know it, too, from my own very plain *buon giorno* and the exuberant response from the Italians, with several lifts and slides of sound. Italian spoken by a native English speaker is much easier for me to understand — the pacing is still in English even when the words in Italian are grammatically perfect. Catching the rhythm — that's the hardest part. The lucky few who have a natural grasp of *ritmo* are understood by Italians even if their grammar isn't so hot.

Too bad you can't take a language in a series of injections labeled 'indirect pronouns,' 'the pronunciation of *glielo*,' and 'tile installation terminology.' But I tell myself, *Roma non fu fatta in un giorno*. Dante, the five-year-old son of an American mother and Italian father, moves easily, thoughtlessly, back and forth between English and Italian. I can't fool him on the phone into thinking that I'm Italian. I say '*Posso parlare con la tua mamma*,' May I speak with your mother, and he says, 'Sure, she's right here.'

I recently read in the paper that those who acquire multiple languages when they're young learn them in the same thimble-sized spot in the brain. Those of us who try to learn later must locate the new language in an entirely different territory. The new area must be something like frozen tundra. As I study Italian, I can feel that journey. The new words buzz to the real language spot – top center – for translation, then slide back to the new one, which is being chopped out somewhere in the obdurate back right corner. On the way, many new words fall off into lost canals and abysses. Some do make it all the way back to the new quarry. They become natural. *Gioia* is no longer joy, it's the buoyant feeling of *gioia*. Hundreds of other words are now themselves. Still, I pick up a novel by Pavese and I'm sunk by the third paragraph. *Piano*, slowly, *piano*, I tell myself, there's no exam coming. As if there will be a final, I compulsively concentrate on what I don't understand. I make lists of *all* the cases when the imperfect is used, spending hours writing examples for each of the cases I don't understand and neglecting to reinforce examples of what I do.

★

Besides the luxury – and necessity – of being able to

converse easily, I am desirous of another literature. My long habit of browsing in bookstores and leaving with a nice sack of books has been stymied in Italy. I have become a great appreciator of cover designs.

Travelling or living here as a foreigner, I experience the life force of Italians acted out every day on the streets, in the cafés, and on the roads. As I walk by open windows, I'm transfixed by the aroma of *ragù* and the cascades of con-current voices. So often I'm bearing witness to the rich *outer* life of Italians, knowing that the direct route to the inner life always is literature. Novels, essays, books of place, the philo-sophical treatises, poetry – here's the big news of the place, the territory most hidden from me in my friendships and brief sojourns in this *bel paese*.

Gradually, my summer reading has shifted to native Italian writers: Eugenio Montale, Umberto Eco, Italo Calvino, Natalia Ginzburg, Primo Levi – all the heavy-hitters whose work appears in English. Sometimes I've bought a difficult book in Italian, as one might buy a skirt a size too tight, hoping to lose the ten pounds by summer.

First, their guidebooks. All the Slow Food Arcigola Editore books, especially the yearly guide *Vini d'Italia*, quickly convinced Ed that the Italians' own perspective on food and wine was the one we wanted. The Gambero Rosso guides to restaurants and hotels led us to uncrowded places of intrinsic character. They're easy to follow because of clear ranking symbols.

Then we began to pick up poetry, simply for the pleasure of reading it aloud, even if we mispronounced the author's name, as we did with Quasimodo for too long. Cesare Pavese revealed all the dark and melancholy layers of the countryside that I missed in my own elation over the landscapes straight out of Piero della Francesca and Perugino. Leonardo Sciascia's stories gave me the heart of Sicily, which I otherwise would have encountered with a raft of fears and assumptions. 'Once there was a special room in old Sicilian houses that was called "the *scirocco* room." It had no windows, or any other communication with the outside other than a narrow door opening onto an inside corridor, and this is where the family would take refuge against the wind.' That is the way I went into Sicily – an island where weather rules and the isolation of geography is reflected in the microcosm of the family. Thank you, Leonardo; I did not focus overly on the Mafia when I was there but on the wind in the thousands and thousands of palms.

The lavish Italian sense of design extends to books as easily as it does to shoes and cars. I found the art books irresistible, the crisp, fresh colors in both the cheap booklets on individual artists and in the grand tomes of the Uffizi Gallery and the Vatican collections. Paperback novels attracted me most. I took them down one by one, staring at the cobalt covers, each with a small reproduction of a painting tipped onto the cover. These books lead me farther into the language. To sit in a café with a cappuccino, a book, and a dictionary is not a bad way to spend an hour or two in the morning. Of course, I bought Dante. How can you not buy Dante in Italy? I had a dark secret – I'd never read Dante, except in snatches. Translating a few stanzas provides an instant cure from the textbook tedium of: The tide was ebbing. She dreaded snakes and spiders. The servicemen are on furlough. The fair was rained out. Their behavior will improve. She was looking very coy. I was a fool from the beginning. Precisely so!

★

Since I have been coming to Italy for so many summers,

my friends assume that my Italian is completely fluent. 'Oh, you pick up Italian,' they say flippantly. 'It's so close to Spanish.' Well, I never picked up Spanish that easily. From a summer of studying in San Miguel de Allende, most of what I remember is going off-road in a taxi with my instructor whose passionate interest was Chichimeca pottery. He responded to my interest in the culture more than to my need to translate the story of the little mouse. We searched through middens for bits of black-painted pottery and I came home with more shards than words.

But my friends are right; you travel to Italy, you pick up a few phrases. Italians are so courteous and responsive that you're lulled into thinking, *This is a cinch.* I have long since spoken restaurant-Italian, travel-Italian, shopping-Italian, and a lot of house-restoration Italian. But I never have 'picked up' the imperfect subjunctive or the past remote. I have not learned to understand the various dialects spoken around Tuscany, not to mention the rest of Italy. I read in *Italian Cultural Studies* that dialects are used by sixty percent of Italians, and are spoken exclusively by fourteen percent. Since we've learned on the fly, our vocabularies are unholy mixes of dialect words and the Italian we've learned in classes. The local dialect often changes the 'ah' sound to 'eh,' producing a harsher sound. We don't always hear the difference. Our store of curses is rather vast, since hauling out stone and digging trenches and wells elicits those from workers. *Madonna cane*, *Madonna diavola*, Madonna-dog, Madonna-devil, are two drastic curses. The use of some expressions we've picked up still escapes us. *Non mi importa una sega,* Don't bring me a saw, ac-companied by a sawing motion, has something to do with masturbation.

Some aspects of this amazing language confound me. I admitted to myself recently that I am going to give up on the idiomatic and incomprehensible use of the invariable pronoun 'ne'; whatever Italian I speak will have to be without this protean word. I have not admitted this to Amalia.

★

American friends say with modesty, 'I did quite well in Spain,' or 'It's amazing how it all comes back.' Comes back from where? I've travelled with some of those same friends, have seen them point at the menu, have seen them meekly hold out their hands for the clerk to take the cost of a purchase from their palms because they get dizzy when *duemilaquattrocentosettantalire* (2470 *lire*) spirals out of the clerk's mouth. One friend belongs to the speak-loud-and-clear-and-they'll-understand-English school. Another, who visited me in Italy, was annoyed that local shop-keepers had made 'no attempt to learn basic English phrases that would help them in business,' not noticing that we are in *their* country, and in a rural area at that.

Even though I 'took' years of French in high school and college, it never really took to me. I never met anyone from France, and my high school teacher believed in the method of a verb workbook, with tiny spaces to write all the conjugations. Even if we had no idea what those con-jugations meant, we still had to write the *passé composé* for hundreds of verbs. For the last half-hour of class she turned on scratchy records of Paris street sounds and stood clasping her hands and looking out the window. We filed out to 'Under the Bridges of Paris,' Carl Twiggs slapping Mary Keith Duffy's girdled bottom and shouting 'Monobuttock,' by far the most inventive linguistic moment of the hour.

In college, the class focused on 'lab' – tapes about *mon moulin*, letters in a crabbed French, which I had to listen to in a cubicle in the gym at seven in the morning. News from a faraway French mill was accompanied by a basketball pounding the gym floor and a wafting odor of pine oil–scented disinfectant. When I was called on to read in class from *Les Misérables*, our endless text, the professor would say with a smirk, 'Miss Mayes speaks French with a Southern accent.' I slammed the book shut and sat down. His Midwestern accent wasn't *magnifique* either.

Later, I took classes in Spanish and German. They all seemed somehow so *fake*. Surely these people went home at night and spoke English. A friend who has had similar experiences says she would like 'I studied languages' carved on her tombstone. I endured German even through a bout of explosive flatulence from the instructor. '*Pflaumenkuchen*,' plumcake, he explained and continued with *Es war einmal ein junger Bauer*, There was once a young farmer. The day I dropped out of German was when I came across the word for nipple: *Brustwarze*. A glance, and even I translated 'breast wart.'

*

Several local people speak many languages. Isabella, a neighbor, speaks eight; her son, a journalist, also speaks eight, but not exactly the same eight. She is in her seventies. 'I tried to learn Greek a couple of years ago,' she tells me, 'but it's getting hard. I used to learn a language in three weeks. If you know Russian, Polish is easy. English and French I spoke as a child . . .' I walk home sulking after this conversation. I still am having trouble learning the uses of the simple word '*ci*,' a chameleon of a word that shifts meaning shamelessly, while she picked up French like a warm croissant. She arrives at dinner and surveys the other guests. 'What language are we speaking tonight?' she asks brightly. At one party she and her Danish, Dutch, and Hungarian friends began to recite French poetry. They all knew the same poems by heart. Then they moved on to Latin poems.

In a dream, I am sitting by a window, writing on pale blue paper. Reading the wet ink as I write, I see that I am writing a poem in Italian. But maybe I am not this person. Could I be? The blue-black ink fluidly moves into words, phrases, lines – even my handwriting is better in this dream – and the woman I am or am not has on a wool sweater, a dark dress. Her hair is twisted up, like Maria's, like Anna's, like Isabella's, like the older women I know here, all of whom are at home in wider worlds than I have known. This is a poem to be sung, I can tell, the shiny ink, the wind lifting the edge of the paper, my hand moving rapidly, yes, my hand.

Bergson says the present does not exist; it is always disappearing as the past gnaws into the future. With my own language and now with the vast voyage into Italian, this feels true as well. *The past gnaws at the future.* What to say always disappears into the saying, leaving me wanting to say more. *Gnaws*, there's that word again. To gnaw the stalk to topple the corn. To gnaw: *rosicchiare*. Language: the house that Jack built.

Since language always has been crux and core for me, I was pleased to discover that we could make friends when we knew very little. My mother always thought that attraction was based on smell. Those good flashes of energy between people can supersede words. At the *frutta e verdura*, Rita was welcoming me with a hug before I could talk to her. At the same time, our neighbor invited us to dinner. We wanted to refuse. We imagined three hours of halting words and awkward silences. '*Grazie, mille grazie, ma non parliamo bene italiano.*' Thank you, but we don't speak Italian well, we apologized. 'Later, when we speak better . . .'

He looked incredulous. His eyebrows shot up. 'You eat, don't you?'

another boat.

ANSELMO'S IDEA OF TOMATOES

'Do you have the beans of Sant'Anna?'

'No, they were in season *last* week.' Matteo points to
the fresh *cannellini*. 'These are ready now. From all over –
Roma, Milano – they come to Tuscany for these beans.' I
know the *cannellini*. Simply dressed with oil, sage, salt, and
pepper, they have restorative powers beyond all other
beans. I've seen Ed eat them for breakfast. They are
Tuscan comfort food.

When I walk out of the *frutta e verdura*, I'm struck. He
said the Sant'Annas were *in season last week*. I had these
skinny string beans once. Now they're gone for a year.
With Anselmo's garden burgeoning, I've hardly been
shopping. The cookbook watchword 'seasonal' has taken
on an immediacy I've never dreamed possible. Ed and I
take the baskets up on the terraces late in the day and pick

dinner. Anselmo has sown waves of lettuces all summer, providing tender salads constantly. We can't eat enough; when it bolts, Beppe wields his sickle and bundles the greens for his rabbits. When we cut the *bietole*, chard, it comes back. I like the Italian word for that, *ricrescere*; it sounds as though the stalks are crashing upward through the soil. We give sacks and sacks away. Fortunately, Anselmo planted a lot of cantaloupe and watermelon. Even with the gnawing animal raiders, who take one hunk from a melon, we have plenty. I try to give them to Giusi but she has her own garden. As a crop finishes, Anselmo stomps down the remaining plants and stalks, letting them decay into the ground. I'm delighted to pick eggplant and zucchini while they are small. His one flop is celery; the stalks never developed.

In the spring, we were convinced he was planting too much, and we were right. It's divine. We never have eaten so well in our lives. Or as simply. As it turns out, Anselmo's idea of tomatoes is my idea of tomatoes. I am up to my knickers in tomatoes and I love it. Every day, a heaping basket of perfect, absolutely perfect, red, red tomatoes. I look on these brimming baskets with more pleasure than I felt when I saw my new car last year. Not a bug or a blemish. He planted three kinds. A plain round tomato he calls *locale*. This local favorite is the kind to bite into while picking – a sweet, dripping, crisp, paradigm tomato. For sauce, he planted the ovoid San Marzano, with a meatier texture and less juice. For salads, we have cherry tomatoes, tight little balls that explode with flavor.

Once upon a time, Italy had no tomatoes. Imagine the poor Etruscans and Romans, the centuries of people who lived before the New World was explored. Their garlic and basil went unpaired with tomatoes. Now, so many people grow up thinking those pallid blobs arriving in supermarkets all year are tomatoes. They should have another name. Or perhaps a number. I'd hoped to pair our Italian tomatoes with American sweet corn. What could be better? Since the animals discovered this new-on-the-mountain crop, our yield from the two packets of seeds I sowed was only three scrawny ears. Anselmo had disregarded my corn plot. 'Pig food,' he pronounced.

★

The giant sunflowers I planted along the edges of several terraces are in bloom. I'm cutting a bunch early, before they have a chance to droop from heat. Suddenly, from behind my circular 'room' of sunflowers, a small woman emerges. I recognize her immediately from Ed's description as the forager of daffodils and asparagus. '*Buon giorno, signora*,' I greet her and introduce myself. Even in summer, she is wearing a dark cardigan.

'*Venga*,' she invites me. Her basket is heaped with the yellow flowers of wild fennel. She leads me up one terrace to a spot behind some broom. A dozen or so tall fennel plants are untouched. She has come prepared with scissors. She clips off the flowers and tells me to spread them under the sun to dry, then to rub them between my hands to remove the flowers from the stems. She pulls a plastic sack from her pocket and begins to snip some for me. She points up to the ridge of locust and oak trees. 'In autumn, you find the *porcini* there.'

'And truffles?'

'Never. But you find other mushrooms, too. I will show you after the rains.'

'We'll be gone, unfortunately.'

'*Peccato*,' too bad. 'You will go back to Switzerland?'

'No, the United States. We live in California.' I remember she seemed not to believe Ed when he

274

told her he was not a Swiss professor.

She shakes her head. '*Arrividerla, signora.* The fennel you will use with all the meats, with rabbit it is very good and always with roast potatoes.' She starts to head down the terrace path, then turns back. 'I like the house now.'

★

I've reverted to another old love. I could have fried tomatoes for breakfast, lunch, and dinner. Cream, an almost forbidden ingredient now, is so good with them that I risk a blip in the next cholesterol count. Heresy to some Southern cooks, I prefer fried red tomatoes over green ones. I like them sliced about ½-inch thick. I pour some flour on a piece of waxed paper and turn the tomato slices to coat them lightly then fry them on both sides in a hot skillet with 3–4 T. of peanut or sunflower oil. Then, as my mother before me and hers before her, I turn the heat to low, pour on heavy cream to cover the bottom of the pan. Shake to blend, grind a lot of black pepper over the tomatoes, salt to taste, and add a little thyme or oregano. I find them best eaten alone. Willie Bell would sometimes coat the slices in cornmeal and fry them in hot, hot oil so that they're crisper. With a plate of fried tomatoes in front of me, I feel a longing for Willie Bell's fried chicken, especially for her cream gravy over mashed potatoes, and her creamed corn. Why were we not huge from all the pints of cream that went into most meals? She always cut the kernels off the cob and cooked them with onion and chopped peppers, then stirred in cream. Longing for these brings the memory of her yellow squash casserole, too. Southern summer food rivals Italian food in my affections. Willie Bell and my mother would sit all morning shelling the delectable tiny lady finger peas, which I've never seen outside the state of Georgia.

When Ed grills, he tosses on thick slices of tomato just before we eat, just for a little smoky taste. Nothing surpasses a plain tomato sandwich if the *focaccia* is made in heaven, as it is here in Cortona. The chewy flat bread with crackly sage and sea salt on top lifts the sliced tomato into the realm of gastronomic highs. How long would it take for us to tire of fresh tomatoes? Simple stuffed tomatoes, what's better? Only one thing – the addition of chopped hazelnuts. Anselmo alerted us that ours are ready to pick. We cracked and roasted about a cup, mixed them in equal part with bread crumbs, chopped some parsley and stuffed four big tomatoes. On top, a pat of butter and a square piece of cheese such as *tallegio*, which melts in the oven. Supper is a zucchini *frittata* and these tomatoes, along with a Southern touch, a pitcher of iced tea sweetened with a little peach juice.

*

On a Tuesday after siesta, the dazzling heat of the morning abates. I decide we should go to Deruta, majolica *paradiso*. An English guidebook to Umbria dismisses Deruta, 'You will probably not wish to linger in Deruta, the center of Umbria's majolica industry, whose approach roads are lined with shops selling all manner of hideous ceramics.' Is the writer crazy? My new kitchen shelf was built especially to display all the platters I've found irresistible. Some Deruta majolica is hideous, but much of it is based on traditional regional designs and is delightful. I wonder what the English writer's breakfast dishes look like. Mine from Deruta have hand-painted Tuscan fruits and a yellow border, something that certainly could cheer up a drear English morning.

In Italy, I've learned the art of serving on platters. Along the stone wall I place one for roasted vegetables, one for cheeses, one for breads, another for the main course. Every night during this season, we have a platter of plain sliced tomatoes. They can be passed family-style or guests can get up from the table under the trees and help themselves – again and again. Pitchers, too, pitchers for iced tea, wine, water. The hand-painted majolica suits the casual and abundant Tuscan style of dining. I love the colors. Some bright, others slightly muted and soft, like fresco colors. Setting the yellow table outside, or my round dining room table in San Francisco, the table comes to life instantly. True or not, it appears that a great meal will arrive.

I bought cups with pink flowers for cappuccino at Christmas, and hope now to find breakfast plates to match. Deruta must have a hundred shops selling handmade majolica gaily painted in traditional designs.

'Which shop was it?' Ed asks. 'How can you remember? There are so many.' His enthusiasm for Deruta is limited.

'The one on the corner, right where the street ends.' No other town looks like Deruta. Church, fountain, façades are decorated with tiles. This has been a hub of this ancient craft for centuries.

'*Ah, sì signora*,' of course. The shop owner calls a friend who will bring the plates I want from the studio. While we wait, we wander to three other shops on the main street and in one we find a lamp for Ed's desk. There must be other stores in Deruta: hardware, grocery, shoes – but somehow I've never noticed them. We stop and watch a woman painting geometric designs on small saucers. At the bar, a very old man in wide suspenders, which hold his pants almost up to his armpits, asks where we're from. San Francisco sets him into a frenzy – he was there on a ship in 1950. He remembers the *strada del mercato*. Market Street. He insists on buying our coffee. Yes! The water was right at the end of the street. When his friend comes in, he introduces us as though we were visiting relatives. The instant bond of San Francisco, a place Italians love.

Many of the ceramic shops are just outside town on Via Tiberina. My sister and I have shipped home whole dinner sets for ourselves and for my daughter, Ashley. Only one cup was broken. They pack not in plastic bubble wrap but in wet straw. Shipping is expensive but not nearly as expensive as buying Italian ceramics at home, even if you could find the variety that is available here. Choices are staggering. Most popular is the sunny yellow and blue Raphael design, a stylized dragon in the center of each piece. I don't fancy seeing a dragon as I eat, even a benign one like Raphael's.

Bisected by the Apennines, many areas of Italy developed their own designs, as well as their own dialects and habits. In Deruta they make the rooster of Orvieto, the bluebird of Amalfi, the black Siena pattern taken from the cathedral floor mosaics. There's an effort toward contemporary designs as well. Some are garish; others are playful and bold, pleasing to hold, hang on a wall, or punctuate a glass coffee table. You even can design your own dinner service, with your monogram or flowers you like. My sister chose a pattern with a blue and yellow border and Ashley loved the white set with a grape-and-vine embossed border. When I chose mine, with a pomegranate, cherries, or blueberries painted in the middle of each dish, I asked, 'What is the name of the pattern?'

He lifted his shoulders, '*Frutta.*' Glad I asked. Three months later – my order was individually made and painted – the dishes arrived in San Francisco. They translated perfectly into my American kitchen.

Today I am looking for a wedding present for a friend's son. Espresso cups? A teapot? A wonderful salad bowl? Ed looks rather wild-eyed after three or four of these majolica stops. 'Everyone likes a teapot,' he insists. 'Let's just get one.'

'Which one do you like?' I like one that is all tiny flowers and green leaves. Also a white one scattered with sprigs of spring flowers.

He picks up the white one. 'Let's go.'

I look longingly at my other favorite shops on the way to the highway but Ed has his foot firmly on the accelerator. 'We might run over to look at ceramics in Gubbio and Gualdo Tadino one day soon. We could go to both places on the same day.' Is he just being nice?

★

On the way home, we stop in Assisi in spite of the tidal waves of tourists. My favorite paper store is on the main *piazza*, across from that mysterious church which began as a temple to Minerva. I need a new gift supply of hand-printed stationery, beautiful pads, note cards, and blank books to take home. In San Francisco, I almost never have time to go shopping. These forays for *things* are a treat. Ed wants to pick up a few bottles of Sagrantino, his favorite Umbrian wine, which we usually can't buy in Cortona.

We walk past the delicate roseate church of Santa Chiara, the houses of amber and pearl stone with faded blue shutters. As usual, two dogs are sleeping on either side of the door to the paper store. After I stock up, we walk, as we always do, to the Chiesa di San Rufino – the opposite direction from the undertow of tourists headed toward the famous Giotto (or according to many, school of Giotto) frescoes at San Francesco – to look at its almost primitive Romanesque facade of gargoyles and animals of the imagination. It faces a blessedly empty *piazza* with a fountain. No number of tourists can totally destroy the enchantment of Assisi. We've lingered until seven-thirty, might as well have dinner at a favorite resturant where the roasted rabbit is superb.

★

I forget the heat that comes every August. As I finish cleaning a room, I close the windows and inside shutters three-quarters of the way. Air still comes in, if any is moving, but the direct hit of the sun is closed out. My coolest white linen dress touches me only at the shoulders. It hangs like a nightgown. Emily Dickinson wore only white. I can see her point. Sometimes even that is too hot and I unbutton it all the way down, then when the heat seems to bank against me late in the afternoons, I throw it off and read in my underwear with the fan blowing straight on me.

The day we make tomato sauce must be the hottest of the summer. After several trips to the *orto*, we've filled the sink and a laundry basket with ripe tomatoes. Ed cores, I seed. We don't peel because the skin is thin, unlike commercial tomatoes which often seem to be encased in rubber. When I splash juice on my blouse, I take it off and throw it in the washing machine. Ed already is down to shorts. Soon juice is running over the chopping boards, onto the floor. We're chopping heads of garlic, a whole braid of onions, stripping leaves off the thyme, snipping basil, and tossing a handful of salt into the cauldron. The kitchen sweats with the aroma of cooking onions; we sweat with the aroma of cooking onions. In go the gallons of chopped tomatoes. Ed empties a bottle of local red wine. Everything is from right here. All year we, and our guests when we're in California, will feel the July sun in every spoonful. We put the cauldron on to simmer and start to mop.

'I have a taste in my mouth, a wonderful taste.'

'What is it? Do you smell the tomato sauce? Maybe it's that.' But I don't smell anything. We're out in the Lime Tree Bower recovering, reading after lunch, and trying to catch a breeze.

'It's a taste I can't describe. It's like the song you can't get out of your head. I've had it for two days.'

'Is it like mint or honey or iron or salt?'

He shakes his head. He's watching an ant carrying a rose petal, a coverlet for his worker-comrade. The ant falters and struggles on. 'The taste, I think it's happiness.'

We walk up two terraces to the tree laden with Golden Delicious apples. No crunch. Delicious they are not, except in their mellow color. 'Next year, let's plant more apples.' I throw mine in the bushes. 'They would make decent apple butter.' After the tomato frenzy, I don't think I'll be making apple butter. 'I can imagine a whole row along this terrace, companions for this poor stunted Golden Delicious.'

'It's not stunted; it's a dwarf tree.' Ed is filling his shirt front with apples. 'Maybe a small batch of apple butter.' He adores apples. A favorite memory of his is of an apple-picking job he had in Iowa one fall. 'I read about a man near Rimini who grows the *limoncella*, a small apple with the flavor of lemon, and one called *pum sunaja*. The seeds inside are loose and rattle like maracas. This man has 300 kinds of apples, lost varieties he's bringing back.' From his tone, I know that we will be journeying to meet this fascinating person.

★

My original desire to live here came partly from a belief that Italy is endless and could never be exhausted — art, landscape, food, language, history. Changing the direction of my life by buying and restoring this forsaken house, committing a portion of every year to life in a foreign country, seemed like acts of high risk if not madness. At that time, I wanted to accomplish something I did not know how to do. I thought – and now know – that Italians claim more time for their lives. After a long marriage and a horrid divorce, I thought Italy certainly would be a more than adequate replacement for just one man. I wanted a big change.

I had no concept of just how lucky my primary instinct was. At home in California, time often feels like a hula-hoop, a ceaseless whirl on a body fixed but rocking in place. I could kiss the ground here, not to feel myself in that tight space where the past gnaws the future but in the luxuriant freedom of a long day to walk out for a basket of plums under the great wheel of the Mediterranean sun. At the tail end of the century, continual splashes of new-ness: Eight summers here and still we're babes. What luck.

I stuff two shopping bags with potatoes, onions, chard, melon, tomatoes and drive them down to Donatella in the valley. Earlier this summer, the boars destroyed her garden in one full-moon orgy. She's not home so I leave the bags under her arbor of Virginia creeper, just on the edge of a carefully tended olive orchard. Crossing the valley floor as I leave her place, I look up and catch a glimpse of Bramasole. I stop, amazed to see the house as a peach-colored smudge against the steep hillside, with the Etruscan and Medici walls above it. Far away, it stands totally within its own green landscape of terraces and trees, clouds and sky. No sign at all that we have been there or will be there. As I drive on, a spur of hillside suddenly cuts away the view.

COLD

On an early October morning in San Francisco, Ed puts aside a stack of student papers and begins to look through an Italian guidebook. I am busy, super-busy, in my study – eleven graduate theses, memos, letters of recommendation, and a pile of overdue correspondence. Tomorrow, meetings of the laborious sort and appointments in three corners of the city. These madhouse weeks seem both to stretch endlessly and to fly. Ed turns on the espresso machine, still reading. My study is across the hall from the kitchen, which is why I don't get as much done as I could. Anyone cooking or wandering in for a snack naturally visits with me. Kitchens develop powerful magnetic fields around them and pull all humans and animals within the four walls their way. My theory is proven by my black cat, Sister, who perpetually lies on the black-and-white kitchen tiles right in the center of the floor.

'Don't you think it would be a perfect gift to go back to Venice for Christmas?' For several years, since we bought Bramasole, we've endured the twenty-hour trip from California across the waters for the brief winter season at Bramasole, when we harvest our olives, feast with our friends, and escape the frenetic pace of our usual holidays.

'Um, oh, yes,' I answer. Soon I hear him dial a long telephone number, then request a room with a balcony on the Grand Canal for December 23, 24, and 25. The heaps of paper start to look less and less formidable.

★

We arrived in Cortona early this morning from Rome. We are spending a week here, just enough time for our favorite December activities, then we'll drive to Venice. Arrival at Bramasole is easy now. What a marvel, everything works (for now); heat, hot water − what luxury. We even have neatly stacked firewood − one of the bonuses of pruning olive trees.

While I unpack, Ed starts right in picking olives, a wicker basket strapped around his red wool sweater. After the sun drops behind the hill around 4 p.m., a chilly wind comes up. He drags a sack into the *cantina* then runs hot water over his hands a long time to warm them. 'Two more days,' he says, 'with both of us working. There are a lot of olives.' We make a quick supper of *tagliatelle con funghi porcini*, thin pasta with mushrooms sautéed in our oil. Ed builds a fire and we sit in front of it, eating on trays. Tomorrow we will pick all day then go up the mountain to a favorite *trattoria* for pasta with wild boar sauce. The day we take the olives to the mill for pressing, we'll celebrate the new oil with a feast for friends. We feel compelled to drive over to Assisi to find out how the violent earthquake has changed that place of peace. Then it will be time to get ready for Venice, where it may be colder. We have coats, boots, gloves, and I bought a delicious cut-velvet scarf in dark, dark green, as green as a Venetian lagoon. I hope for snow in Piazza San Marco. Ed has a special wine to take. I have ginger-lily soap, and lilac-scented candles to burn in our room. We promised to buy only one gift for each other since the main gift will be Venice. I have a sumptuous yellow cashmere sweater for Ed, with a volume of W. S. Merwin's poems tucked under the sleeve. His box for me, glimpsed in his luggage, looks intriguingly small.

Around eleven the phone rings. Since we've bought this house I've hated the sound of the telephone. It reminds me of workers calling to say a pump did not arrive or the sandblaster is extending his vacation at the beach. In bed, cozy in flannel sheets, with jet lag just about to pull me under, I'm finishing the novel I started on the plane. I hear Ed answer 'Hey, how are you?' enthusiastically, then his voice drops. 'When? No. No. How long?'

He sits down on the end of the bed, frowning, his shoulders hunched. His mother has been taken to the hospital and is in grave condition. 'I don't get it. Two weeks ago she was baking bread. She's strong. My sister said myo-something, a blood disease. I got the doctor's number.'

★

In the morning, we repack and take the train back to Rome. Beppe and Francesco will pick the olives for us and take them to the mill. The doctor was more definite than Ed's sister. 'Come at once,' he said when Ed called him. 'It could be anytime. Today, a week, could be a month.' Reboarding and flying, practically meeting ourselves coming over, seems surreal. Sometimes the weather has a way of reflecting emotional states. When the skies neatly express emotions in my students' poems I always write, *Beware of the pathetic fallacy; it's a weak gesture*, but here we are tossing across the Atlantic, seatbelt sign blazing. The storm finally grounds us in Philadelphia. All connecting flights into Minnesota are canceled. We load our luggage onto a cart and walk through malls to an airport hotel. We spend a long night watching the storm worsen on the TV weather station. Why do people die at Christmas? A strange call to pull the family home again? My father died on a December 23, when I was fourteen. The pink net dress I was to have worn to the dance that night hung on the back of the closet door until it looked limp. The Christmas tree was taken down.

During a break in the storm, we fly out and are greeted in Minneapolis by the coldest temperature on record for that day. At the rental car desk we run into Ed's sister Sharon and her husband and daughter, just in from southern California. They're heading straight for the hospital, too. His brother, Robert, and other two sisters, Anne and Mary Jo, already are there. We step out of the airport into crusty snow and ferocious wind chill, a cut-glass air. My thin boots seem like no more than socks. Ed has to chip the car out of a block of ice. We take off for Winona, two hours south, on plowed roads through snowy fields which look to my new eyes like the absence of everything. I do not know Ed's mother well, only through one visit and through telephone chats on Sundays. I know that she raised Ed to be the person he is and therefore I feel immensely grateful to her.

★

She has rallied with the excitement of all her children returning at once. Mary Jo has put lipstick on her and she's sitting in a chair. Seeing her is easy; unbelievable that she is in danger. But she tires and, back in bed, her long frame looks gaunt, her breathing sounds scary. The children set up a rotation so that someone always is with her. His sisters are staying at his mother's house so we go to a generic motel. Ed keeps flashing on the unreality of Venice – how we had expected, at this moment, to be reading aloud from Shelley or Mann in a great bed above the immortal waters. Now his mother, whom he loves easily and unequivocally, is sliding by the moment away from him.

Days are long. Back and forth to the hospital. Visitors tiptoeing in, the IV tubes, the imperial visits of the doctor, the little errands. The sisters are busy with the house, trying to give away, sort, and deal with the contents so the work won't be left to Mary Jo and Robert who live there. Not that there is much. Opening drawers and cupboards, I see how clearly his mother's life was not about acquiring things. Her name is Altrude, one I've never heard. The connotations of altruism fit well; she is a woman given to her five children. In the afternoons, we take long drives. Ed knows the weather intimately, having grown up loving winter camping, cross-country skiing, and snowshoeing, and all those foreign – to me – activities of a cold climate. With absolute wonder, I keep asking him, 'Why would anyone choose to live here? It hurts.'

'No, you just have to get into the rhythm of it. Watch – if it ever gets above freezing, there's a Minnesotan obligation to put on a pair of shorts and a T-shirt and pretend it's warm.'

Ed is driving, the mid-sized heater blaring. I'm looking out the window. *In Venice, the aroma of fried calamari drifting from a window, a dusting of snow on the lions of San Marco, a thick hot chocolate at Florian's where they're playing schmaltzy music.* But no, here's the purity of an emptier landscape. A rust-red barn etched against a faint sky, a forest of iced birch trees glittering fantastically, a deer running across a frozen lake, his hooves sending up puffs of snow. We pass small huddled towns, the farms where his parents grew up. *His family's place, the place that formed him. He saw fish swimming under clear ice. His life before he knew who he is. A place of overwhelming winter, a death-grip that releases a poignant, intense spring.*

'What will you do for Christmas?' his mother asks. 'You're all together.' She does not say *probably for the last time* but everyone knows that. Mary Jo, a nun for thirty years, gives her communion every day and they talk bluntly about death. Seeing Ed at her bedside gives me new glimpses of the sweetness of his character. He is simply there. He feeds her, washes her face, talks about her graham cracker pie, her ritual of putting up beets, about the neighbors' ugly garage, and about his father, who died two years ago.

★

In the closet of Ed's old room, the sisters pull out a box of his books and Anne holds out a dusty copy of Mann's *Death in Venice.* 'What's it like?' she asks. Italy has become interesting to them by osmosis. And they've learned, from reading what I wrote about our lives there, things about us they never knew. Living in scattered places with vastly different lives, these five have grown apart, after a childhood intensely close together in this small house. Now the walls come alive; synapses reconnect; everyone tells their stories. Mary Jo's reinvention of a life outside the order, Sharon's complex family, Anne's relocation to Stillwater and her juggling of job and mother to two boys dressed in grunge with earphones perpetually beating into their ears, Robert's unconventional life of refusal 'to work for The

Man.' The whispers, *She was prom queen, he tiled his bathroom with rejects of all colors, she wants the sofa but he doesn't want her to have it, look at how dignified Mom looked in her wedding dress, we only got one game at Christmas, how could you have married that creep, I don't remember it that way at all.*

Ed goes to the hospital at six-thirty every morning, cherishing quiet hours with his mother. And 'What will you do for Christmas?' she had worried. When in doubt, cook. On Christmas Eve morning, Ed and I scour the grocery stores of Winona, buying olive oil and wine, garlic, a mounded cart we push through the frozen ruts of the parking lot. His mother is remote today, far into her dying. We visit the lawyer; the family puts the house on the market. We rush into the florist's, stunned by the humid warmth and the perfume of roses and lilies. Candles and flowers for her room. There is so little to *do*. The temperature falls; how low can it go? Another new record. We take a two-block walk and I am afraid we won't get back without lost fingers and toes.

The one luxury in the plain motel is the Jacuzzi tub. *Ya-coot-see*, the Italians say. Back in the room, after a last late visit to the hospital, we empty the complimentary vial of bubble bath into the water, light a candle and lie in the swirling hot water, finally warm.

On Christmas morning, Ed's mother feels well enough to be wheeled to the lobby to watch the thumb-sized yellow birds in the aviary. I wonder what it is like for her to see gathered around her bed the five children she raised, all now forty to fifty years old, living their lives, health all over each of them, and strong good looks and bodies.

Too cold to go anywhere. Most of us are at the house all afternoon. Going through kitchen drawers, the sisters find the famous family recipe for graham cracker pie and the three − all self-proclaimed non-cooks − launch into baking, consulting with each other over the consistency of the custard and when to stop beating the egg whites. Meanwhile, Ed and I make little pasta rolls with spinach and cheese, a grand beef stew with carrots, potatoes, and red wine. We make broccoli (one of the few fresh vegetables we could find) purée, and, for an Italian note, we'll serve *bruschette*, grilled slices of bread rubbed with garlic.

At dark, we take Ed's mother's dinner on a tray to the hospital. She eats most of the slice of graham cracker pie, giving it high praise, even though we all know the custard could have been a little firmer. As we drive back, snow starts again, bringing down its dazzling silence.

At dinner Ed puts on a tape of Puccini arias. Everyone gathers around Altrude's table. I look out the window at the lights of the house falling in gold squares on the snow, a scene repeated all over the white town. We pour the wine. 'Cheers.' 'To Mother.' *'Salute.'* The parents are absent and the house is poised to roll under into memory. Dinner is ready. We are hungry and we eat.

*

Graham Cracker Pie

This favorite pie in Ed's family is a mid-century classic. In my family the same pie was flavored with lemon.

Crush 12 graham crackers into fine crumbs with a rolling pin. Mix with 1 t. of flour, 1 t. of cinnamon, and ⅓ c. of sugar. Melt ⅓ c. of butter and mix with the crumbs. Press into pie plate.

For the custard, blend ½ c. of sugar with 2 T. of cornstarch. To 2 c. of milk, add 3 beaten egg yolks. Mix with sugar and cook on moderate heat, stirring constantly, until the mixture thickens. Whisk in 2 t. vanilla. Beat 3 egg whites until stiff. Whisk in 1 T. sugar. Pour custard into the pie shell, top with meringue and bake at 350 degrees until meringue has toasted.

RITMO: RHYTHM

In the midst of the torrential El Niño winter in San Francisco, we decided to move. I was reading the paper one Sunday and saw a small drawing of a Spanish/Mediterranean house with two balconies and what looked like a tall palm in front. 'Look at this house — doesn't it remind you of Bramasole?'

Ed stared. 'I like it. Where is it?'

'It doesn't say. Isn't the balcony nice? You could line it with those yellow orchids that seem to grow everywhere in San Francisco.' Ed called the listing agent and found out the house was sold.

Living at Bramasole makes us want to import into our American lives as many Italian elements as we can. More urgently, the death of Ed's mother in January heightened our sense of *carpe diem*. Our flat, which I bought as my former marriage slowly dissolved, is the third floor of a large Victorian house. I loved the coved ceilings and moulding and all the light flooding through skylights and thirty windows. The dining room looks out into trees and then onto a city view, with a slice of the bay in the distance. After years there, every room reflected the way we live. The kitchen I'd remodeled the year we bought Bramasole. Black and white tile, mirror between the glass-fronted cabinets and counters, and a six-burner restaurant stove with an oven where I easily could roast two geese and a turkey. What we began to miss was living outdoors. Stepping outside as though it were inside, stepping inside as though it were outside. Suddenly, I needed herbs in the ground and a table under a tree. Besides, it's good to move. I throw away all the accumulated junk – jars, papers, shoes in the back of the closet, black-splotched cookie sheets, tired towels. Remembering every move, I see that a new period of my life began with each change of house. Is the irrational instinct to move now (the flat is large and pretty and in a great location) also a pre-knowledge of change, or a readiness for the new?

We began to circle ads for houses in the paper, to drive around on Sunday afternoons to open houses, to look at neighborhoods we hardly knew, since our own Pacific Heights neighborhood was not remotely affordable, given what we wanted. The real estate market was wild: Asking price turned out to be a base in what quickly became an auction. Houses were selling for up to a hundred thousand dollars over the list price. Confusing. John, our agent, agreed. And we weren't finding anything we especially liked. I wanted the *this is it* feeling I experienced when I first saw Bramasole.

We'd give up for a couple of weeks, then John would call and say we might drive by a certain address, we might like this ranch house with a large garden with redwoods and a greenhouse. As we were driving toward the peninsula one day to see a Carmel-type cottage, we followed an open house sign and turned into a wooded area of San Francisco originally landscaped by the Olmstead firm, designers of Central Park. The houses live among trees and lawns. The Tudor house for sale was in 'original' condition, meaning every plank and pane needed attention. We started talking to the agent, and told him we were about to give up for a year or so, until things calmed down. 'I have a house I think you might like. Meet me at four and I'll show you.' We drove on to see the overly charming cottage, where multiple offers were being made during the first hour.

When we pulled up at the address the agent had given us, I recognized the house I'd seen in the paper, the one that had set me dreaming about moving. 'We saw this house advertised and called about it. We thought it was sold.'

'It was, but the deal fell through. It's not yet back on the market.' Steps curve up to a tile veranda with a large arched door from the dining room opening to it. Three upstairs balconies and a sunroom with eleven windows – the house is speaking my language. I can see Sister moving from one sunny patch to another in this light-flooded house.

We bought it. Even though we'd not even listed our own flat, we had to act quickly. I started sorting through letters and sweaters. My daughter became engaged. We were getting to know Stuart, her fiancé. Ashley and I began to plan their wedding. Visits to photographers and florists were fitted between trips to the hardware store to find hooks and doorknobs. She was studying for her PhD qualifying exam, then her orals. High panic set in. Several of her classmates had failed the year before. We listed the flat and it sold within three days. We closed on the new house and ripped out miles of thick white carpet, blotched with spills. Underneath, the seventy-five-year-old herringbone hardwood floors were intact. Dirty but intact. We found a brick stairway spattered with paint, which had to be stripped. We began having the floors refinished, new wiring and alarm system installed, the interior painted. We had to have a new tile roof put on. While I was out, the wrong room was painted yellow. Ashley and I looked at wedding dresses – she quickly decided that she wanted the floating-cloud variety – and invitations and bridesmaids' dresses. We met with caterers. Ed went to Italy to prune during his spring break. I was running between the flat and the house, dealing with workmen who spoke no English. The people we hired to work spoke English but when the actual labor began, they sent workers newly arrived from Cambodia, Malaysia, Korea, and all parts of South America. Often, they couldn't even talk to each other. Restoring Bramasole was so much easier! One Honduran painter locked a bedroom door from the inside and closed it as he came out. When I showed him that the door wouldn't open, he looked at me with great brown eyes and sadly uttered his only two American words, 'Fook sheet.' I looked at him for a moment before those popular expletives registered.

Blithely, I'd said I loved to move. It would be fun. When the truck loaded our furniture and boxes for an entire day, I wondered how we ever would unpack. Sister yowled all the way from our flat, which she'd lived in always, to the new house. The bookshelves we bought – and painted three coats – did not begin to accommodate all our books. Sixty boxes were stored in the new basement. In the large living room, our sofa and chairs looked like dollhouse furniture. The men set about unpacking but

I didn't know where vases and platters and paintings should go. They were left in stacks and heaps on the gorgeous new floors. We were happy with the house every step of the way. Our bedroom has a fireplace and floor-to-ceiling windows opening onto a balcony, tropical trees, and then, in the distance, the Pacific Ocean. I had the walls painted a color called 'Sicily,' a faint shade of peach. Studies for both of us, extensive storage, a little walled garden, and a bougainvillea that must have been planted when the house was new – we were too thrilled to be overwhelmed by our dawn-to-midnight days. Ed came back from two weeks of solid work at Bramasole. Re-entry was rude. A pipe burst and the basement started to flood. He was up to his ankles in water, telephone in one hand, a box of books under the other arm. Two plumbers worked for eleven hours and finally found the leak. I travelled three times to southern California to give talks. Locally, I spoke at several events. We had a new window made for the stair landing, replacing with clear glass a pair of staring, stained-glass owls on a limb. We had a gardener hacking ivy, a reminder of buying Bramasole. The entire garage door had to be replaced. Oh, and I was teaching full time. I had ten MFA theses, classes, and meetings.

We decided to get married. We told no one. I recalled my primitive instinct that moving is a signal that one is ready for change. I ordered two cakes from Dominique, my favorite pastry maker, we sent invitations for a house-warming to about thirty of our closest friends. Then I told Ashley and two friends. We dashed downtown for the license, which was shockingly easy to obtain. Twelve dollars, sign on the line.

All the years after my divorce, I had avoided the subject of marriage. Even when it was clear that Ed and I would be permanently together, I'd say, 'Why bother?' Or, 'I'm not in the important business of raising children anymore. We're adults.' I feared my friend who said, 'Marriage is the first step toward divorce.' To myself I'd say, *I don't want to put my hand down on the hot burner twice*. Also, I never wanted to be financially dependent ever again. My former years of writing poetry while my husband worked, I'd paid for dearly. I knew I'd never marry without stepping into it with full financial freedom. Miraculously, and thanks to my own writing hand, I felt secure.

A carload of flowers, a big board of cheeses, straw-berries, the cakes, *gelato*, champagne – no wedding ever was easier. Our friends arrived bearing soaps, plants, bowls, and books to warm the house. Our close friend Josephine, a licensed minister, called everyone together in the living room for a blessing of the house. We stood beside her in front of the fireplace. Ashley and Stuart stood with us. And then Josephine said, 'Dearly beloved, we are gathered . . .' Our friends gasped and clapped. She talked about happiness. Ed and I read poems to each other. That was it.

The next day we were back into unpacking boxes and changing locks and arranging insurance. But we were breaking into big smiles at the mailman, and now and then dancing in the hallway.

Most of the arrangements for Ashley's August wedding were finished. She did well on both exams and had a paper accepted for a conference. Stuart broke away from his company and started a new business. They moved his office and hired people. He talked on the phone as we drove to restaurants. Who could cook? We were all so far beyond the beyond that we seemed calm. They brought us a grill and one night we managed to burn both steak and vegetables. Changes, changes, changes. The house looked spare but settled. We lived there two weeks. I never knew where the forks were or how the new washer worked. We'd compressed a half-year of house restoration into six weeks, thanks to our Italian training. Sister looked at us accusingly and wouldn't budge from the top of Ed's suitcase. We were searching for tax papers, having filed extensions during all the confusion. We filled in final grade sheets and cleared up our school offices. It was June. The house sitter arrived. Time to move to Italy.

★

On Italian time I wake up by the sun, not by my alarm clock. In shock from the chaotic spring, I look blankly out the window. Ed has risen in the dark, only to fall asleep on the sofa. We have come back to Bramasole for summer. I wonder if we could stare into the trees without speaking to anyone for at least a week. I would like a nurse in the hallway, a silent white-uniformed presence who would bring in crescents of melon on thin plates, her pale hand soothing my forehead. The first week of June – odd, the garden is at prime bloom. Even the yellow lilies are open. The linden trees Ed and Beppe pruned in March have spread umbrellas of fresh leaves. Some roses already are waning from their first flush of flowers.

Beppe arrives and Ed steps out barefooted and shirtless to say hello. Beppe hands him a sack. '*Un coniglio per la signora, genuino.*' In its seventy days on earth, the rabbit has eaten nothing but greens, salad, and bread. I look in the bag and see the head. 'Put the head in sauce,' he tells me. 'The meat of the face is . . .' He makes the corkscrew gesture of rotating his forefinger against his cheek, signaling a fine taste. Beppe says rain fell every day in spring and all the plants are two weeks early. The air feels heavy with moisture and it seems that I'm looking through a green lens at the wet light over the valley. He tells us he has planted the *orto* because Anselmo is sick again. When we call Anselmo later, he sounds weak but says he'll be well in a couple of weeks. Ed makes coffee and we lower ourselves into chairs outside in the sun, ready to let the rays restore us. We're discussing symptoms of post-traumatic stress disorder and whether we have them.

Primo Bianchi drives up in his battered blue Ape. As we walk down to meet him, we see him limping badly. He's dressed in pressed gray pants and loafers, not in his usual work clothes. Immediately he sits on the wall and slips off his shoes. Even through his socks, his ankles look swollen. He grimaces every time his foot touches the ground or moves. 'Gout, perhaps gout. I have not been able to work for a month. And the pills they give me are bad for my liver.'

We are poised to finish the bathroom project we started last summer, which had to be aborted when the Sicilian tile ended up in the sea. We also plan to build a stone terrace and grill in front of the *limonaia* and to make a pergola of grapes, a continuation of our garden master plan. He tells us he spent the entire rainy spring reconstructing a stairwell in a *palazzo*. On his knees on damp brick, pouring cement and hauling – no wonder his feet rebelled. Maybe we should find someone else, he suggests. 'No, no, we'll wait until you are ready,' Ed tells him. 'We like your work and your men.' We're crazy about him, too. He knows how to do anything. He looks at a problem, moving his head from side to side, pondering. Then he looks at us with a smile and explains what we will do. When he works he sings tuneless songs like those I've heard on a tape of traditional Tuscan and Umbrian farm music. The songs don't seem to venture far from three or four notes endlessly repeated in a humming drone. His blue eyes have a far sadness in them which totally contrasts with his immediate smile. He hoists himself up and promises to call when he can begin.

Although we are worried about his feet, we are ecstatic over the delay. Now a few weeks of *dolce far niente*, the sweet to do nothing, which we love most. It seems accidental that we keep falling into enormous projects. The sweetness of the early summer is intense. The double-time, triple-time rhythm of the past few months suddenly starts to fade and the long, long Tuscan days present themselves like gifts. Even the Mad Spring was motivated by our desire to bring a piece of our lives here to San Francisco, although at this moment that seems like bomb-the-village-to-save-the-village thinking.

Reliving the spring, we ask each other what we could have done differently. And what *can* we take back to our lives in the new house? What accounts for the dramatic shift in our minds and bodies when we live here? And, in California, aren't we frequently out of control? When over-commitment kicks in, I feel my concentration start to flit. After a few days here, my scattered consciousness gradually melds, mends. Even that seems a level of happiness: the absence of anxiety. Clearly, factor one is not working at our jobs in summer. But we like teaching and must continue, so, given that, what else?

Here, almost all media are subtracted from daily life. I notice the enormous difference immediately. The habit I have, of turning on the radio news as I drive to work, comes to mind as a destroyer of the natural rhythm of the day. Subtle, because flicking on the radio *seems* almost an automatic gesture, a neutral gesture. But in the half hour from my flat to the parking lot at school, drug lords are shot, children are abused by those who are supposed to protect them, car bombs go off, houses are carried off by floods, and my waking psyche has absorbed a load of the world's hurt. The bombardment of frightening, disturbing images assaults any well-being that might have accrued from a lovely night's sleep. TV probably would be worse; I rarely watch TV news except for reports of earthquakes and dire events. At school, I get out of the car already tense and not knowing why. The constant overload of re-current horror on the news and in the papers we assume is normal until we live without it. Has any study focused on the correlation of anxiety and level of exposure to news? I read the paper here two or three times a week, enough to more than keep up with crucial events. 'I'll start the day without that negative drone,' I tell Ed. 'On my own terms.'

'I do like the traffic report, though. All the words rush together; it sounds like a Dylan Thomas poem. Instead of the news, try the Bach cello suites.' He is normally not as pushed as I am because the teaching load at my university is double that at his. 'Taking buckets of time back is the main thing.'

'In the new house let's get up early and walk, the way I do here. Another way of starting out on our own terms. We could walk to the ocean.'

'If only we could take back the siesta – free hours in the middle of the day.'

'Wouldn't you like to call one friend and say "How are you?" and not hear the answer, "I'm so busy"?'

'Well, "I'm busy" means several things – partly it means "I'm important." But maybe living life is so important that we shouldn't be busy. At least not busy, busy, with that buzz-buzz sound.' Ed tells his students to figure out how many weekends they have left, given the good fortune of normal life expectancy. Even to the young it's a shock to see that there are only 2800 more.

That's it. Done for. *Carpe diem, sì, sì*, grab the days.

★

We decide on hedonism. After two days of stocking the house with essentials, planting the last annuals we can grab before the nurseries are emptied, and just breathing in the life we know so well here, we start taking long walks. The wildflowers must be at the peak of the century. All that spring rain coaxed every latent seed, and from the fire roads around the hills we see meadows knee-deep in bloom and hillsides golden with *ginestre*, the broom sending its scent down the breezes in rivulets. We gather strawberries the size of two-carat rubies and sit in long grass eating them. We drive around in Umbria, looking at antiques, hoping to find a desk. One shop owner tells us, 'I can find anything you want; just tell me what you want.' I flash on the grandiose promises of my father when I was a child. 'You can have anything in this world. Just tell me what you want.' I could never think of anything except a swimming pool, to which he'd say, 'You don't want that; you just think you want that.' We travel to San Casciano dei Bagni, where the Romans bathed, and eat pigeon ravioli at the restaurant on the main street, then on to Sarteano and Cetona, with meandering drives around the blissful countryside.

When the exhaustion we brought over finally disappears, we go up to Florence and spend the night. I must find a dress to wear to Ashley's wedding in August. Already the browns, plums, and grays of fall are on view. Ed slips easily into a fall mood and finds two soft-style sport coats. When we have shopped in Florence before, I never bought anything except shoes and handbags. Especially when Jess (Ashley's former boyfriend and now our friend) visits, Ed loves a day in the men's stores. He and Jess incite each other and I'm the spectator. Now Ed visits shop after shop with me. I'm getting used to the Italian mode of shopping. You say what you are looking for and they show you. It's a mistake just to browse through what's out, since many shops only have one size on display. The salespeople are there to be of service. The self-service we are used to is still unusual here. As soon as I say I want a dress for my daughter's wedding, everything in the shop comes forth. They understand totally that the occasion is *molto importante*. Most brides' mothers, I think, do not want a mother-of-the-bride dress. All the lavender lace and beige crêpe dresses designed with that in mind must go unsold. The suit I finally choose at a small shop, which makes everything especially for the customer, is orange. I never have had an orange dress in my life. It's a frosty silk orange, which requires two fittings. My sister will loan me her coral and pearl necklace. I find beautiful dull gold shoes with high heels that could kill. The wedding will be wonderful. The hitch being that I will see my former husband for the first time in years.

★

Vittorio calls to invite us to a dinner on a boat. The Lago Trasimeno wine consortium has arranged for a ferry to take a group on what we used to call a 'progressive dinner,' a different course in four places around the lake. We meet at Castiglione del Lago on Sunday at noon. When we arrive, glasses of *prosecco* and plates of *bruschette* with tomatoes and basil are being passed. We're given a wine glass and a pouch to wear around our necks where we can store the glass when we're not drinking. The crowd is larger than we expected. We find Vittorio and Celia, their children, and several friends of theirs. Maybe two hundred people are piling onto the ferry, with a bar set up at the entrance. People are drinking more *prosecco* as we pull away from the dock. I love boats and islands and the sky shifting as we ride the rises and falls of the water. We disembark on Isola Maggiore, and the hotel staff serves us pasta with the roe of carp and baskets of excellent bread. The workers of the wine consortium of the lake area generously pour all their whites. After the pasta, there's time for a hot walk along the beach. Back on the ferry, we move farther into the lake toward Isola Polvese.

The red wines are open. Various *crostini* are passed. The lake silvers under the flaring white sun. The children start to tire but a band begins to play and some people are dancing. I'm ready to go home but there is no exit. We've been gone four hours. An empty island for birds and small wildlife, Polvese has grassy beaches full of people over for the Sunday afternoon in the sun. One man spread out on a towel has turned so red he looks like an *écorché*, a body without skin. We troop across the island to long outdoor tables. We're served carp cooked in the style of *porchetta*, grilled and stuffed with herbs and salt, and also wrapped in *pancetta*. It's rich, meaty.

On the boat again, I realize that the Italians have had long training for this kind of day. All the first communions, baptisms, weddings, and other *feste* totally prepare them for the long celebrations. We've had steady wine poured into our glasses all afternoon. Faces are glazed with sweat. The bar is popping cork after cork. The band cranks up its speakers and the singer in a slinky dress starts in on 'Hey, Jude,' then speeds up to Italian rock. Suddenly everyone is dancing. The boat is swaying. Could we tip? A retarded man is dancing with his mother, grannies are swinging their hips, a man twirls his three-year-old daughter. The drummer announces a soccer score into the microphone and everyone jumps up and shouts so loud I

303

think the boat will sink. We disembark again at Passignano for dessert. Children turn cranky. But back on board the wine keeps pouring, spinach and cheese crêpes are passed around, and we enter our eighth straight hour of eating and drinking.

Finally, the ferry heads back toward Castiglione del Lago. We see the other two Americans on board; he looks stony and she looks as if she could cry. The sun falls low and the sherbet colors of the sky reflect on the water. We lean over the rail, watching the wake while all the Italians join with the band singing *like a bridge over troubled waterrrr, I will lay me down* in English, and then Italian songs everyone knows. As we gather our sunscreen and camera, we hear several groups talking about where they will go for dinner. They have a secret gene that we don't have.

*

Beppe's *fagiolini*, the green beans we call Blue Lake at home, are ready. Tender and small, they don't even need topping and tailing but I do it anyway. Steamed just to the right point, their full flavor emerges. Underdone, they squeak when you bite them and taste slightly bitter. We eat them alone, with just a little oil and salt and pepper. They're not hurt by toasted chopped hazelnuts, or a little sautéed onion, or by my old favorite, sliced fennel and black olives. My mother liked green beans with tarragon, oil and vinegar, and crumbled bacon. I remember what a fine thing we thought that was, since beans usually were cooked to pieces with a hunk of fatback. In memory of that ultra-sophisticated recipe, I clip branches from my tarragon, which has turned into a towering bush. I'm searching my books for ways to use it, other than plunging the wands into vinegar. Medieval pilgrims to the Holy Land put sprigs inside their shoes to give energy and spring to their feet. I'd like to try that.

Green beans are the one vegetable Anselmo did not plant last year when he established our garden. Beppe's garden thrives, though he has narrowed Anselmo's scope. We have onions, potatoes, green beans, lettuces, garlic, zucchini, and tomatoes. Anselmo's artichokes and asparagus gave us several treats just after we arrived. Beppe plans to plant fennel, and to reseed the lettuces every few weeks. We miss Anselmo — his ironic humor and bossy control of the garden, as well as his adventuring spirit which landed us in new situations constantly. When we call to check on him, we're told that he has been taken to the hospital.

We pick a bunch of lavender and tie it to a jar of honey. How strange to be going back to the hospital. He's a vigorous man, full of opinions and laughter. He'll have his swollen leg propped up, saying '*Senta, senta,*' listen, listen, into his *telefonino*. Ed parks and goes to the machine to get a parking receipt. I walk on toward the hospital, pausing to wait for him.

I glance up at the black-bordered *manifesti funebri*, funeral notices, posted on the wall. Anselmo's name. I scan it, unbelieving. I force myself to focus. Read. *Yesterday, with all the religious comforts . . . funeral tomorrow . . . no flowers but good works . . . Anselmo Pietro Martini Pisciacani.* . . . Unlike the other plain notices, his pictures a sappy pastel Christ in a crown of thorns, upturned eyes, surrounded by roses. Because he would have mocked it, I think there must be a mistake. He was not a churchgoer. He could not be dead. But then no one else could have that name. As Ed approaches, I shake my head and point. 'No. How can this be?'

We walk on up to the hospital. At the front desk Ed says, 'We have a friend who was a patient and we're afraid he has died. Is he still here? Anselmo Martini.'

He finds no record — maybe there's a mistake but then I remember 'Pisciacani,' the name he hated and dropped after his mother died, was on the death notice. Pisciacani means dog piss in dialect. 'Pisciacani,' I say.

'Yes, I am sorry, he is in the chapel. If you die in hospital, you must remain for twenty-four hours.' He leads us downstairs. Ed waits at the door and I walk in. There lies Anselmo on a stone slab, dressed in his brown suit, his feet splayed and a little dust on his shoes. Four women in black pray around him. I put down the honey and lavender at the door and flee.

At home the land feels charged with Anselmo's presence. He rebuilt that stone wall, he cleared two terraces for the *orto*, he planted the grass in the Lime Tree Bower. The potted lemons and the three roses the color of dried blood and the wine press — he gave us these with few words but I could tell with immense pleasure. On the third terrace he planted two apricots, and, near the road, two pears. For all the years we will have here, we still will be enjoying the literal fruits of his labors. In the *limonaia*, his red beret hangs on a nail.

We feel we've lost a good uncle. Ed is still reeling from his mother's death. Anselmo's brings a double rush of grief. The hurt of loss is too hard, then there's the incomprehensible fact that the loved person simply is erased from the planet. The basic facts of birth and death I've never remotely been able to fathom. *The prenatal abyss, out of it you came, into the tumult of life, light, and on to the other void* . . . I hope to be dazzled by the news of an afterlife, when the last plug is pulled on me. *I can't take non-life.* Anselmo stood at the Thursday market with fifty or sixty men every week for decades, talking weather, business, jingling change in his pocket. In his office on Sacco e Vanzetti, he always dropped everything when we walked in. I quizzed him about the farms for sale in photos on the wall, and if one looked wonderful, he'd say 'Let's go look,' and grab his hat. He had all the time in the world. Now, none. *'There's no one hundred years guaranteed or life cheerfully refunded, young lady,' my grandfather warned.*

People are crammed into the church. We stand in the doorway. Out on the porch, thirty or so men smoke and talk during the funeral mass, just as though they were at the market. I recognize many of them. Their sunbaked faces attest to work in the fields. The older ones are short, dressed in suits too thick for the brutal July sun, the younger ones are taller, beneficiaries of post-war nutrition, and wear pressed short-sleeved shirts. Inside, heat and incense swirl. Who will faint? Family members support each other as they walk by the casket for communion. It's hard to grasp that Anselmo lies inside that box. The wailing Catholic hymns drag on forever. The casket is loaded into the hearse. We have seen these processions before. Now we join the crowd walking behind the hearse up to the cemetery. I hope he is not going into one of those thirty-year slots that look like dresser drawers in a wall. No, there's the raw hole. He is going into the earth, this man of the earth. No ceremony, he's just lowered by ropes into the ground. Not even a thud. When my father was buried, the ground was so saturated that the coffin floated for a moment before whooshing down into water. *'That's not true at all,' my sister says. 'They didn't even lower the coffin when we were there.'* She's wrong. *I see the red rose blanket slide off into the arms of the undertakers and the bronze box start to sink. 'You were dreaming,' she insists.* His family steps forward and everyone throws on a handful of dirt. No denying that he will be in the ground. We talk to the family. Everyone leaves quickly. There's no dinner or visiting. Monday, back to work.

At home, Beppe is tying grape vines to wires. We tell him about Anselmo, how quickly he was gone, and he stands up slowly, saying nothing. He takes off his hat and his eyes fill with tears. He shakes his head and goes back to the vines.

★

When the excitement of death is over, the shock and disbelief subside quickly and we're left with the fact of absence. A funeral cools emotion because it leaves not a doubt. It's over — the traditional sacraments are wise ways to instantly internalize the major events of life. Now we begin to say, *His first night in the ground, the men at the market are gathering around a space that was his, look, Anselmo's pears.* The last work of his life was here on this land. He had the oldest knowledge of what grows where and when. Did we ever thank him enough for finding Bramasole for us?

'Hearse is a strange word,' Ed says. We are walking home from town over the Roman road. 'In Middle English it's *herse* — I know this because it came up in a poem I wrote when my father died. *Herse* comes from Latin *hirpex*, meaning "harrow." You know how the harrow has all those prongs — in Italian they call them *quarante dente*, forty teeth. Well, *hirpex* reaches way back to the Oscan *hircus*, which means wolf, a connection to teeth. It felt strange to follow that hearse.'

'Show me the poem again.'

★

SCORPIONS

The heaving, sweating, *cento per cento* heat broke
    today,

308

as if it can break as unexpectedly as a car breaks,
or as the large glass demijohn that shattered on the
    tiles
when I bumped into it while carrying an armload of
    books
from one bookcase in one room to another bookcase
in another room: the heavy inhale of heat into my
    own lungs,
my bare feet surrounded by sharp glass. Which
brought
    me
to 'booklungs' (what the dark hollow lungs of
    scorpions
are called), lined up in their own bodies like blank
    books.
All week, an inch-and-a-half long black scorpion
has stayed in the shower, not because of the heat but
    because
it has eaten a slightly smaller scorpion, who had come
    in earlier,
perhaps looking for water. The one ate *all* of the
    other,
except for three of its eight legs, still scattered on the
    porcelain.
I remembered hearing the woman at the restaurant,
her overly large white teeth crunching through a
    plateful
of chitinous shrimp. The scorpion carries its carapace,
    too.
It too proved it could continue to eat, to chew
    through shell,
to decisively end its quarrel with the other, which
    was surely
over nothing important enough to die for. The one

has the other
completely inside itself, is running on two histories.
I was reminded of Kronos eating his own children,
    lungs and all,
crunching through skull, into brains, and then Zeus
    tricking him
into vomiting them all whole and alive. But the
    proof is
in the eating – better to eat than not to. Which brings
    me
to my father, who ate his last on August 8th, and felt
    his lungs,
sacks of cheap cloth, let all the air out. Now the coffin
    is his new
carapace, shiny steel – we could see our faces distorted
    in it.
Here I hear pears drop in late August, skins pierced
by sharp wasps and armored iridescent beetles, and
there's a heavy sweetness under the tree when I rake
    up
the bruised fruit: *Rake*, as in *harrow*, as in *hearse* (the
    one
I followed August 12th) from the Oscan for wolf –
because of its teeth, strong enough even to break
    through bone.

We have had not a drop of rain all summer. The flamboyant flower garden I had last year has limped through the hottest summer on record. 'I can eat only watermelon and *gelato*,' la signora Molesini in the grocery store tells us. No matter how much we water, the grass burns. The voluptuous roses of early June gradually have shed their leaves. The tiny buds they send out refuse to open.

    The year we bought the house it was the same. Clouds

would gather over the house and thunder practically shook the fillings out of our teeth – but no rain. Our well went dry and I remember thinking in the middle of the night, *I must be certifiably insane. I have no idea what I'm doing.* The singed oaks and locusts defrocked early, leaving dead-looking trees all over the hills. The next summer was soft, with wildflowers spilling over every terrace. We slept under a light blanket until July. We love living close to the pulse of the seasons, even the searing dry heat, which has sent foxes and wild boar into our yard for the first time. I hear the *cinghiale* snorting across the lawn at night, making their way to the faucet where they lap water from the stone basin. They scuffle with, what – squirrels and porcupines? Then they thunder off with their strange 'ha-ha' cries. They have not managed to get through Beppe's fence around the vegetables but they find plenty to love in the fallen plums.

★

At the beginning of August, we return to foggy, cold San Francisco for Ashley's wedding. All my Southern relatives are arriving – the clan is stomping. My college roommates and their husbands are coming, Ashley's New York friends from her artist life, Stuart's friends, family. Ashley and her bridesmaids arrive at the house with the wedding dress and hang it in front of one of the many still-bare windows, where it drifts on its own, bringing home the reality of the wedding. Ashley suddenly is struck with the magnitude of what's coming. She comes into my room while I'm unpacking and throws herself on the bed. 'Any advice for me?'

I remember asking my mother the same question. She thought a minute then said, 'Don't ever wear old under-wear.' I tell Ashley I'll try to come up with something better but I'm not sure I can. She's very grown, as is Stuart, and they seem to be entering this marriage not only with love and excitement but with enormous relief to have found each other after a lot of false starts. Ashley is one of the most decisive people I've ever known; when she makes up her mind there's an iron will behind her.

We're having all the out-of-town people over for drinks, and my family will stay afterwards for dinner. At this party, one of the strangest things of my life happens. Ashley looks glorious in a short red dress. Two waiters are passing champagne and Ed is going over the toast he's about to give. My sisters, brothers-in-law, nieces, and nephews are in full reunion mode. Ashley is in the foyer greeting guests. I'm talking to friends in the living room when I see my nephew arrive in the crowded foyer. As I walk toward him, I introduce myself to the man talking to Ashley. 'Hello, I'm Frances, Ashley's mother.' I shake his hand and see the startled look on his face. 'And I'm Frank,' he answers with a laugh. My former husband. Ashley's father. We were married for a lifetime. I do not recognize him. He thinks I am surely joking. Of course, I am distracted with all the arrivals, trying to circulate among the guests – still, I look straight at him and do not know him. Once he said to me, *I'd know your hand in a bucket of hands,* one of the strangest intimacies I have heard. I step outside and take big breaths of air and try to adjust to the jolt – the snap of that imagined entwined umbilical of the past. He doesn't even look that different. I've seen him in my mind and in dreams many times over the years. I'd expected a flash-flood of memories, a by-pass connection to the now historical past. Looking at him, I used to feel I was looking in a mirror, my equal-opposite. For a long time, I will be feeling my hand go out to shake that of a stranger.

The garden wedding is at an inn in the wine country, a dreamy dream of a wedding, with pink and apricot roses everywhere, a golden light over the vineyard hills, a bride descending as though from a cloud, a groom with the heart to cry as she walks toward him, and the tenor sealing us all together with 'Con te partirò,' With you I will go. Her veil catches on a rose thorn and tears, her father frees her, takes the torn piece of veil into his pocket, and they walk. A moment, and of such moments myths are made.

For dinner, candles all over the garden, and a Tuscan feast. As we sit down a snowy egret flies over and lands on the feathery top of a tree. 'A great omen,' someone says. 'No, the stork,' someone else answers. For my toast, I remember a line from Rilke, 'Love consists of this, that two solitudes protect and touch and greet each other.' Her father gives an eloquent toast about the enormous support the presence of all the guests will give to Ashley and Stuart. Soon Ashley is dancing, floating under the full moon, then everyone is dancing. Ed is smoking a big cigar. I wish everyone would stay all night.

The newlyweds take off for hot tropical islands. My sisters and their families leave over the next few days, we see friends, adjust to the decrescendo, pack, pack, pack again, and board the plane for the long haul back to Bramasole, taking a duffle of books, fall clothes, and a handful of moments to last a lifetime.

★

The end of August and still no rain. In earlier times, farmers prayed to saints. If no rain came, the statue of the saint might be flogged, thrown into a river, dragged out, and stuffed in the mouth with salty sardines to make him thirsty. Whatever rituals occur now, they're private.

For nine summers I've lived on this hillside in Tuscany.

I've spent scattered winter and spring holidays here, and last year had the great boon of a whole spring. I am about to spend my first fall. The *feste* of August – beefsteak and *funghi porcini* – are over; the streets are emptying by the day as tourists head home. The sun has been tamed, softening the evening light to rose-gold. An early fall; truffles and mushrooms and sausages will be coming. Already we're peeling the green Sicilian tangerines, exactly the color of a parrot, and buying apples that taste like our earliest memories of apples. Primo has left a load of cement and sand; in a week he will begin the project. Beppe today has planted *cavolo nero*, the black winter cabbage, and has set out fennel for next year. He picked the last little bunch of beans and another basket of tomatoes. All summer we eat outside in the long twilight, now the days are short enough that we set out lanterns for dinner.

Vittorio, always with his taste buds anticipating the season, calls to invite us to a goose dinner, the last feast of the summer. His voice is the siren's call. Our Slow Food group has just celebrated the foods and wines of the Verona area at an eight-course dinner. 'I think of goose as a Christmas treat,' Ed says.

'No, you do not eat the white geese after summer. They are too old, too fat. The flavor is best now.' So we wind far into the mountains to a *trattoria* where we gather at two long tables near the fireplace. Vittorio is pouring the wine, his treat, the Avignonesi reds we love. We see Paolo, the winemaker of that noble vineyard, at the other table and toast him. The *antipasti* begin, the usual *crostini*, served with the special stuffed goose neck. The pasta with rich *ragù d'oca*, goose sauce, is followed by roast goose, easily the best I've ever tasted. The noise level rises until it's impossible to hear what anyone is saying. That's OK.

We just eat. The baby in the stroller at the end of the table sleeps through everything.

★

Margherita, daughter of signora Gazzini, forager *par excellence*, stops by to introduce herself. Driving by, she happens to witness the felling of the dead palm. We waited all summer while it shed dry fronds one by one. We hate to cut it, especially since its thirty-foot mate on the other side of the house still thrives, but the completely bare trunk, like a giant elephant leg, looked bizarre. She watches from below as I watch from the window. Heavier and denser than they thought, Ed and Beppe both yell as the palm starts to fall off-course, crashing into a pot of geraniums.

Margherita lived at Bramasole as a child, when the palm was small. I am stirred to hear that she still dreams of the rooms and land she knew at four years old. From my first glance, Bramasole always has been a house of dreams. Coming upon it now, I see that it belongs to the Etruscan Bramasole wall, to Torreone, to Cortona, to Tuscany. Beyond my possession, still it is mine – the contraries meet – and transitory as my tenure may be, it is a fierce and primitive tenure. 'Don't give up the house, no matter what happens,' I recall a friend advising another friend, who was divorcing. 'You're discovering the irrational power of a woman's domesticity,' my friend Josephine tells me. 'Possession always has a secret root.'

I don't say any of this to Margherita. Since I've just met her I don't want her to think I'm some sibyl of the mountain. While Ed and Beppe cart away the carcass, she tells me that her mother stays out for six or eight hours some days. Not only does she gather lettuces, asparagus, snails, and mushrooms, she cuts greens for her rabbits. 'She's a person who likes to live outside,' she explains. 'We don't know where she goes – sometimes she's just roaming the hills. She's been roaming this mountain for a lifetime.'

★

I understand the impulse. Walking the ridge road toward the Porta Montanina gate to town, I'm reading Keats's ode 'To Autumn' and feeling how closely his words anneal to the subject. Of all the poems about the season, his brings me the closest to the unsayable sensation I experience as summer circles toward the autumnal equinox. The internal clock turns, too, a visceral knowledge of change. Earlier, the pale dog-roses bloomed along the road; today the branches are studded with bright orange rose hips. The air seems to hold a calming sense of peace as the landscape turns toast, amber, wheat, and the grasses dry to – what? The shade of lion's fur, the tawny crust of bread, the gold of a worn wedding ring. A moment ago the grasses were a fervent green. 'Season of mists and mellow fruitfulness,' Keats writes, and I see the valley mists and laden branches of pear blotched and gnawed and bumbled by birds, bees, and worms. I like the idea of the season conspiring with the sun to 'load and bless' the fruit and vines. I taste his phrases: 'hair soft-lifted by the winnowing wind,' the furrows 'drowsed with the fume of poppies,' 'fill all fruit with ripeness to the core.' And yes, we do think 'warm days will never cease,' that first moment in the poem when the innocence of the perspective gently darkens. The resonant hint of change and cold trip easily along the tongue. And that's his skill, to tinge the mind with knowledge, while simultaneously reveling in the season when gold ingots of light fall across the road. Entering the Etruscan gate into upper Cortona's immaculate streets, I see a woman setting out small cyclamen plants in a pot by

316

her front door. Pink, white, magenta, she's mixed all the colors into a little blaze to warm her during the cold months. Beautiful, I tell her, and she points to dark green spikes and a tight yellow bud pushing through the ground. 'This kind of crocus comes back in autumn, but only briefly, only a few.' *We're riding the earth, she and I.* Sitting on the front steps of San Francesco, listening to the bells early Sunday morning, I don't want anything more than this poem rolled in my hand, 5000 *lire* in my shirt pocket for coffee and pastry, my new red loafers which navigate the stony streets so well.

★

I wander at night, too. Ed and I have walked into town for a *gelato* and he starts a long conversation with Edo about installing lawn irrigation. Our wild-herb lawn has not survived the summer drought, though fall rains will bring back the green hills. Out of chat, I start back, walking over the Roman road with a flashlight, then down onto the cypress-lined road toward home. Before it was paved, the white pebble *strada bianca* used to reflect the moonlight. Now with the asphalt and the *luna nera*, black moon, the road is dark, the cypress trees seeming to gather into their massive shapes all the light from the stars. I have the ambition to see every cypress tree in Tuscany. Like the California oaks in the Bay Area countryside, the cypresses seem to speak for the landscape. The bare oaks of California interact with light, giving their skeletal shadows to the hills and their silhouettes to the sky.

But the cypresses play no games with light. If they were in the sky they would be the black holes and if I were in America, I would be petrified to be alone on a deserted road at night. Because each of these trees was planted for a local boy who died in World War I, they are huge presences, not only in form but in a silence stopped inside their fixed curves, something of the unlived life of each boy. The tips, pointed like sable paintbrushes, wave back and forth against the stars.

Hot from the climb over the hill, I unbutton my blue linen dress all the way down and let it lift behind me. *Oh, for a life of sensation,* our friend Keats also told us. The cypress trees are grand companions. If anyone were coming, I would hear them because sound carries along the mountain, like the last sigh of the gladiator in the amphitheater heard on the last row. Around the curve, the house rises above the road, a rough translation of my body into a mute language of windows, doors, and stone. Ed, I think, is translated by the olive trees and vines, which now droop with dusty purple grapes.

From the yard above the road, I see the cypresses graph a rise and fall against a sky blown clean of clouds by this afternoon's wind. Stars are shooting over the valley, stars that fell even before the Etruscans watched from this hillside. I recognize the cadence of Ed's step below in the road. 'Are you home?' he calls up to me. Five, six, stars streak across the sky. I hold out my hand to catch one.

Under the Tuscan Sun
by Frances Mayes

'A glorious book – seductive, sensuous, beautifully crafted ...
With a poet's economy of language, she tells of heat rising
from white-washed stones, of grapes still warm from the
vine, of pottery bowls of Etruscan design filled with the first
wild greens of spring' *Elizabeth Luard*

Frances Mayes – widely published poet, gourmet cook, and
travel writer – opens the door on a wondrous new world when
she buys and restores an abandoned villa in the spectacular Tuscan
countryside. She finds faded frescoes beneath the whitewash in
the dining room, a vineyard under wildly overgrown brambles
– and even a wayward scorpion under her pillow. And from her
traditional kitchen and simple garden she creates dozens of
delicious seasonal recipes, all included in this book.

In the vibrant local markets and neighbouring hill towns, the
author explores the nuances of the Italian landscape, history and
cuisine. Each adventure yields delightful surprises – the perfect
panettone, an unforgettable wine, or painted Etruscan tombs.
Doing for Tuscany what Peter Mayle did for Provence, Mayes
writes about the tastes and pleasures of a foreign country with
gusto and passion. A celebration of the extraordinary quality of
life in Tuscany, *Under the Tuscan Sun* is a feast for all the senses.

'An intense celebration of what [Mayes] calls 'the
voluptuousness of Italian life' ... appealing and very vivid ...
the kind of thing you'd tuck into a picnic basket on an
August day ... or better yet, keep handy on the bedside table
in the depths of January' *New York Times Book Review*

A Bantam Paperback

0 553 50667 6